# LANDSCAPES

SENIOR AUTHORS

**Virginia A. Arnold**     **Carl B. Smith**

AUTHORS

**James Flood**     **Diane Lapp**

LITERATURE CONSULTANTS

Joan I. Glazer     Margaret H. Lippert

**Macmillan Publishing Company**
New York

**Collier Macmillan Publishers**
London

Parts of this work were published in the first edition of CONNECTIONS.
This work is also published in individual volumes under the titles *Enterprises, Frontiers, Encounters,* and *Forces,* copyright © 1989 Macmillan Publishing Company, a division of Macmillan, Inc.

Macmillan Publishing Company
866 Third Avenue
New York, N.Y. 10022
Collier Macmillan Canada, Inc.

Printed in the United States of America.

ISBN 0-02-174870-5

9 8 7 6 5 4 3 2

# ACKNOWLEDGMENTS

*The publisher gratefully acknowledges permission to reprint the following copyrighted material:*

"The Art of the Old West" from THE ART OF THE OLD WEST by Shirley Glubok. Copyright © 1971 by Shirley Glubok. Edited with permission of Macmillan Publishing Company.

"A Bat Is Born" (originally titled "Bats") from THE BAT POET by Randall Jarrell. Copyright © Macmillan Publishing Company 1963, 1964. Reprinted with permission of Macmillan Publishing Company and Penguin Books, Ltd.

"The Best Kind of Book" is adapted from SEVEN-DAY MAGIC by Edward Eager. Copyright © 1962 by Edward Eager. Reprinted by permission of Harcourt Brace Jovanovich, Inc.

"The Big Wave" is an adaptation and abridged selection from THE BIG WAVE by Pearl Buck (John Day). Copyright 1947 by Curtis Publishing Company. Copyright 1948, 1976 by Pearl Buck. Reprinted by permission of Harper & Row, Publishers, Inc., and A. P. Watt Ltd., London.

"Books Fall Open" from ALL DAY LONG by David McCord. Copyright © 1965, 1966 by David McCord. By permission of Little, Brown and Company.

"By the Shores of Silver Lake" is Chapters 24, 25, 26 from BY THE SHORES OF SILVER LAKE by Laura Ingalls Wilder. Copyright 1939 by Harper & Row, Publishers, Inc. Renewed 1967 by Roger L. MacBride. Reprinted by permission of Harper & Row, Publishers, Inc., and Lutterworth Press.

"Caddie Woodlawn" from CADDIE WOODLAWN by Carol Ryrie Brink. Copyright 1935 by Macmillan Publishing Company, renewed 1963 by Carol Ryrie Brink. Reprinted with permission of Macmillan Publishing Company.

"Canyon Winter" is adapted from CANYON WINTER by Walt Morey. Copyright © 1972 by Walt Morey. Reprinted by permission of the publisher, E. P. Dutton, a division of New American Library.

"Cave of the Ancestors" is an abridged and adapted selection from THE TALKING EARTH by Jean Craighead George. Copyright © 1983 by Jean Craighead George. Reprinted by permission of Harper & Row, Publishers, Inc., and Curtis Brown, Ltd.

"The Changing River" is from THIS IS A RIVER by Laurence Pringle. Copyright © 1972 by Laurence Pringle. Edited with permission of Macmillan Publishing Company.

"C. L. U. T. Z." adapted from C. L. U. T. Z. by Marilyn Z. Wilkes. Text copyright © 1982 by Marilyn Wilkes. Reprinted by permission of the publisher, Dial Books for Young Readers. By permission also of Victor Gollancz Ltd.

# Contents

6/16/04

7/15/04

8/11/04 ✓

8/20/04 ✓

13

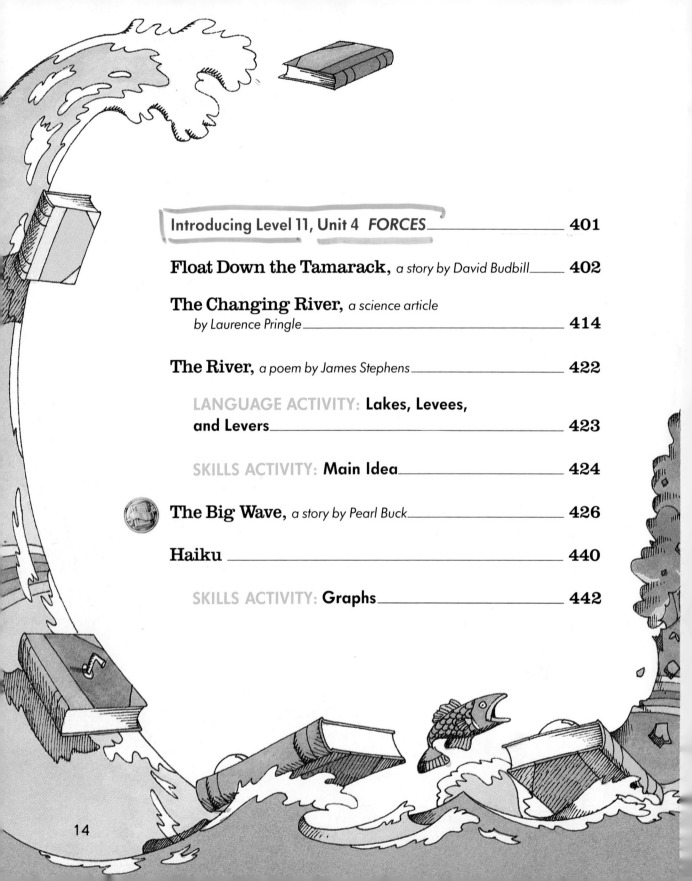

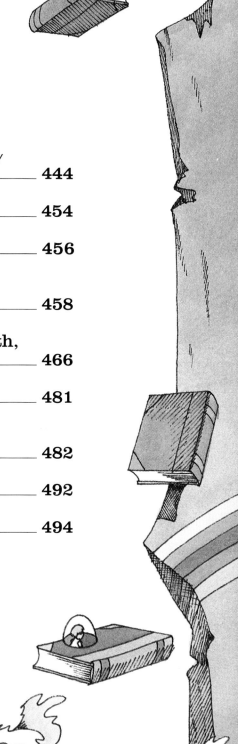

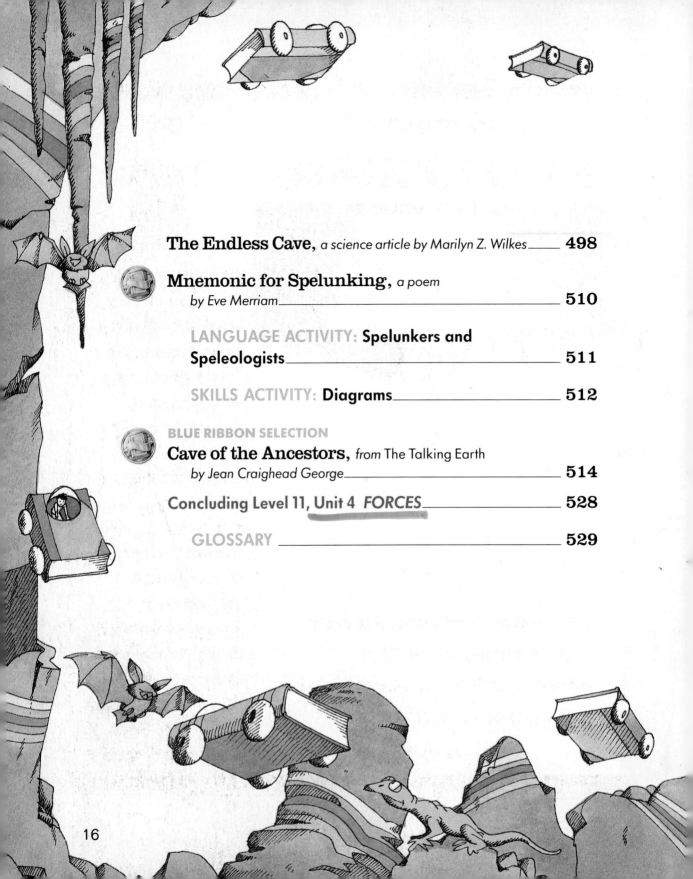

Introducing Level 11

# ENTERPRISES

*Each morning sees some task begun,*
*Each evening sees it close;*
*Something attempted, something done,*
*Has earned a night's repose.*

**Henry Wadsworth Longfellow**

# 1

Many people enjoy the feeling of satisfaction they get from completing a task. In this unit, you will read about people involved in a variety of enterprises: money-making enterprises such as running an "odd jobs" business or selling a new toothpaste, and writing ventures such as a travel journal or newspaper column. What skills do people need to make their enterprises successful?

# KID POWER

## SUSAN BETH PFEFFER

*Have you ever wanted to earn money so you could
buy something? In this story, Janie wants to buy
a ten-speed bicycle. She also would like to earn
the money for it. She plans to do odd jobs for the
people in her neighborhood. "I'll advertise," she
decides. "Before too long I should have plenty of
jobs to do." With the help of her sister Carol,
Janie begins her enterprise, but will it work?*

"What do you want this sign to say?" asked
Carol.

"I don't know," I said. "I guess it should have
my name and phone number on it, so people will
know who to call."

"It's going to need more than that. You're going
to have to say what you do, or else nobody will call."

"But I don't know yet what I do. I'll do whatever
people hire me to do."

"Then you need some sort of all-purpose name. Something catchy. You need a slogan, too."

"I figured one out already. 'No job too big or small.'"

"That's not bad. You should let everybody know you're just a kid, too."

"KID POWER," I said. "No job too big or small."

"Perfect!" Carol said. "Kid Power it is."

That's how it all started.

First thing next morning, I put my Kid Power sign up on the supermarket bulletin board. I knew people looked there a lot. Then I went home and called Grandma. She said she'd be delighted to have some help with the attic, so I took the bus to her house.

I helped her for three hours, carrying boxes out of the attic and helping her decide what to keep and

what to throw out. I carried practically as much back to the attic as I'd taken out. But Grandma claimed we'd done a lot of good work that day, and insisted on paying me my three dollars. I offered her a special family rate, but she said she wouldn't hear of it.

I didn't get home until pretty late in the afternoon. When I did, I found Mom in the kitchen.

"There you are," she said. "You got a call for Kid Power. I took the woman's name and number down and said you'd call her back just as soon as you got in."

"Where is it?" I shouted. Somehow a job from your grandmother doesn't count the way a job from a stranger does.

"Calm down," Mom said. "Right here." She handed me a scrap of paper with "Mrs. Dale, 555-4456" written on it.

I called the number, and took a deep breath.
That's a trick my father taught me. It makes your
voice sound deeper and it relaxes you.

"Hello?"

"Hello, Mrs. Dale?"

"Speaking."

"This is Janie Golden of Kid Power calling."

"Oh, yes," Mrs. Dale said. "I saw your poster in
the supermarket today, and I was wondering if you
could help me. I'm having a yard sale on Saturday.
Your sign made me think it would be a good idea if
I had someone at the sale just to look after the kids
people bring with them."

"Kind of like day-care?" I asked.

"Exactly," Mrs. Dale said. "Do you think you
could fit me into your schedule?"

"I'm sure I could," I said, pretending to look at a
calendar. "What time would you want me there?"

"The sale is scheduled to start at ten," she said, "which means the first customers will be there by eight-thirty. It's supposed to end at four."

"No problem," I said. "I'll be there at eight-thirty."

"What do you charge?" she asked.

I breathed deeply. "A dollar an hour," I said.

"Oh, that's quite reasonable," Mrs. Dale said. "I'm sure if someone is there to watch the children, their parents will be more likely to buy things."

"There is one more thing," I said.

"Certainly," Mrs. Dale said. "What is it?"

"Kid Power is just getting started, and I could use some free publicity. Would you mind if I put up a little sign at your yard sale?"

"Of course not," Mrs. Dale said, "I like an enterprising young woman. I'll see you Saturday then—120 Woodhaven Road."

"Saturday," I said, writing down the address.

"Thank you, Janie," she said, and we hung up.

"I got a job!" I hollered, running over to hug Mom. "Eight-thirty to four. At a dollar an hour, that's $7.50. And I earned $3.00 at Grandma's. I'm going to be rich!"

I spent the rest of the day reading *A Child's First Book of Investments,* and munching celery. I'd just taken a bite when the phone rang. "Hello," I said, swallowing rapidly.

"Is this Janie Golden?" the voice asked.

"Yes," I said.

"This is Emma Marks," the woman said. "I was wondering if you could tell me what dress size you wear."

"Size 12," I said.

"That's just perfect. I have a little job for you, if you could take it."

"Sure. What?"

"I have a granddaughter who lives in Oregon. I just love sewing things for her, but it's not easy since I don't have her around to try things on. I was wondering if you'd be willing to model the clothes for me while I sew them. How tall are you?"

"Five feet," I said.

"Harriet is four-foot-eleven," she said. "This sounds just ideal. Could you come over tomorrow?"

"Sure," I said. "What time?"

"How about after lunch? I live at 22 Curry Road."

"I know where that is," I said. "I'll see you at one then."

"Fine," she said. "Thank you, Janie."

"Thank you," I said and hung up.

"It certainly sounds like you're going to have a busy summer," Mom said.

Cleaning the attic with Grandma was a snap. Even being fitted by Mrs. Marks for dresses for her

granddaughter wasn't too bad. But babysitting for a bunch of kids at a yard sale was my first real challenge. I hoped I was up to it.

First of all I insisted that Carol letter another sign for me, and she did, for a dollar. I wasn't too thrilled about paying her at all, but she pointed out if I wanted to be paid for my labor, so did she.

"You're going to have to spend some money, you know," Carol told me a few nights before the sale.

"Why?" I asked.

"People who are in business always have to spend money. It has to do with gross and net."

"Gross and what?" I asked.

"Gross and net," she said. "That means you have to spend money to make money."

"That doesn't make any sense at all," I said, and walked over to where Dad was reading a book.

"Dad, may I ask you a question?"

"Sure," he said and put his book down.

"What's gross and net?" I asked.

"Gross and net are business terms," he said. "Let's take that job you did for Grandma. How much did she pay you?"

"Three dollars," I said.

"Okay, your gross profit was three dollars. But it cost you fifty cents to take the bus there and back, right?"

I nodded.

"So if you subtract the fifty cents from the three dollars, you have a net profit of $2.50. The net profit is the gross minus expenses."

"There have to be expenses?"

"Yes," Dad said. "Alas."

I went back to Carol. "Tell me about spending money to make money," I said. "How much do I have to spend?"

"That depends," she said. "Now take this yard sale business. If I were in charge of the kids, I'd make sure they had something to keep them busy."

"I've already thought about that," I said. "But if I bring some of my own toys, they might think they're for sale."

"Then bring something else," she said.

"Like what?"

"Like food. Everybody loves food."

"That's certainly true," I said.

"Of course, it'll cost you some money," she said. "But it'll make your job easier, and then you'll do it better, and then other people'll be more likely to hire you. That's what I mean by spending money to make money."

"What kind of food do you think I should bring?" I asked. I was hoping she'd suggest something inexpensive.

"I make really good oatmeal cookies," she said thoughtfully.

"They are good," I said. "Carol, would you bake me some?"

"Sure," Carol said.

I got up and hugged her. "Carol, you're the greatest big sister in the whole world!"

"A dollar a batch," she said coolly.

I broke away from her. "What?"

"You heard me," she said. "After all, I should be paid, too. How many batches do you want?"

"How many cookies are there to a batch?" I asked.

"A couple of dozen," she said.

I did a little mental arithmetic. "I'll take three batches at fifty cents a batch," I said. "I won't pay for any burnt cookies, and you have to give me my money back for any cookies I don't sell."

"I will not," she said. "A dollar a batch and you keep what you get."

"Fifty cents and I'll let you make a sign saying you made the cookies," I said. "You might get some business that way."

"A dollar and I get to have the sign anyway," she said.

"I think we need a mediator," I said.

Carol and I crossed the room and explained our problem to Dad. "How does this sound?" he asked. "Seventy-five cents for each batch, no burnt cookies allowed. Carol gets to advertise, and Janie's responsible for any extra cookies."

"That sounds okay to me," I said.

"I guess it'll be okay," Carol said. "But I want to make four batches instead of three. All I'd have to do is double the ingredients."

"Are you willing to order another batch?" Dad asked me.

"Okay," I said. "But only if Carol throws in two free pitchers of homemade lemonade."

"I get to advertise?" Carol asked.

"Absolutely," I said.

"Deal," she said.

So Carol made a sign that said, "Homebaked Oatmeal Cookies by Carol Golden." The next day she made the oatmeal cookies. I packed them into a paper bag and stuck in a couple of paper plates to put them on. Carol said she'd make the lemonade after supper.

The next morning Mom drove me and the cookies and the lemonade and the signs to Mrs. Dale's

house. I could see Mrs. Dale setting out her merchandise on folding tables. There were already people there watching as she unpacked boxes.

"Hello," I said, walking over to her, holding the pitchers of lemonade carefully. "I'm Janie Golden of Kid Power."

Mrs. Dale smiled at me.

"Is there any place I could put my stuff?" I asked. "I brought cookies and lemonade for the kids."

"That's a great idea," she said. "There should be some space at that end of the table. Why don't you put your things there?"

I went to where she pointed and set up. I taped my sign and Carol's sign to the edge of the table.

"Do you think you should make another sign telling the kids the cookies are for them?"

"I already did," I said and took out another pair of signs. One read, "Kids' Cookies. Free for all kids

12 and under." The other read, "Adult Cookies. 5¢ each."

Mrs. Dale laughed, and handed me a nickel. "I'll have one adult cookie please," she said. "You'll probably make more money today than I will."

"Just trying to build up my net profit," I said.

It was a long, hot, and tiring yard sale. The kids stayed away from their parents and stuck to the cookies and me. The lemonade didn't last the morning, but Mrs. Dale sent me inside to make some more. When I came back with a fresh pitcher, a lady walked over and asked for an adult cookie. I gave her one and she gave me a nickel.

She ate it very carefully. "This is an excellent oatmeal cookie," she said when she finished. "I'll take a dozen."

Mrs. Dale walked over to the table. "Janie, you'll be a millionaire before you're twenty-one!"

## Thinking and Writing About the Selection

1. What jobs was Janie hired to do?

2. Janie had to spend money to make money. How much money did Janie spend for the yard sale? How much did she make?

3. Is advertising an important part of running a business? Why or why not?

 4. Janie's slogan was "No job too big or small." Make a list of slogans used by companies that advertise in newspapers and magazines, or on television and radio. Choose the slogan that you think is best and write a short explanation that tells why you think it is a good slogan.

## Applying the Key Skill
### Context Clues

Read the sentences below. Use context clues to choose the correct meaning of the underlined words. Write the words and their meanings.

1. Janie wanted to make money, but she just couldn't decide what to do. It wasn't long before she found a solution to her quandary.
   a. a state of unhappiness
   b. a state of anger
   c. a state of relief
   d. a state of confusion

2. To figure out her net profit, Janie had to take her gross profit and deduct all of her expenses.
   a. to add
   b. to subtract
   c. to multiply
   d. to divide

3. Instead of using a calculator, Janie decided she would figure out her expenses by using mental arithmetic.
   a. done on paper
   b. done quickly
   c. done in the mind
   d. done by estimating

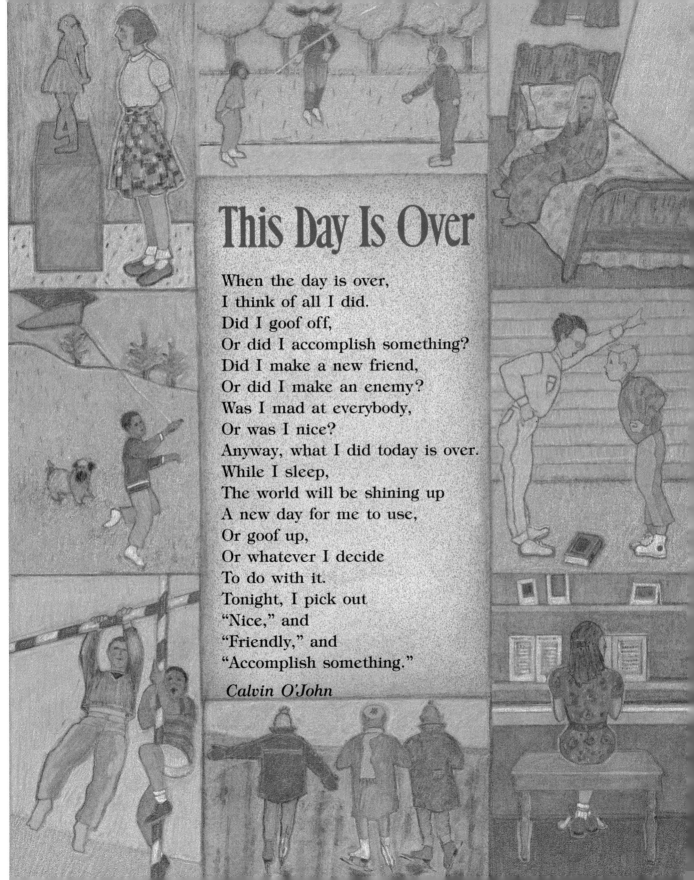

# This Day Is Over

When the day is over,
I think of all I did.
Did I goof off,
Or did I accomplish something?
Did I make a new friend,
Or did I make an enemy?
Was I mad at everybody,
Or was I nice?
Anyway, what I did today is over.
While I sleep,
The world will be shining up
A new day for me to use,
Or goof up,
Or whatever I decide
To do with it.
Tonight, I pick out
"Nice," and
"Friendly," and
"Accomplish something."

*Calvin O'John*

# YOU CAN GET A JOB!

Have you ever wondered what kind of work you would be good at or would like to do? Perhaps you have wanted to work but haven't known how to get started. The article you are about to read is from *Penny Power*, a consumer magazine for young people. The article describes the work experiences of more than a hundred students who responded to a *Penny Power* questionnaire. It may answer some of the questions you have about the world of work.

34

Kids have always worked. They've taken care of younger brothers and sisters, helped with the laundry, run errands. But work that you get *paid* for is something special. It's a job.

Can a kid handle a job? You bet! We asked students in fourteen classes across the country to tell us about jobs they'd done, summer or not. Almost all the 173 students who sent back the forms had earned some money working. Most were very eager to hear about ways to earn more! Maybe what we learned from them will answer some of the questions you might have about getting a paying job.

## " *What job can I do?* "

There were seven jobs that kids listed most often: babysitting, mowing lawns, shoveling snow, delivering newspapers, running errands, walking dogs, and cleaning house. Runner-up jobs included washing cars, taking out the trash, and caring for animals.

A few wrote about unusual jobs. One boy fixed bikes. A girl washed dogs. Two kids made money stacking firewood.

Their answers show that jobs can be found anywhere. Look around you. See a dirty car that could use a wash? A peeling fence that would look better with a new coat of paint? A garden full of weeds? You're looking at jobs! After all, a job is simply something that someone else can't do, or doesn't want to do. So he or she will pay *you* to do it.

There are some jobs you won't be able to do simply because you are too young to be hired. Some states have strict laws that won't permit businesses and stores to hire children.

## " *Who will hire me?* "

Someone who believes you can do the job, whatever it is, will hire you. Most kids start out working for their parents, family friends, or close neighbors. These people know you best and will trust you to do a good job. People who don't know you quite so well might have to be convinced about your skill, perhaps by someone who has already hired you.

Susan Staich of Lexington, Ohio, got her first babysitting job from her aunt. Her aunt liked the way Susan took care of her child, so "she told others about me." This is called "word of mouth" recommendation. Asking satisfied customers to tell their friends about your work is one of the best ways to find more work!

Sometimes you may be lucky enough to take over someone else's job. Steve Weber of Montrose, Iowa, wrote: "My friend had the paper route. Then my brother. Then my other brother, and now me."

Christopher Daley of Detroit, Michigan, used the direct approach. "I started going around and asking, 'Do you want me to mow your lawn?'"

A good thing to do when you are looking for customers is to take a piece of paper and neatly print on it the sort of work you do, your pay rates, your name, and telephone number. You can tack this up in your apartment lobby or neighborhood store. Or you could make copies and hand them out to your neighbors when you ask them for work. That's called advertising— and it works!

We don't think kids should work for strangers, though, unless their parents check out the strangers and the job.

## " How much will I get paid? "

Deciding what pay is fair can be one of the stickiest parts of starting work. It helps to find out what other kids in your area are charging for the same sort of work. One neighborhood might be used to paying $5 for a car wash, but on your street the going rate might be $2.50 for the job.

36

Most of the kids we asked were pleased with their earnings, but the pay they reported earning varied widely. Babysitters usually charged between $1 and $2 an hour. But three said they worked for only 25¢ an hour, and one girl earned $3.50 per hour.

The amount of reponsibility you have can affect how much you charge. Walking three dogs is a lot more work than walking one, although it might take the same amount of time. Some babysitters think preparing a meal for little children is an extra chore. They charge extra for it.

One out of seven kids was disappointed with the amount of money he or she earned. One sure way to avoid being disappointed is to discuss pay rates with your employer before you start work. You might be paid by the hour or by the job. Agree on the rates beforehand. If you decide you need to change your rates, it's time for another discussion with your employer.

Don't be afraid to ask for what you think your work is worth. If people think your work costs too much, they can tell you so. Then you might want to suggest a lower price. That's called "negotiating," and it's a normal part of business.

## " Will they like my work? "

They'll like it if you "do it right the first time," suggests Kelly Buchanan of Vandalia, Ohio. Kenneth Waters of Detroit, Michigan, adds: "Be polite and ask what they want done. Don't just go to work and not know what to do."

Kids who have worked will tell you that following this advice isn't always easy. Many jobs are much more difficult than they look. When Shelly Flores of Los Angeles, California, wanted to earn money by bathing dogs, she decided "to watch my mom do it and learn to do this job the right way."

Annette Homes of Wakarusa, Indiana, had to mow a few

lawns before she was sure she could do a good job. "Don't skip corners," she advised. "Be careful of flowers. And do it as often as the lawn needs it—not whenever you feel like it."

You can't pick up that sort of information unless you get out and try the job yourself. Practice on your own lawn, wash the family car, or have your mom or dad show you how to weed a garden the right way, before you hire yourself out.

Jodi Parsons of Lexington, Ohio, tells future babysitters, "You should like little kids and meet them before you start the job." We think that finding out as much as you can about the job *before* you start is good advice for most jobs.

## " Will I like my job? "

You probably will, judging from the kids who filled out our forms. Most of them said they'd like to continue doing the jobs they had. But Asif Sheikh of Herndon, Virginia, wanted to warn kids that just about any job is both "fun *and* boring, sometimes."

Chris Deever of Beaumont, Texas, agreed with Asif. He liked mowing, but "it's hard when the weather is hot, and I get sweaty after ten minutes. The grass grows thick in Texas!"

Several students reminded kids to take the responsibilities of their jobs seriously. Keith Morgan of Vandalia, Ohio, said, "Sometimes you have to work while your friends are playing. You have to be responsible."

Now and then, of course, a job just doesn't work out. Terry Hale of Waltonville, Illinois, didn't like cutting and stacking wood. He wrote, "Try to avoid this job! You get splinters."

But most kids reported that they enjoyed getting paid for a good job, well done. Amy Schult of Wakarusa, Indiana, added something else she liked about her babysitting job: "It's fun to watch the expression on their faces when you help them do something and it turns out right."

## Thinking and Writing About the Selection

1. What should you find out from your employer before you start a job?

2. Why is it important to practice doing a job before you try to do it for an employer?

3. What do you think are some of the advantages of having a job in the summer? What are some of the disadvantages?

 4. Write an ad for a job you would like to have. Be sure to include all the information an employer would want to know.

## Applying the Key Skill
### Summarize

Write the answers to the following questions about "You *Can* Get a Job!"

1. Which of the following sentences best summarizes the fifth paragraph under the heading "Who Will Hire Me?"

   a. Advertising works.

   b. A good way to find customers is to put up signs or hand out announcements. Your advertising should tell about the work you do and the rates you charge, and give your name and phone number.

   c. If you want a job, you can put up signs in your apartment lobby or neighborhood store. Handing out copies to your neighbors is a good idea, too.

2. Summarize the last paragraph under the heading "How Much Will I Get Paid?" in two sentences.

# DICTIONARY

When Janie, one of the characters in "Kid Power," didn't know the meaning of *gross* and *net*, she asked her father. Asking people is one way to find out word meanings. Another way is to look up the words in the dictionary.

A **dictionary** is a book with information about words. In addition to telling you the meanings of words, a dictionary also shows you how to spell them and how to pronounce them. Most dictionaries have other useful information about words, too. But in order for the dictionary to be helpful to you, you must know how to use it.

You know that the words in a dictionary are listed in alphabetical order. Use the sample dictionary on the next page to review other important dictionary features.

**Guide words** are the first and last entry words on a page. *Nest* is the first entry word and *neuron* is the last entry word on the sample page.

An **entry word** is printed in bold-face type and is divided into syllables by dots. Remember that many words that end in *s*, *es*, *ed*, *er*, *est*, or *ing* are not listed as entry words. To find any of these words, you must look up the base word. For example, *nestled* is not an entry word. To find it, you must look for the base word *nestle*.

The **pronunciation** of a word is given in parentheses following its entry. The special symbols used to show you how to pronounce words are explained in the **pronunciation key. Accent marks** indicate which syllable or syllables to stress. A heavy accent mark is used for primary stress, and a lighter one for secondary stress.

| | |
|---|---|
| **guide words** | |
| **entry word** | |
| **sample sentence** | |
| **pronunciation** | |
| **part of speech** | |
| **definitions** | |

**nest** (nest) *n.* **1.** a place or structure built by a bird for holding its eggs and raising its young. **2.** a place or structure used by insects, fish, turtles, or other animals for laying eggs or raising young: *a hornet's nest.* **3.** a group of birds, animals, insects, or other animals living in a nest. **4.** a cozy place or shelter. **5.** a place where something dangerous, bad, or illegal takes place: *a smuggler's nest.* **6.** a set of similar objects made so that each fits into the next largest one. —*v.* to build or live in a nest: *The robins nested in the oak tree.*

**nest egg 1.** a natural or artificial egg left in a nest to persuade or encourage a hen to continue laying eggs on the nest. **2.** money saved for an emergency or some future need.

**nes·tle** (nes' əl) *v.* **nes·tled, nes·tling. 1.** to press or lie close; snuggle, cuddle: *The foal nestled up to its mother.* **2.** to settle oneself snugly and cozily: *We nestled by the fire.* **3.** to be located in a snug and sheltered place: *The cabin nestled among the trees.*

**nest·ling** (nest' ling) *n.* a bird too young to leave the nest.

**net¹** (net) *n.* **1.** any of various fabrics made of thread, cords, or ropes that are knotted, twisted, or woven into an open, crisscross pattern. **2.** Something made of such a fabric, used to catch, hold, or protect: *a badminton net, a butterfly net.* —*v.* **net·ted, net·ting. 1.** to catch with a net: *to net a fish.* **2.** to make into a net: *to net string.*

**net²** (net) *adj.* remaining after all deductions have been made: *net income, net profit.* —*v.* **net·ted, net·ting.** to produce or earn as a final yield or profit: *After taxes John nets $10,000 a year.* —*n.* something that remains after all deductions have been made: *The business produced a yearly net of more than $750,000.*

**neth·er** (neth' ər) *adj.* lying below; lower.

**net·tle** (net' əl) *n.* any of a group of weedy plants whose leaves are covered with tiny hairs that sting the skin when touched. —*v.* **net·tled, net·tling.** to cause annoyance to; irritate; rile.

**net·work** (net' wėrk') *n.* **1.** any system of lines or structures that cross: *a network of highways.* **2.** a group of radio or television stations connected so that they may all broadcast the same program.

**neu·rol·o·gy** (nü rol' ə jē, nū rol' ə jē) *n.* the branch of medicine concerned with the nervous system and its disorders.

**neu·ron** (nür' on, nūr' on) *n.* the basic unit of the nervous system, consisting of a cell body and its fibers. The neuron receives nerve impulses and sends them to other cells.

a bat, ā cake, ä father, är car, âr dare; e hen, ē me, ėr term; i bib, ī kite, ir clear; o top, ō rope, ô saw, oi coin, ôr fork, ou out; u sun, ů book, ü moon, ū cute; ə about, taken

| |
|---|
| **pronunciation key** |

The **part of speech** is given by abbreviations. The abbreviations for the parts of speech are listed below.

| | | |
|---|---|---|
| *n.* noun | *prep.* preposition | *conj.* conjunction |
| *adj.* adjective | *v.* verb | *interj.* interjection |
| *pron.* pronoun | *adv.* adverb | |

The **definition** is the meaning of the word. Many words have more than one definition.

A **sample sentence** is sometimes included. It is an example of actual use that can often help you better understand the meaning of the word.

**ACTIVITY A** Number your paper from 1 to 5. Write the answers to the questions on your paper.

1. Which word would appear first in the dictionary?

    a. gross      b. grosgrain      c. grotesque

2. *Profit* would appear on a dictionary page with which guide words?

    a. process/profession   b. profiteer/project   c. profile/progress

3. Which word would be found on a dictionary page with the guide words *silly/simplify*?

    a. silver      b. silk      c. simply

4. What entry word would you look for to find out about *contracting*?

    a. contract      b. contractor      c. tractor

5. What do accent marks show?

    a. stressed syllable    b. first syllable    c. number of syllables

**ACTIVITY B** Number your paper from 1 to 8. Use the sample dictionary page to answer the questions below. Write the answers on your paper.

1. How many syllables does *neurology* have? Which syllable is accented?

2. Which syllable of *network* receives primary stress? Which receives secondary stress?

3. What word in the pronunciation key has the same vowel sound as the second *o* in *neurology*?

4. What is the meaning of each underlined word as it is used in the sentence?

   a. Ted hauled in the fish with a <u>net</u>.
   b. The students had a <u>net</u> profit of $15.00.

5. What is the part of speech of each underlined word as it is used in the sentence? What is its meaning?

   a. Pamela put the <u>nest</u> of boxes inside one another.
   b. A family of wrens <u>nested</u> in the old barn.

6. Which definition of *network* explains how the word is used in the following sentences?

   a. Underneath the floor of the computer room was a network of cables.
   b. The major networks agreed to broadcast the speech.

7. What words are synonyms for *nettle* as a verb?

8. Why might someone want a nest egg?

# THE DOUGHNUT MACHINE

## ROBERT McCLOSKEY

*Homer Price has a knack for getting into sticky situations. Yet, he always manages to come up with a plan. Even a disastrous situation becomes a very successful enterprise for Homer.*

When Homer and his mother got to Centerburg they stopped at the lunch room, and after Aunt Agnes had come out and said, "My, how that boy does grow!" which is what she always said, she went off with Homer's mother in the car. Homer went into the lunch room and said, "Howdy, Uncle Ulysses!"

"Oh, hello, Homer. You're just in time," said Uncle Ulysses. "I've been going over this automatic doughnut machine, oiling the machinery and cleaning the works . . . wonderful things, these labor-saving devices."

"Yep," agreed Homer, and he picked up a cloth and started polishing the metal trimmings while Uncle Ulysses tinkered with the inside workings.

"Look here, Homer," sighed Uncle Ulysses. "You've got a mechanical mind. See if you can find where these two pieces fit in. I'm going across to the barber shop for a spell, 'cause

47

in the machine? You could turn the switch and make a few doughnuts to have on hand for the crowd after the movie . . . if you don't mind."

"O.K." said Homer. "I'll take care of everything."

A few minutes later a customer came in. Homer looked up from putting the last piece in the doughnut machine and said, "Good evening, Sir, what can I do for you?"

"Well, young feller, I'd like a cup o' coffee and some doughnuts," said the customer.

"I'm sorry, Mister, but we won't have any doughnuts for about half an hour, until I can mix some dough and start this machine."

"Well, Bud, I'm in no real hurry so I'll just have a cup o' coffee and wait around a bit for the doughnuts. Fresh doughnuts are always worth waiting for is what I always say."

"O.K.," said Homer, and he drew a cup of coffee from Uncle Ulysses' super automatic coffee maker.

"Nice place you've got here," said the customer.

there's somethin' I've got to talk to the sheriff about. There won't be much business here until the double feature is over and I'll be back before then."

Then as Uncle Ulysses went out the door he said, "Uh, Homer, after you get the pieces in place, would you mind mixing up a batch of doughnut batter and putting it

"Oh, yes," replied Homer. "This is a very up and coming lunch room with all the latest improvements."

"Yes," said the stranger, "must be a good business. I'm in business too. A traveling man in outdoor advertising. I'm a sandwich man, Mr. Gabby's my name."

"My name is Homer. I'm glad to meet you, Mr. Gabby. It must be a fine profession, traveling and advertising sandwiches."

"Oh no," said Mr. Gabby, "I don't advertise sandwiches, I just wear any kind of an ad, one sign on front and one sign on behind, this way . . . Like a sandwich. Ya know what I mean?"

"Oh, I see. That must be fun, and you travel too?" asked Homer as he got out the flour and the baking powder.

Just then a large shiny black car stopped in front of the lunch room and a chauffeur helped a lady out of the rear door. They both came inside and the lady smiled at Homer and said, "We've stopped for a light snack. Some doughnuts

and coffee would be simply marvelous."

Then Homer said, "I'm sorry, Ma'm, but the doughnuts won't be ready until I make this batter and start Uncle Ulysses' doughnut machine."

"Well now aren't *you* a clever young man to know how to make *doughnuts*!"

"Well," blushed Homer, "I've never done it before but I've got a recipe to follow."

"Now, young man, you simply must allow me to help. You know, I haven't made doughnuts for years, but I know the best recipe for doughnuts. It's marvelous, and we really must use it."

"But, Ma'm . . ." said Homer.

"Now just *wait* till you taste these doughnuts," said the lady. "Do you have an apron?" she asked, as she took off her fur coat, her rings, and her jewelry and rolled up her sleeves. "Charles," she said to the chauffeur, "hand me that baking powder, that's right, and, young man, we'll need some nutmeg."

So Homer and the chauffeur stood by and handed things and cracked the eggs while the lady mixed and stirred. Mr. Gabby sat on his stool, sipped his coffee, and looked on with great interest.

"There!" said the lady when all of the ingredients were mixed. "Just *wait* till you taste these doughnuts!"

"It looks like an awful lot of batter," said Homer as he stood

on a chair and poured it into the doughnut machine with the help of the chauffeur. "It's about *ten* times as much as Uncle Ulysses ever makes."

"But wait till you taste them!" said the lady with an eager look and a smile.

Homer got down from the chair and pushed a button on the machine marked *Start*. Rings of batter started dropping into the hot fat. After a ring of batter was cooked on one side, an automatic gadget turned it over and the other side would cook. Then another automatic gadget gave the doughnut a little push and it rolled neatly down a little chute, all ready to eat.

"That's a simply *fascinating* machine," said the lady as she waited for the first doughnut to roll out.

"Here, young man, *you* must have the first one. Now isn't that just *too* delicious!? Isn't it simply marvelous?"

"Yes, Ma'm, it's very good," replied Homer as the lady handed doughnuts to Charles and to Mr. Gabby and asked if they didn't think they were simply divine doughnuts.

Homer poured some coffee for the lady and her chauffeur and for Mr. Gabby, and a glass of milk for himself. Then they all sat down at the lunch counter to enjoy another few doughnuts apiece.

"I'm so glad you enjoy my doughnuts," said the lady. "But now, Charles, we really must be going. If you will just take this apron, Homer, and put two dozen doughnuts in a bag to take along, we'll be on our way. And, Charles, don't forget to pay the young man." She rolled down her sleeves and put on her jewelry, then Charles managed to get her into her big fur coat.

"Good night, young man, I haven't had so much fun in years. I *really* haven't!" said the lady, as she went out the door and into the big shiny car.

"Those are sure good doughnuts," said Mr. Gabby as the car moved off.

"You bet!" said Homer. Then he and Mr. Gabby stood and watched the automatic doughnut machine make doughnuts.

After a few dozen more doughnuts had rolled down the little chute, Homer said, "I

guess that's about enough doughnuts to sell to the after theater customers. I'd better turn the machine off."

Homer pushed the button marked *Stop* and there was a little click, but nothing happened. The rings of batter kept right on dropping into the hot fat, and an automatic gadget kept right on turning them over, and another automatic gadget kept right on giving them a little push, and the doughnuts kept right on rolling down the little chute, all ready to eat.

"That's funny," said Homer, "I'm sure that's the right button!" He pushed it again, but the automatic doughnut maker kept right on making doughnuts.

"Well I guess I must have put one of those pieces in backwards," said Homer.

"Then it might stop if you pushed the button marked *Start*," said Mr. Gabby.

Homer did, and the doughnuts still kept rolling down the little chute, just as regular as a clock can tick.

"I guess we could sell a few more doughnuts," said Homer, "but I'd better telephone Uncle Ulysses over at the barber shop." Homer gave the number and while he waited for someone to answer he counted thirty-seven doughnuts roll down the little chute.

Finally someone answered "Hello! This is the sarber bhop, I mean the barber shop."

"Oh, hello, sheriff. This is Homer. Could I speak to Uncle Ulysses?"

"Well, he's playing cards right now," said the sheriff. "Anythin' I can tell 'im?"

"Yes," said Homer. "I pushed the button marked *Stop* on the doughnut machine but the rings of batter keep right on dropping into the hot fat, and an automatic gadget keeps right on turning them over, and another automatic gadget keeps giving them a little push, and the doughnuts keep right on rolling down the little chute! It won't stop!"

"O.K. Wold the hire, I mean, hold the wire and I'll tell 'im." Then Homer looked over his shoulder and counted another twenty-one doughnuts roll down the little chute, all ready to eat. Then the sheriff said, "He'll be right over . . . Just gotta finish this hand."

"That's good," said Homer. "G'by, sheriff."

The window was full of doughnuts by now so Homer and Mr. Gabby had to hustle around and start stacking them on plates and trays and lining them up on the counter.

"Sure are a lot of doughnuts!" said Homer.

"You bet!" said Mr. Gabby. "I lost count at twelve hundred and two and that was quite a while back."

People had begun to gather outside the lunch room window, and someone was saying, "There are almost as many doughnuts as there are people in Centerburg, and I wonder how in tarnation Ulysses thinks he can sell all of 'em!"

Every once in a while somebody would come inside and buy some, but while somebody bought two to eat and a dozen to take home, the machine made three dozen more.

By the time Uncle Ulysses and the sheriff arrived and pushed through the crowd, the lunch room was a calamity of doughnuts! Doughnuts in the window, doughnuts piled high on the shelves, doughnuts stacked on plates, doughnuts lined up twelve deep all along the counter, and doughnuts still rolling down the little chute, just as regular as a clock can tick.

"Hello, sheriff, hello, Uncle Ulysses, we're having a little trouble here," said Homer.

Uncle Ulysses groaned and said, "What will Aggy say? We'll never sell 'em all."

Then Mr. Gabby, who hadn't said anything for a long time, stopped piling doughnuts and said, "What you need is an advertising man. Ya know what I mean? You got the doughnuts, ya gotta create a market. Understand? It's balancing the demand with the supply. That sort of thing."

"Yep!" said Homer. "Mr. Gabby's right. We have to enlarge our market. He's an advertising sandwich man, so if we

hire him, he can walk up and down in front of the theater and get the customers."

"You're hired, Mr. Gabby!" said Uncle Ulysses.

Then everybody pitched in to paint the signs and to get Mr. Gabby sandwiched between. They painted "SALE ON DOUGHNUTS" in big letters on the window, too.

"I certainly hope this advertising works," said Uncle Ulysses, wagging his head. "Aggy'll certainly throw a fit if it don't."

The sheriff went outside to keep order, because there was quite a crowd by now—all looking at the doughnuts and guessing how many thousand there were, and watching new ones roll down the little chute, just as regular as a clock can tick. Homer and Uncle Ulysses kept stacking doughnuts. Once in a while somebody bought a few, but not very often.

Then Mr. Gabby came back and said, "Say, you know there's not much use o' me advertisin' at the theater. The show's all over, and besides

almost everybody in town is out front watching that machine make doughnuts!"

"Looks like you will have to hire a truck to waul 'em ahay, I mean haul 'em away!!" said the sheriff who had just come in. Just then there was a noise and a shoving out front and the lady from the shiny black car and her chauffeur came pushing through the crowd and into the lunch room.

"Oh, gracious!" she gasped, ignoring the doughnuts, "I've lost my diamond bracelet, and I know I left it here on the counter," she said, pointing to a place where the doughnuts were piled in stacks of two dozen.

"Yes, Ma'm, I guess you forgot it when you helped make the batter," said Homer.

Then they moved all the doughnuts around and looked for the diamond bracelet, but they couldn't find it anywhere. Meanwhile the doughnuts kept rolling down the little chute, just as regular as a clock can tick.

After they had looked all around, the sheriff cast a suspicious eye on Mr. Gabby, but Homer said, "He's all right, sheriff, he didn't take it. He's a friend of mine."

Then the lady said, "I'll offer a reward of one hundred dollars for that bracelet! It really *must* be found! . . . it *really* must!"

"Now don't you worry, lady," said the sheriff. "I'll get your bracelet back!"

"This is terrible!" said Uncle Ulysses. "First all of these doughnuts and then on top of all that, a lost diamond bracelet!"

Homer sat down and thought hard. Before twenty more doughnuts could roll down the little chute he shouted, "SAY! I know where the bracelet is! It was lying here on the counter and got mixed up in the batter by mistake! The bracelet is cooked inside one of these doughnuts!"

"Why . . . I really believe you're right," said the lady through her tears. "Isn't that *amazing*? Simply *amazing*!"

"I'll be durn'd!" said the sheriff.

"Ohh-h!" moaned Uncle Ulysses. "Now we have to break up all of these doughnuts to find it. Think of the *pieces*. Think of the *crumbs*! Think of what *Aggy* will say!"

"Nope," said Homer. "We won't have to break them up. I've got a plan."

So Homer and the advertising man took some cardboard and some paint and printed another sign. They put this sign in the window, and the sandwich man wore two more signs that said the same thing and walked around in the crowd out front.

THEN . . . The doughnuts began to sell! *Everybody* wanted to buy doughnuts, *dozens* of doughnuts!

And that's not all. Everybody bought coffee to dunk the doughnuts into. Those that didn't buy coffee bought milk or soda. It kept Homer and the lady and the chauffeur and Uncle Ulysses and the sheriff

FRESH DOUGHNUTS
2 FOR 5¢
$ WHILE THEY LAST
$100.00 PRIZE
FOR FINDING
A BRACELET
INSIDE A DOUGHNUT
P.S. YOU HAVE TO GIVE THE
BRACELET BACK

busy waiting on the people who wanted to buy doughnuts.

When all but the last couple of hundred doughnuts had been sold, Rupert Black shouted, "I GAWT IT!!" and sure enough there was the diamond bracelet inside of his doughnut!

Then Rupert went home with a hundred dollars, the citizens of Centerburg went home full of doughnuts, the lady and her chauffeur drove off with the diamond bracelet, and Homer went home with his mother

when she stopped by with Aunt Aggy.

As Homer went out of the door, Uncle Ulysses was saying, "The rings of batter kept right on dropping into the hot fat, and the automatic gadget kept right on turning them over, and the other automatic gadget kept right on giving them a little push, and the doughnuts kept right on rolling down the little chute just as regular as a clock can tick—they just kept right on a comin', an' a comin', an' a comin'."

## Thinking and Writing About the Selection

1. What two things did Uncle Ulysses ask Homer to do while he was gone?

2. Why did a crowd begin to gather in front of the lunch room?

3. Was the doughnut machine really a labor-saving device? Why or why not?

4. List five things Homer and Uncle Ulysses could have done with the doughnuts if they hadn't sold them.

## Applying the Key Skill
### Drawing Conclusions

Use complete sentences to answer the following questions about "The Doughnut Machine."

1. Why did Homer conclude that Mr. Gabby's job was advertising sandwiches? What did Mr. Gabby really do?

2. When the doughnut machine kept on making doughnuts, what did Homer conclude had caused the problem?

3. What information did Homer use to conclude that the lady's bracelet had been cooked inside of a doughnut?

# ROBERT McCLOSKEY

*"It is just sort of an accident that I write books. I really think up stories in pictures and just fill in between the pictures with a sentence or a paragraph or a few pages of words."*

For someone who says he only "accidentally" writes books, Robert McCloskey has done rather well for himself. Of his first six books, two won the Caldecott Medal and two were runner-ups!

As a boy growing up in Hamilton, Ohio, before World War I, McCloskey was interested not only in art, but also in music and inventions. The influence of all these hobbies later led to an after-school job at the YMCA teaching other boys how to play the harmonica, make model airplanes, or do soap carving. It's easy to see how these experiences played a part in the creation of the Homer Price stories.

McCloskey played oboe in high school and was an artist for the school newspaper and yearbook. After three years of study in Boston, he called on a children's book editor, who told him he needed more training in drawing. After two more years of study, his first book, *Lentil*, was accepted by that same editor.

Robert McCloskey has many interests but art and design remain his chief concerns. "I should like to clamor for the teaching of drawing and design to every child, right along with reading and writing," he has said.

**More to Read** *Homer Price, Centerburg Tales*

# CONTEXT CLUES

When you come across a word you don't understand, you know that you can ask someone to explain it to you or that you can look it up in the dictionary. There is another way you can discover word meanings—by using context clues. **Context clues** can be other words that you do know in a sentence. Other sentences can also provide you with context clues.

Read the sentences below from "The Doughnut Machine," and pay particular attention to the word *calamity*.

> By the time Uncle Ulysses and the sheriff arrived and pushed through the crowd, the lunch room was a calamity of doughnuts! Doughnuts in the window, doughnuts piled high on the shelves, doughnuts stacked on plates, doughnuts lined up twelve deep all along the counter, and doughnuts still rolling down the little chute, just as regular as a clock can tick.

If you don't know the meaning of the word *calamity*, you can figure it out from the context clues provided by the second sentence. The description of the room with doughnuts everywhere and more doughnuts still coming out of the machine should help you realize that *calamity* means "a disaster" or "an event that causes great misfortune."

Of course, you may still want to check the definition you come up with against that in a dictionary. But you will find that using context clues to figure out meanings of unknown words as you read will add to your enjoyment of the story. You can continue reading without interruption and not lose the thread of the plot.

**ACTIVITY A** Use context clues to help you choose the correct meaning of each underlined word. Write the word and its meaning on your paper.

1. Automobiles came to a halt as the traffic light turned red. When it flashed "walk," <u>pedestrians</u> scurried across the street.

   a. children    b. carts    c. walkers

2. Jake <u>sauntered</u> down the street, hands in his pockets and whistling. He didn't seem in any hurry to go anywhere.

   a. walked slowly    b. raced    c. rode

3. Mark's letter was hardly <u>legible</u>. The *d's* looked like *l's*, and many words seemed to run together.

   a. worth anything    b. easily read    c. very interesting

**ACTIVITY B** Write a meaning for each underlined word on your paper. Check your definition in a dictionary. Then write a sentence of your own using each underlined word.

1. Every time Barbara brought up the question of having a pet, her parents said, "No." At last they <u>relented</u> and agreed that she could have a bird or a fish.
2. The soldiers wore <u>khaki</u> uniforms that blended with the color of the ground and the vegetation.
3. The metal <u>android</u> was programmed to count the cars that passed by the highway marker.
4. Several people responded to the school's <u>plea</u> for used automobile tires.
5. The <u>maximum</u> number of people who could attend the banquet was 75 because the dining room was not very large.

61

# THE Toothpaste MILLIONAIRE

## The Joe Smiley Show

A one-act play by Susan Nanus
based-on the novel by Jean Merrill

*Rufus Mayflower was a young man with ideas who became a millionaire. He didn't set out to build a successful enterprise. He just had the initiative to put his ideas, himself, and his friends to work. Rufus became quite a celebrity. In this play, he is being interviewed by talk-show host Joe Smiley.*

## CHARACTERS

Joe Smiley
Rufus Mayflower ✓
Kate MacKinstrey
Mr. Conti
Clem
Josie ✓
Lee Lu
James
Auctioneer ✓
Customer #1

Customer #2
Customer #3
Hector
Josh
Sharon
Members of
  the Class
Mr. Perkell
Mr. Perkell's
  Secretary

*A long bench is set up across the center of the stage. A large portable chalkboard is behind the bench. Downstage left is a long table with several bowls on it. Downstage right is a smaller table and two chairs.*

*As the curtain opens, JOE SMILEY and RUFUS are seated at the small table.*

**JOE**: Welcome to the Joe Smiley Show! Today we have a fantastic young guest who has used his fantastic young brain to become a millionaire! Meet Rufus Mayflower of East Cleveland, Ohio.
(*to Rufus*) Welcome, Rufus!

**RUFUS**: Thank you, Mr. Smiley.

**JOE**: Now, Rufus, my first question is one that I know everyone wants to ask. How did you figure out how to make so much money?

**RUFUS**: Well, I wasn't trying to make money, just to make toothpaste.

**JOE**: All right, Rufus. What gave you that brilliant idea?

**RUFUS**: It all started when I was doing some shopping for my mother at the Cut-Rate Drugstore with my friend Kate.

(*KATE comes out and stands in the middle of the stage.*

*RUFUS joins her. KATE panto-
mimes pushing a shopping
cart, while RUFUS pulls out a
list.)*

**RUFUS**: Now, let's see. I need
toothpaste.

**KATE**: Here it is.

*(She pretends to hand him a
tube.)*

**RUFUS**: One dollar and thirty-
nine cents for a six-inch tube
of toothpaste? That's crazy!

**KATE**: It's better than this
other one for a dollar and
eighty-nine cents.

**RUFUS**: That's even crazier!
What can be in those tubes,
anyway? Just some peppermint
flavoring and some paste.

**KATE**: Maybe the paste is
expensive to make.

**RUFUS**: Who knows? I never
tried, but I bet it isn't hard.
Put that tube back.

**KATE**: But Rufus, your mother
said to get toothpaste. You
can't help it if it's expensive.

**RUFUS**: I'll make her some. I
bet I can make her a gallon for
less than a dollar.

*(KATE goes and sits on the bench. RUFUS returns to the small table to continue the interview with Joe Smiley.)*

**JOE**: Fantastic! I suppose you stayed up day and night creating your secret formula.

**RUFUS**: No, I just used some stuff anybody can buy for a few cents and mix up in a few minutes. The main ingredient was plain old baking soda.

**JOE**: What happened next?

**RUFUS**: The next morning, Kate stopped by on the way to school.

*(RUFUS goes over to the long table with the bowls. KATE joins him.)*

**KATE**: What are you making?

**RUFUS**: I already made it.

*(He hands KATE a spoonful.)*

Don't eat it. Rub a little on your teeth.

*(KATE tries some.)*

**KATE**: What's in here?

**RUFUS**: A drop of peppermint oil. I've got enough for forty tubes of toothpaste here!

**KATE**: Wow! Wait until we tell the kids at school! Come on, Rufus.

*(KATE and RUFUS hurry to the bench and sit down. CLEM, JOSIE, and LEE LU come out and join them. They face MR. CONTI, their math teacher, at the chalkboard.)*

**MR. CONTI**: All right, class, take out your math books.

*(RUFUS passes a note to CLEM, who hands it to JOSIE, who hands it to LEE LU, who hands it to KATE. KATE opens the note.)*

**MR. CONTI**: Kate MacKinstrey, would you please bring me that note?

**KATE**: Well, it's not exactly a note, Mr. Conti.

**MR. CONTI**: I see. I suppose it's a math problem.

**KATE**: It looks like a math problem, Mr. Conti.

**MR. CONTI**: (*reading*) There are about 226 million people in the United States. Each one buys about ten tubes of toothpaste a year. That's two billion two-hundred-sixty million tubes of toothpaste a year! If an inventor made a new toothpaste, sold only *one* billion tubes, and made a one-cent profit on each tube, how much would he make? (*looking up*) Well, class, what would you do to figure it out?

**CLEM**: You'd have to take one billion times one cent or .01. That comes out to . . .

**ALL**: Ten million dollars!

**JOSIE**: Did you invent a toothpaste, Rufus?

**CLEM**: What's it called?

**LEE LU**: How much does it cost?

**MR. CONTI**: All right, class, quiet down.

*(RUFUS gets up and goes back to sit at the small table with JOE SMILEY.)*

**RUFUS**: I called it *Toothpaste.*

**JOE**: Not *Sparkle* or *Shine*?

**RUFUS**: No. Just plain *Toothpaste.* Kate and I packed it into sterilized baby jars, and we delivered them to customers on our bikes.

**JOE**: How much did you charge?

**RUFUS**: It cost me two cents to make, so I charged three cents unless I had to mail it somewhere out of town. Then I included postage. In a couple of months, I had so many customers that my math class had to help me out.

*(RUFUS, KATE, CLEM, JOSIE, and LEE LU go over to the long table with the bowls. They pantomime filling the jars with toothpaste.)*

**CLEM**: Rufus, what would you do if you had to pay us to do all this work?

**JOSIE**: We spend hours washing out baby jars and filling them with *Toothpaste.*

**RUFUS**: I don't have any profits to pay anybody yet. I've got to use the money I'm making to buy more stuff for *Toothpaste*. But I'll tell you what. I'll give you stock in my company.

**CLEM**: Stock? What good is that?

**RUFUS**: At the end of the year, every stockholder will get a share of the year's profits.

**KATE**: Like in that game you have called "Stock Market"?

**RUFUS**: Right. Anybody who puts in a hundred hours helping me make *Toothpaste* gets a stock certificate, which will entitle him or her to a share of the company's profits. I'll use the stock certificates from my game.

**KATE**: Well, I've already worked more than two hundred hours.

**RUFUS**: So you are the first stockholder.

*(RUFUS returns to JOE SMILEY to continue the interview.)*

**JOE**: This is mind-boggling! What happened next?

**RUFUS**: The next part of the story belongs to Kate.

*(KATE talks to LEE LU, CLEM, and JOSIE who are still working at the long table.)*

**KATE**: You know, I wish we had real tubes instead of these baby jars.

**LEE LU**: It sure would look better.

**KATE**: I wonder if I can find any.

**CLEM**: I bet they'd be expensive even if you could.

**KATE**: I'm going to start looking around.

*(She looks at her watch.)*

Oh, oh, I have to get home for supper. See you tomorrow.

*(KATE leaves the long table and goes back to the bench.*

*Her brother, JAMES, comes out reading a newspaper and sits on the bench.)*

**KATE**: Hi, James.

**JAMES**: Don't bother me, I'm reading.

**KATE**: Well, excuse me! I don't call that reading. It's just another list of companies going out of business.

**JAMES**: It can be very informative. Now, let's see . . . *(reads)* . . . Complete furnishings of ice cream parlor . . . Ferris wheel swings . . . 15 trailer trucks . . . 50 gross high-quality aluminum tubes . . .

**KATE**: Did you say *tubes*? Let me see.

**(She looks at the paper.)**

It doesn't give the price.

**JAMES**: Of course not. You have to go to the auction and bid on them.

**KATE**: An auction? Where?

**JAMES**: At Pulaski Brothers Warehouse. Somebody with a lot of tubes just went out of business.

**(JAMES walks off. KATE goes behind the bench. Several CUSTOMERS come on stage and stand near KATE at the**

68

auction. *The AUCTIONEER comes out and faces the CUSTOMERS and KATE.*)

**AUCTIONEER**: Item Number 76: aluminum tubes, 50 gross. How much am I bid by the gross? Bidder takes the lot.

**KATE**: How much is a gross? I can't remember. Let's see 50 dozen is 600 and that's already a lot.

**(to AUCTIONEER)**

Excuse me, sir. Can I just bid on a couple of dozen?

**AUCTIONEER**: The bid is for the whole lot. Who'll bid five cents a gross?

**CUSTOMER #1**: Five cents!

**KATE**: Six cents!

**AUCTIONEER**: Six cents for the lady.

**CUSTOMER #2**: Seven cents!

**KATE**: Eight! We really need those tubes.

**AUCTIONEER**: Anyone for nine?

**KATE**: TEN!

**CUSTOMER #1**: I give up.

**CUSTOMER #2**: Me, too.

**AUCTIONEER**: Sold to the lady for ten cents a gross.

**KATE**: Oh, well, I guess we'll use up six hundred tubes.

**CUSTOMER #3**: Six hundred? You just bought seven thousand two hundred tubes.

**KATE**: Seven thousand two hundred!

*(The CUSTOMERS and the AUCTIONEER exit. KATE goes back to the long table with JOSIE, LEE LU, and CLEM.)*

**KATE**: I forgot that a gross is a dozen dozen. Twelve times twelve times fifty is what I bought.

**LEE LU**: Isn't there some kind of machine for filling tubes?

**CLEM**: What about the place that all these tubes came from?

**KATE**: Let's see if there's a name on the box.

*(She pantomimes looking at a box and reads:)* Happy Lips Lotion Company.

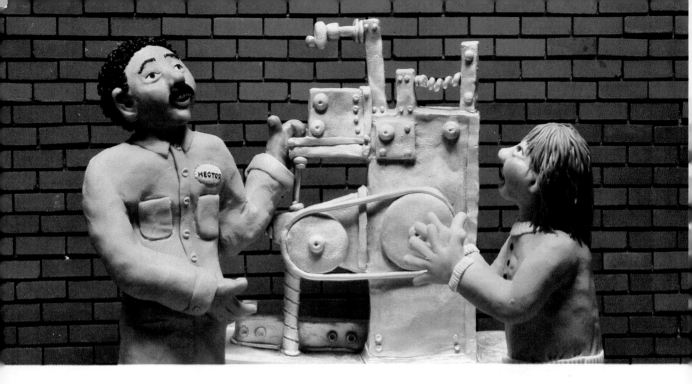

**KATE**: I am going to the Happy Lips Lotion Company to check it out.

(*HECTOR comes out on stage. He moves away the bench and brings the chalkboard downstage. He flips the chalkboard around to display a diagram of a complicated machine.*)

(*KATE comes up to HECTOR.*)

**HECTOR**: Can I help you?

**KATE**: No thank you. I'm just looking.

**HECTOR**: Oh?

**KATE**: For a machine. I have a friend who needs a certain kind of machine for filling toothpaste tubes.

**HECTOR**: Did you say toothpaste tubes?

**KATE**: Like this.

(*She pulls out a tube and shows it to him.*)

**HECTOR**: Oh, sure, that's the Number 5 aluminum round-end.

**KATE**: Are you in the toothpaste business?

**HECTOR**: No. I was a mechanic for the Happy Lips Lotion Company. Is *your* friend in the toothpaste business?

**KATE**: Yes. Is there a tube-filling machine still in there?

**HECTOR**: Is there! It's the most beautiful piece of machinery you ever saw.

**(HECTOR shows KATE the machine on the chalkboard.)**

**HECTOR**: The Happy Lips Lotion Company owed the owner of the building so much rent that they had to leave him this machine. The owner is paying me a small salary to keep an eye on the factory.

**KATE**: It looks like a wonderful machine.

**HECTOR**: Yes, ma'am. If your friend rented the place and hired me to look after the machinery, we could be in full production tomorrow. Have you got a lot of orders?

**KATE**: More than five thousand.

**HECTOR**: Do you think you can swing it? The rent's about three-hundred dollars a month.

**KATE**: The rent? Oh. I forgot about that. And how much would *you* want, Hector?

**HECTOR**: I was getting eight dollars an hour from Happy Lips. I guess that much would be fine.

**KATE**: Hmm. I think we better have a stockholders' meeting.

**(The interview continues. RUFUS is talking with JOE SMILEY.)**

**RUFUS**: So we all got together and discussed it. By now, we had a lot of other kids working with us, too.

**(CLEM, JOSIE, and LEE LU remove the bowls from the table. They bring in chairs. KATE and RUFUS each sit at one end of the long table. CLEM, JOSIE, LEE LU, JOSH, SHARON, and other MEMBERS OF THE CLASS sit around the sides.)**

**RUFUS**: Let's see, I'd say we need about $15,000.

**LEE LU**: Well, where do we get that? Just walk into a bank and ask for it?

**RUFUS**: Why not? Isn't that what other business people do? I'll just go down to Everybody's

Friendly Bank and borrow the money!

(*MR. PERKELL and the SEC-RETARY move the bench in front of the chalkboard. The SECRETARY sits at one end of the bench, MR. PERKELL at the other. KATE and RUFUS leave the long table and approach the SECRETARY.*)

**SECRETARY**: May I help you?

**RUFUS**: Yes, we'd like to see Mr. Perkell, the Vice President, please.

**SECRETARY**: I'm sorry, Mr. Perkell has an appointment at four o'clock.

**RUFUS**: I know. My name is Rufus Mayflower, and I'm Mr. Perkell's appointment.

**SECRETARY**: *You're* Mr. Mayflower?

**MR. PERKELL**: (*comes to the SECRETARY's end of the bench*) Hello. What can I do for you?

**RUFUS**: You can lend us money for the business I'm starting. I have a product called *Toothpaste*.

**MR. PERKELL**: Ah, yes, I've heard of you. Just plain toothpaste, the kind that gets your teeth clean.

**KATE**: That's us! Can you lend us the money?

**MR. PERKELL**: I'm afraid not.

**KATE**: Why not? Your commercials say you lend money to everybody.

**MR. PERKELL**: Well, not exactly *everybody*.

**RUFUS**: In other words, not kids.

(*MR. PERKELL and the SEC-RETARY walk off. RUFUS and KATE go back to the long table. HECTOR brings a chair and joins them.*)

**HECTOR**: I can't believe it! Just because you're under age, they turn you down! We have the machine. We have the product. We can make it big!

The Joe Smiley Show

**RUFUS**: I believe you, Hector. I believe you would even lend me the money, if you had it.

**HECTOR**: You bet I would!

**RUFUS**: Great! Hector, you can go to Mr. Perkell and ask him to lend you the money.

**HECTOR**: Me?

**RUFUS**: I'll hire you as manager of the toothpaste factory. The money you borrow will be used to pay your first year's salary, to pay the rent, and to buy more tubes. I'll also give you shares of stock in the company.

**HECTOR**: You mean I'd own part of the business? That would be beautiful!

*(RUFUS goes back and sits with JOE SMILEY.)*

**JOE**: Absolutely fantastic! And did you get the money?

**RUFUS**: We sure did. Then we had to find more customers. So we decided to advertise. My friend Lee Lu had a movie camera, so we all got together and decided to create the Absolutely Honest Commercial.

*(CLEM and JOSIE and KATE move stage center. LEE LU is*

*on his knees in front of them pantomiming shooting a movie camera.)*

**LEE LU**: Okay, action!

**CLEM**: No fancy names.

**JOSIE**: No fancy promises.

**KATE**: All *Toothpaste* claims to do is clean your teeth.

**CLEM**: We make it as cheaply as possible so we don't have to charge you very much.

**KATE**: That's why *Toothpaste* comes in a plain cardboard box. All to keep the prices low.

**JOSIE**: We only make a one-cent profit on a tube, but we think it does the job as well as the more expensive kinds.

**LEE LU**: CUT!

*(JOE SMILEY continues the interview with RUFUS.)*

**JOE**: How big is this business now?

**RUFUS**: Let's put it this way. We had to order three more machines and hire ten people to work full time.

**JOE**: Fantastic! Well, Rufus, it looks like you really are a *Toothpaste* Millionaire. What's your next step? Do you have any new ideas up your sleeve?

**RUFUS**: *(smiles)* Not yet. But I'm not worried. All I have to do is walk into another store, or take a ride on my bike, or just keep my eyes and ears open and my brain working. Something will come to me.

**JOE**: Isn't he *fantastic*?

the end

## Thinking and Writing About the Selection

1. What made Rufus decide to get into the tooth-paste business?
2. Why did Rufus issue stock certificates?
3. How was the commercial for *Toothpaste* different from commercials you have seen?
4. Rufus took an ordinary product and found a way to make and sell it very successfully. If Rufus asked you for an idea for his next enter-prise, what would you suggest? How would you "sell" him on the idea?

## Applying the Key Skill
### Facts and Opinions

Write these three headings on your paper: Fact, Opinion, and Part Fact/Part Opinion. Then read the sentences below. Write each sentence under the proper heading.

1. One six-inch tube of toothpaste at the Cut-Rate Drugstore costs one dollar and thirty-nine cents.
2. The prices at Cut-Rate Drugstore are certainly not cut-rate.
3. Rufus came up with the fantastic idea of making his own toothpaste.
4. *Toothpaste* was less expensive than other brands.
5. Unlike other commercials, the commercial for *Toothpaste* was absolutely honest.

# AD IT UP!

In "The Toothpaste Millionaire," Rufus and his friends decided to advertise to find more customers for *Toothpaste*. Some of the things they said in their commercial were **facts**. For example, *Toothpaste* comes in a plain cardboard box.

Some of the things said in the commercial were said in order to **persuade**, or convince, people to buy *Toothpaste*. For example, We make only a one-cent profit on a tube, but we think it does the job as well as the more expensive kinds.

When reading advertisements, it is important to recognize the difference between language that is used to state facts and language that is used to persuade.

Read the advertisement below. Find the sentences that state facts. Then find the sentences that are used to persuade.

Citizens' Bank is the friendliest bank in town! You will find it very convenient to bank with us right here in Pleasantville. If you open an account with us this month, you will receive a free gift. Not only that, but there is no charge for the checks you write. We will also be happy to talk to you about a loan. We lend money to everyone who has a need. We can arrange convenient terms if you need money for a new home, for home improvements, or for your business. We are open Mondays through Fridays, from 9:00 A.M. until 3:00 P.M.

# FACTS AND OPINIONS

Read the sentences below about "The Toothpaste Millionaire." See if you can decide how the kinds of statements they make are different.

• Joe Smiley interviewed Rufus Mayflower on his talk show.
• Joe Smiley did a good job interviewing Rufus Mayflower.

The first sentence states a fact. **Facts** are statements that can be checked and can be proven to be true. You can check the first statement by reading the play.

The second sentence states an opinion. **Opinions** are statements that express personal feelings. Opinions cannot be proven or disproven. When people give an opinion, they often begin with the words *in my opinion*, or *I think*, or use such words as *should*, *ought*, *must*, *best*, *most*, *least*, and *all*.

**ACTIVITY A** Number your paper from 1 to 5. Read each sentence below and decide whether it is a fact or an opinion. Write **Fact** or **Opinion** next to each number.

1. People work at many different kinds of jobs.
2. Everyone ought to have a job.
3. Babysitting is the best job for students.
4. Many jobs require special training.
5. With the right training, anyone can get the job he or she wants.

Some statements *seem* to be facts. But are they? Read the sentences below.

- "The Toothpaste Millionaire" is the title of a play and a book.
- "The Toothpaste Millionaire" is an essay about advertising.

One of these statements is true, and the other is false. You can find out which is true and which is false by checking in your book.

Sometimes sentences make statements that are part fact and part opinion.

- Joe Smiley said that Rufus had the most fantastic brain of any young person in the country.

It is a fact that Joe Smiley spoke and made the statement about Rufus. But the statement he made is an opinion.

**ACTIVITY B** Number your paper from 1 to 5. Read each sentence below and decide whether it is a fact, an opinion, or part fact and part opinion. Write **Fact**, **Opinion**, or **Part Fact/Part Opinion**, next to each number on your paper.

1. Mrs. Oliver said she thought it would snow.
2. Two feet of snow fell on the city and surrounding area.
3. Nobody was happy about the heavy snowfall.
4. The newspaper had a really terrific story about the storm.
5. The story was on the front page of the newspaper.

Whenever Henry and Midge get together, something interesting always happens. They discovered that last summer when Henry spent his vacation with his aunt and uncle in Grover's Corner, New Jersey. That's where he met Midge. It's summer vacation time again, and Henry is looking forward to another visit with his aunt and uncle. Only a few hours ago, he was in Singapore, where he lives with his parents. Now he's on his way to San Francisco, California. Midge and her parents are already there. Together they will drive across the United States to New Jersey. Henry has decided to keep a journal as he travels, but he can tell you about that.

# June 15th - En route to San Francisco

My name is Henry Harris Reed, and this is my journal. Last year I kept a journal of what I did and used it as a report when school opened. I got an "A" on it. Miss Prescott, my English teacher, said it was very good, even though she did complain about the pages being sort of grimy. Probably what upset Miss Prescott was the angleworm that got pressed between pages 42 and 43. I remember using a worm as a marker, but I wouldn't have closed the notebook on it. I wonder if Midge could have done that? That's the sort of trick she'd think was hilarious.

Midge Glass was my partner in a research business in Grover's Corner last summer. We got to be good friends.

Mr. Glass is a research chemist, and he is attending a convention in San Francisco. Midge and Mrs. Glass are with him, and they are all going to drive back to New Jersey. The trip is their vacation. Since I was due to arrive in San Francisco at the same time they planned to be there, I was invited to drive back with them. That was a lucky break for me. I haven't seen much of the United States.

I went to the library and got out all the travel books I could find. None of the guidebooks had the really important information that someone my age needs. After about three days of reading, I could see that there is a crying need for a topnotch travel book about the United States. I am going to keep this journal, and when the trip is over I'm going to edit it and publish it.

## June 16th - San Francisco

I arrived in San Francisco this morning. Midge and her mother met me at the airport. I didn't think they would recognize me, because I've grown a lot and look much older and more experienced. They did though.

This afternoon was pretty dull. Mr. Glass attended meetings with all the other chemists. There was no sign that the rain would stop, so there wasn't much to do. Midge and I went down to the hotel lobby and wandered around. Then we each bought a book and sat down in the lobby to read. After half an hour or so, the rain turned to a damp drizzle.

"It doesn't look too awful," I said. "Maybe we could walk over to Chinatown."

"I think we'd better ask Mom and Dad first," Midge said.

"How are we going to do that?" I asked. "Your dad's got meetings all afternoon, and your mother is out."

"We'll get permission from Dad. There's a break about every hour and a half. We can go sit outside the hall and read. Then we'll catch him when he comes out."

The meetings were being held in a small auditorium on the ground floor. Outside the auditorium there is a little reception room, so we sat down on the sofa in the corner and began to read. We had just found our places when a tall, thin woman with a high, orange hat hurried in. Trotting behind her without a leash was a miniature French poodle. There was a woman's shoe in its mouth.

"Oh, hello there," the woman said to Midge. "You don't happen to know if Professor Atkins has started his paper on amino acids or not, do you?"

"I don't know who Professor Atkins is," Midge said. "There's a man with a white goatee and a shiny, bald head talking now."

"That would be Mr. Durfee," the woman said. "Professor Atkins must be next."

"Your dog has somebody's shoe," I told her, trying to be helpful.

"Yes," she said, without even glancing at the dog. "Amy always has a shoe. All my friends give her their old shoes. She's forever hiding them in the strangest places."

Amy wagged her tail, put the shoe in front of Midge, and then lay down contentedly.

"She likes you," the woman said. "Would you mind keeping an eye on her?"

"Sure," Midge answered. "Have you got a leash?"

"You won't need one. Just let her wander around. She'll be all right." She turned to the little dog and spoke to her. "You can stay here with Margaret, Amy. I'll be right in there."

The dog seemed to understand, because she jumped up on the sofa between Midge and me and sat down. The woman then turned and went into the auditorium.

"Who was that?" I asked.

"I think her name is Allison," Midge said. "She's a food chemist. She lives in Philadelphia and has been up to our house several times."

Both Midge and I went back to reading. A couple of minutes later we looked up, and the dog was gone. Her shoe was gone too. I nudged Midge and pointed to the door into the lecture hall. It was ajar.

"I guess Amy went in," I said.

"She won't disturb anyone," Midge said. "She's always quiet." With that she buried her nose in her book again.

Several minutes later I glanced up, and there came Amy trotting through the door of the auditorium, a shoe in her mouth. She came across to where we were and disappeared behind the sofa. However, she didn't stay long. When I glanced up, she was just disappearing through the door into the auditorium again.

I came to a really exciting part of my book, and I didn't pay too much attention to Amy for the next fifteen or twenty minutes. I had a vague impression that she was busily trotting back and forth. When I came to the end of the chapter, I looked up. There was Amy coming back again, her shoe in her mouth as usual.

Midge looked at the dog and then looked again. "Say, something is wrong here. That isn't the same shoe."

"The other one was black and had a
higher heel," she said positively. "It didn't look
a bit like this one."

"Where would she get a different shoe?" I
asked. "She hasn't left the place."

"In there," Midge answered, nodding her
head at the auditorium. "Someone has taken
off her shoe, and Amy has traded with her."
Midge began laughing. "I'd like to see the
woman's face when the lecture's over and she
starts to slip her shoes on again. Amy's shoe
is much smaller than this one."

"I guess the thing to do is to hold on to
this until we find out whose it is," I said,
leaning down to pick up the shoe.

I put the shoe on the sofa; Amy jumped up beside it and promptly went to sleep. Five minutes later the lecture ended, and people began to file out. I picked up Amy so she wouldn't slip away, and Midge carried the shoe. People were still straggling out slowly, but we managed to slip into the auditorium. We thought that whoever owned the shoe would be inside looking for it and we wouldn't have much trouble locating her. It wasn't that easy. There must have been a hundred and fifty people altogether, and sixty or so were still inside. There were a number of women, and many of them were either still seated or looking around with funny expressions on their faces.

"I guess we'll have to announce it," I said. "Why don't you get up on the seat and ask who is missing a shoe?"

"Good idea," Midge said. She kicked off her own shoes and stood on one of the seats. She held the shoe high in the air. "Is anyone here missing a shoe?" she called.

It was noisy, and she had to repeat her question in a louder voice. There was a sudden silence. Finally, after a pause, about fifteen women all answered at once.

Amy had done a thorough job. She had collected every loose shoe she could locate. She took some out to the lobby and hid them and

hid others inside. Doctor Allison realized what had happened and took charge.

"May I have everyone's attention please," she called. "It seems my dog Amy has hidden some shoes. I am certain we can locate them all in a few minutes."

Midge and I found more shoes than all the rest put together. We located five in back of the sofa alone. Altogether it didn't take much longer than ten minutes to get everyone shod again.

We finally located Mr. Glass, and he said that we could walk over to Chinatown. When we got to the front entrance of the hotel, it was raining again, so we didn't go after all. There was a movie down the street, and we went to that instead.

This evening I told Midge about my plan of keeping a journal of our trip and then publishing a travel book. She thinks it's a good idea.

"That will fit right in with an idea I had for our firm," she said. "We'll collect something interesting from every place we visit—a curio or something special from the spot, or maybe something historic. Then when we get home we'll set up a travel museum in the barn and charge admission."

It isn't a bad idea at all. I could sell copies of my travel book at the same time.

## Thinking and Writing About the Selection

1. Why did Henry Reed decide to keep a journal?
2. How would Henry's journal be different from the travel guides he had read?
3. Is it likely that people would not have noticed what Amy was doing? Why or why not?

 4. If you decided to write a book, what kind of book would it be? Would it be fiction or nonfiction? What would be the subject of your book?

## Applying the Key Skill
### Draw Conclusions

Use complete sentences to answer the following questions about "Henry Reed's Journal."

1. Henry Reed concluded that there was a "crying need for a topnotch travel book about the United States." How did he reach that conclusion?
2. Why did Allison conclude that Mr. Durfee was giving his talk?
3. Why did Midge conclude that Amy had "traded shoes" with a woman in the auditorium?

7/15/04

# Metaphor

Morning is
a new sheet of paper
for you to write on.

Whatever you want to say,
all day,
until night
folds it up
and files it away.

The bright words and the dark words
are gone
until dawn
and a new day
to write on.

Eve Merriam

# SKILLS ACTIVITY

## SUMMARIZE

When you tell about something you have seen or done, something that has happened to you, or something you have read, you often mention only the most important facts. You may leave out the unnecessary details. When you describe something in this way, you are **summarizing**. Read the paragraph below from ''Henry Reed's Journal.'' Then read the summary.

> I went to the library and got out all the travel books I could find. None of the guidebooks had any of the really important information that someone my age needs. After about three days of reading, I could see that there is a crying need for a topnotch travel book about the United States. I am going to keep this journal, and when the trip is over I'm going to edit and publish it.

> **Summary:** I found no good guide books about the United States for young readers, so I am going to keep a journal of my trip and publish it.

When writing a summary, remember these rules:

1.  Use as few words as possible.
2.  Include only the most important ideas.
3.  Leave out unimportant details.
4.  Write the ideas in your own words.

**ACTIVITY A** Read the paragraph from ''Henry Reed's Journal'' on the next page. Then read the summaries. Decide which summary is best and write it on your paper.

94

This afternoon was pretty dull. Mr. Glass attended meetings with all the other chemists. There was no sign that the rain would stop so there wasn't much to do. Midge and I went down to the hotel lobby and wandered around. Then we each bought a book and sat down in the lobby to read. After half an hour or so, the rain turned to damp drizzle.

a. There was no sign that the rain would stop, but after Midge and I had read for a half hour, it turned to damp drizzle.
b. The afternoon was pretty dull and there wasn't much to do.
c. While Mr. Glass attended meetings, Midge and I wandered around for a while; then we bought books to read.
d. About a half hour after Midge and I sat down to read the books we had bought, the rain had turned to damp drizzle.

**ACTIVITY B** Read the paragraph below from "Henry Reed's Journal." Then write a two-sentence summary of the paragraph on your paper.

I put the shoe on the sofa; Amy jumped up beside it and promptly went to sleep. Five minutes later the lecture ended, and people began to file out. I picked up Amy so she wouldn't slip away, and Midge carried the shoe. People were still straggling out slowly, but we managed to slip into the auditorium. We thought that whoever owned the shoe would be inside looking for it and we wouldn't have much trouble locating her. It wasn't that easy. There must have been a hundred and fifty people altogether, and sixty or so were still inside. There were a number of women, and many of them were either still seated or looking around with funny expressions on their faces.

# CHILDREN'S EXPRESS

Gail Schiller Tuchman

If you live in Salem, Massachusetts; Charleston, West Virginia; Miami, Florida; or Ventura, California, you may have seen the byline *Children's Express* in your local newspaper. Children's Express is a news service by children for everyone. More than 2,500 newspapers feature columns by the reporters and editors of Children's Express. In this article, you will find out how these columns get into the newspaper. You will also read one of the columns that appeared in newspapers throughout the United States.

## HOW DID CHILDREN'S EXPRESS GET STARTED?

Robert Clampitt is the founder and publisher of Children's Express. In 1975, Clampitt was asked to review a children's magazine. The magazine included drawings, poems, and stories by children. The boys and girls really liked writing stories and seeing their work in print. However, Clampitt believed a magazine could do more for readers. A magazine by children for children seemed like a good idea. But something was missing. Clampitt came up with the idea that interviews with people and stories about real events might interest children more.

Clampitt discussed his idea with many children nine to thirteen years of age. The ones who were really interested in his idea became the first reporters. They also came up with the name "Children's Express."

When *Children's Express Magazine* was started in 1975, it was a news and feature magazine. It looked somewhat like *Time* and *Newsweek*.

A Children's Express reporter interviews news commentator Edwin Newman at the 1976 Democratic Convention. As a result of the convention, C. E. reporters became more interested in politics.

## HOW DID CHILDREN'S EXPRESS GET INTO NEWSPAPERS?

In 1980, a newspaper organization, called a syndicate, asked Clampitt if Children's Express would write a column for newspapers. "That's how we got into the newspaper column business," explains Clampitt.

As a syndicated column, Children's Express was sold to about 85 newspapers. In 1983, Children's Express decided to join United Press International (UPI). UPI provides stories to about 6,000 wire service customers worldwide. It reaches more than 2,500 newspapers.

## HOW ARE THE COLUMNS CREATED?

There are two kinds of Children's Express columns: roundtable discussions and interviews. Roundtable discussions usually include an editor, fourteen to eighteen years old,

and several reporters, thirteen years old and younger. They get together to discuss their feelings and experiences about a variety of topics. One roundtable discussion was about working mothers. Another focused on ideas about what makes a person heroic. As the reporters express their views, comments are put on tape. Later, an adult editor prepares the *transcript*, or written record, of what is on the tape. Then he or she prepares the written transcript for publication.

For interview columns, an editor selects a story idea that has been approved. Then an adult assignment editor gathers background information, sets up the interview, and assembles the reporting team. The reporters who accept the assignment are called together for a meeting called a *briefing*. At the briefing, a teenage editor explains the story idea and gives the background information to the reporters. Then the editor and reporters decide what questions will be asked.

The interview lasts about forty-five minutes to an hour. Everything is recorded on tape. The next step in the process is called a *debriefing*. The debriefing is a meeting between the teenage editor and the reporters. The reporters describe the interview and comment about the answers given by the person interviewed. The debriefing is recorded on tape.

In the last step, the adult editor uses the transcripts from the interview and the debriefing to create the column.

# Winning at all Costs

SOUTH BEND, Ind. (UPI)— When the guest athletes were introduced at the opening ceremonies of the Sears National Junior Olympics, they all got big hands. But when Kurt Thomas was introduced, the audience went wild. Lots of people with cameras and autograph books came running.

Thomas started out in the Junior Olympics and now he's the Junior Olympics spokesman. We were really looking forward to meeting him because he's an excellent gymnast, and we've seen him on commercials and in newspapers.

Thomas is a success story. In the 1975 Pan American Games, he won five medals and became quite famous. Now, he has a gymnastic school, a camp, and a book called *Kurt Thomas on Gymnastics*. He's also a sports commentator for ABC network.

We also went to an interview with him about competition and pressure on young athletes. He told us that he put pressure on himself. He really wanted to succeed in gymnastics.

"In a non-pressure situation I kind of slacked off," he explained. "But when I had to score a certain score or hit a certain routine, I did. That was good for me."

The Thomas Flair is a whirling move on the pommel horse that Kurt Thomas was the first to demonstrate.

But Thomas also said that it's very bad for coaches and parents to put the win-at-all-costs attitude onto their kids.

"Kids want their parents' support," he added. "But they don't want to feel that they *have* to win."

Thomas thinks that a child should feel like he can do it on his own, "that it should come from

# is a Losing Game

within." He also told us that "a lot of the coaches push kids very far."

If a young athlete feels that the coach is pushing too hard, the athlete should say, "back off a little. Pretty soon this is not going to be fun for me. And if it's not fun, I'm not going to participate."

Another really important thing is if opponents make mistakes, an athlete shouldn't be happy and excited. That's not good sportsmanship.

Thomas pointed out that he didn't want to win because his opponent fell down or slipped. He wanted to win when his opponent did his best.

The win-at-all-costs attitude can get kids away from sports.

"You win, and then at the next meet you don't win," Thomas said. "You feel like, 'the whole world's collapsing on me.' You've got to accept failure, although it can be one of the hardest things to do."

Thomas feels that the kind of encouragement young athletes need from their parents, coaches, and friends is "not to be pushed to win, win, win, but to set goals toward winning."

"When I was in my first Junior Olympics," he told us, "I was 13th out of 13—dead last. But that really motivated me to train harder. The next year I placed fourth. I saw that if I could move from thirteenth to fourth, I could move from fourth to first."

"So I worked real hard and I did become first. The next year I slacked off and placed third, but it was another good experience."

"Accept failure," he said, "but let that failure teach you something. Turn the failure into success."

By Glenn Golz, 12; Elspeth Steiner, 13; Matthew Wolsk, 12. Assistant editor: Jennifer Avellino, 15.

Kurt Thomas placed third in the National AAU Junior Olympic Gymnastics Championship in 1974.

## WHAT'S IN THE FUTURE FOR CHILDREN'S EXPRESS?

From C.E.'s headquarters in New York City, Robert Clampitt has started Children's Express bureaus in other cities and in other countries. The first was set up in Salem, Massachusetts, and another in Melbourne, Australia. Still others are planned

Above and opposite: Children's Express representatives received a tour of UPI world headquarters after a press conference at which UPI announced it would carry Children's Express as part of its service.

for Japan and elsewhere. All of the bureaus will be linked by computers.

Mr. Clampitt hopes to have a worldwide network. "We want an exchange of cultural experience," he says. "We're just in the stage of working it all out, but we are going to do it. It's going to work. I know it is!"

## Thinking and Writing About the Selection

1. Who makes up the reporting team for an interview column?

2. How do the roundtable discussion columns differ from the interview columns?

3. What do you think Kurt Thomas meant when he said he wanted to win "when his opponent did his best"?

4. If you were a reporter for Children's Express, whom would you want to interview? What questions would you want to ask?

## Applying the Key Skill
### Summarize

Write the answers to the following questions about "Children's Express."

1. Which of the following sentences best summarizes the first paragraph under the heading "How are the columns created?"

   a. The two kinds of Children's Express columns are roundtable discussions and interviews.

   b. To prepare a column for publication, a transcript, or written record, of a discussion is prepared. The adult editor transcribes the discussion.

   c. One kind of Children's Express column is based on roundtable discussions. An editor and some reporters get together to discuss a topic. Their comments are taped and then transcribed.

2. Summarize the first paragraph under the heading "What's in the future for Children's Express?" in two sentences.

# IT'S NEWS TO ME

In "Children's Express," you learned about the newspaper terms **editor**, **byline**, **column**, and **syndicate**. Those are just a few of the words used in the newspaper business. There are many other terms and expressions that are special to people who work on newspapers. The words or expressions that are used by people in a particular occupation or profession are called **jargon**.

Newspaper jargon may seem like another language to someone who is not familiar with it. The words and expressions have meanings different from the usual ones. Read the sentences on the left that include newspaper jargon. Then read the sentences on the right to find out what is meant.

| | |
|---|---|
| The editor asked for a two-inch headline. | The editor asked for the title of an article to be set in type two inches high. |
| The reporter left to check on a story that was breaking. | The reporter left to check on a story that was developing. |
| The editor shouted, "Cut that headline! Kill that paragraph!" | The editor shouted, "Shorten that headline! Get rid of that paragraph!" |
| The reporter asked his assistant to check something out in the morgue. | The reporter asked his assistant to check some facts in the library of reference books and files of earlier newspaper. |

## ADVICE COLUMN

### Prewrite

Many people read a newspaper each day. News articles report facts about current events, sports, business, and many other topics. Columns such as Children's Express report news and views which interest readers of all ages. Another popular kind of column offers advice to readers. Readers send letters with questions, and the author of the column answers with facts and opinions about the topic.

Suppose you were a writer of an advice column for students of your age. You receive a letter from a student asking for your opinion about young people working to earn money. What is your opinion? What facts could you give to support your opinion?

Before you form your opinion, you need to do some thinking about the topic. The questions below should help you get started.

1. Is it important for students to earn their own spending money? Why or why not?
2. Is it important for students to learn about jobs and work? Why or why not?
3. What kinds of jobs would you suggest for students of your age?

Discuss the answers to these questions with other students. Perhaps you can think of some more questions. Reread the stories in this unit for possible answers. Check newspapers and magazines. Make notes.

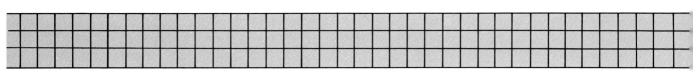

### Write

1. Reread your notes. Write your opinion. List the facts you plan to use to support it.
2. Your answer must be about 300 words long.
3. Your first paragraph should state your opinion and your most important supporting fact.
4. Other paragraphs should present. more facts. You may want to give your opinion about why the facts are important. You may want to tell your readers where you got your facts.
5. Try to use Vocabulary Treasures in your column.
6. Now write the first draft of your column.

> **VOCABULARY TREASURES**
>
> recommendation    attitude
> participate    motivated

### Revise

Read your column. Have a friend read it, too. Think about this checklist as you revise.

1. Did you state your opinion in your first paragraph?
2. Are your facts correct? Where can they be checked?
3. If your column is more than 300 words, you will need to leave out some of your ideas. Which ones will they be?
4. Did you make clear to your reader which of your statements were your own opinions? If you say, "Every student should work," that is an opinion; but it sounds like a fact. You can say, "I believe that every student should work."
5. Check punctuation and spelling carefully.
6. Now rewrite your column to share.

# Mysteriously Yours, Maggie Marmelstein

Marjorie Weinman
Sharmat

**Nobody seemed interested in the newspaper published every month at Maggie Marmelstein's school. The unread papers just piled up. Then Noah, the editor of the newspaper, decided to spice things up. He would hold a contest for a Mystery Person who would write a special column. Maggie knew that she was perfect for the job as she listened to Noah explain the Mystery Person's qualifications.**

"Most of you already know I am starting a new column in the school paper," Noah said. "You know it will be written by an unknown person, a Mystery Person. But *who* will that Mystery Person be?"

Noah went on. "I have made a survey and found that our school newspaper is thoroughly read by only forty-one percent of the students, partially read by twenty-seven percent of the students, and totally ignored by the remaining thirty-two percent. Therefore I have concluded that our newspaper needs a shot of adrenaline."

Noah continued. "Clearly our newspaper should have something new and intriguing to attract all students. An element of mystery. But the Mystery Person must have two qualities. He or she must be a good writer and be a good keeper of secrets. No one must know his or her identity. So anyone here who hopes to become the Mystery Person and then brag about it had better forget the whole idea.

"To continue," said Noah, "any of you who are interested in competing should write something of approximately one hundred words and give it to me within the next two weeks. It can be fiction, nonfiction, a story, a poem, a sample column, anything.

"Please do not reveal any of your mystery ideas," said Noah. "No matter how strange they are. Now, be sure to include your name, address, and telephone number on your entry. There's a chance, I'm sorry to say, that the Mystery Person might not be any of you here this afternoon. But you have the best chance because you cared enough to come."

Maggie looked at Thad. He really hadn't cared enough to come. He had only come because she had. "You're not going to try, are you?" she whispered.

"Are you kidding?" said Thad. "I'm going to write the most exciting, intriguing, mysterious one hundred words I can think of."

Maggie sat at the desk in her bedroom. Now and then she looked up at the pictures of movie actors that were all over the walls. "Cary," she said to her favorite picture of Cary Grant, "I bet you know something mysterious I could write about. Your head must be full of fantastically mysterious things."

For almost two weeks Maggie had spent her spare time trying to think of the approximately one hundred words that would turn her into the Mystery Person. She wrote poems about windowpanes. She wrote a story about a carrot from outer space. She wrote an essay about Falusha Dagwell, a lady who was never born but should have been, according to Maggie.

Maggie had torn everything up. But the deadline for submitting something to Noah was tomorrow. She had to give him *something*.

"My brain has stopped working," thought Maggie. "Maybe it needs some exercise."

Maggie got up, said "I'm exercising" to her mother, and walked down the hall to Thad Smith's apartment. She knocked on the door and Thad opened it.

"I need exercise," said Maggie, walking inside. "So I walked to your apartment."

"I bet you're exercising your head," said Thad.

"About what?" asked Maggie.

"You know," said Thad.

"You mean the Mystery Person?" said Maggie. "Have you thought of anything?"

"Is that why you came over here? To find out what I've thought of?" asked Thad. "Well, I'm not *sure* if I'm even trying. But I won't try hard, if I try at all. Just sort of easy."

"That means you haven't thought of anything," said Maggie.

"I didn't say that," said Thad. "Actually I'm waiting for my ideas to come. Like any minute."

"Oh sure," said Maggie.

"I am," said Thad. "I'm busy waiting. So maybe you could come back when I'm not busy waiting."

"I'm busy, too," said Maggie. "With lots of ideas. So I'll see you when *I'm* not busy. 'Bye."

"'Bye," said Thad.

Maggie walked out of Thad's apartment and down the hall to hers.

She went into her apartment, and to her room. She sat down. "Exercise really helps," she thought. "Maggie Marmelstein is inspired."

Maggie wrote:

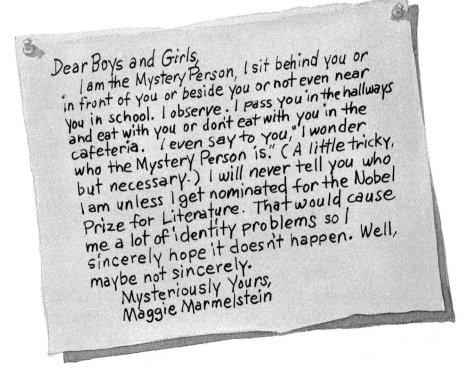

Dear Boys and Girls,
I am the Mystery Person, I sit behind you or in front of you or beside you or not even near you in school. I observe. I pass you in the hallways and eat with you or don't eat with you in the cafeteria. I even say to you, "I wonder who the Mystery Person is." (A little tricky, but necessary.) I will never tell you who I am unless I get nominated for the Nobel Prize for Literature. That would cause me a lot of identity problems so I sincerely hope it doesn't happen. Well, maybe not sincerely.
Mysteriously Yours,
Maggie Marmelstein

"Mistake, mistake," muttered Maggie. And she crossed out *Maggie Marmelstein* and wrote in *The Mystery Person*. Then she counted the words. "One hundred and seven. Well, that's approximately one hundred."

At the bottom of the sheet Maggie printed her name and address and telephone number. Then she went into the kitchen.

"What do you think of this?" Maggie handed her paper to her mother.

Mrs. Marmelstein sat down and read it slowly and carefully. "You wouldn't want a *Nobel Prize*?" she asked. "Your father and I would go to Sweden with you. You could send back picture postcards to all your friends."

"That's true," said Maggie. "But first, do you like this?"

"It has something that I would call flavor," said Mrs. Marmelstein. "Like putting in an extra bit of cinnamon and cloves in fruitcake. It has real flavor."

"Then you really like it?" asked Maggie.

"Really flavorful," said Mrs. Marmelstein. "The highest compliment I can give it. That's my top compliment."

Maggie felt happy. She went to her room and reread what she had written. She copied it in her best printing.

At school the next morning Maggie looked for Noah right away.

"Here's my entry," she said.

Noah looked down at the paper Maggie had handed him. "I'm so glad you decided to try out, Maggie," he said. "I'm certain you wrote something excellent."

"It has flavor," said Maggie.

A line was forming in back of Maggie. Everyone was clutching sheets of paper. "They're lining up for you, Noah," she said.

"Yes, we are the Mystery People," said Ralph Nadesky. "Make way for us."

"I am Cynthia the Mysterious," said Cynthia Stauffeur.

Maggie said good-bye to Noah. "Enjoy your mob," she said to him.

"A mob of mystery, Maggie," said Noah. "Whoever becomes the Mystery Person will have won against a tremendous number of kids."

The next day when Maggie got to school, she noticed a crowd around the bulletin board. Everyone was pushing close to read it. She rushed to join the crowd. Noah had put up a notice! Maggie read it silently.

There is a winner!!! Of course I can't tell you who it is, but this notice is to thank all of you aspiring Mystery Persons. All the entries were interesting, but one in particular had a certain irresistible flavor. The person who wrote it is going to be the Mystery Person. Thank you very much. I sincerely hope you will enjoy the column and think of it as a part of your lives.

P.S. Please do not follow me to see whom I talk to today. I know its an intriguing notion to think I'll lead you to the Mystery Person. But I won't. The Mystery Person already knows, simply by reading this notice, that he or she won. Don't ask me how. That's part of the mystery flavor.

Maggie stared at the bulletin board. "The winner knows by reading the bulletin board. Hmmm." She was talking to herself. Everyone was talking to no one in particular. Maggie read the message again. She stopped at the words *irresistible flavor*. And then at the last line: That's part of the mystery *flavor*. "Flavor again," she thought. "That's it! I told Noah my entry had flavor. Now Noah is telling me that I won!! Me!!"

Maggie wanted to shout, "I won!" But she didn't. This was the beginning of her big secret. She made up her mind that she would keep it no matter what.

Maggie went to class. The classroom was buzzing with Mystery Person talk. "All about me," thought Maggie. It was hard to concentrate on schoolwork. She saw Noah a few times during the day, but he merely said hi and walked on.

When school was over, Maggie ran home. Her mother was sewing a curtain in the kitchen. "How are things in the world of mystery?" she asked.

Suddenly Maggie realized that she couldn't tell her mother that she had won. She had to keep the secret from everyone.

"Somebody won," said Maggie.

The telephone rang.

"The door opens, the telephone rings," said Mrs. Marmelstein. "One minute it's just stitch, stitch, and the next all excitement."

Maggie answered the telephone. "It's Noah," said the voice on the line.

Maggie looked at her mother.

"Your face says private," said Mrs. Marmelstein. She picked up her sewing and left the room.

"Hi," Maggie said into the telephone. "I can talk."

Noah said, "I timed how long it would take you to get home if you ran, and I knew you would run, that walking wouldn't adequately express your feelings of winning. So hello, full of flavor. Congratulations."

"I won!" said Maggie. "It's really true!"

"Shh," said Noah. "Remember that 'Shh' has to become a habit."

"I'll remember," said Maggie. "It's just that I'm so excited. I filled my wastebasket with ideas before I wrote the winner."

"It had such a sense of intrigue," said Noah. "It was just what I was looking for."

"My mother would be so happy if I could tell her," said Maggie. "But of course I won't."

"You won't have to tell her," said Noah. "I'm sure she'll know. But that's okay. She'll keep your secret, and in addition, she can give her opinion on whether your columns are sufficiently flavorful. Think of her as an invaluable consultant as well as your mother."

"Invaluable consultant. I'll remember," said Maggie.

"Do you have any ideas for your first column?"

"My first column?"

"Your deadline is next Thursday," said Noah.

"So soon?" said Maggie.

"That's almost a week away," said Noah. "You'll have a week's worth of ideas to work with."

"Right now I don't have a minute's worth," said Maggie. "I'd better hang up and start thinking."

"I have every confidence in you," said Noah. "Good-bye, Mystery Person."

"Good-bye," said Maggie. She hung up.

Maggie went to her room. "Tomorrow is Saturday. No school. But I will get up early, I will sit down at my desk and immediately write the entire column. I just know it will happen that way." Maggie looked up at her picture of John Wayne. "I have nothing to worry about, John."

On Saturday Maggie got up early. Her mind was blank. "This is a Saturday-morning disaster," she thought. Then she smelled something good coming from the kitchen. "Empty stomachs lead to blank minds." Maggie went into the kitchen.

"I'm baking Mystery Muffins," said Mrs. Marmelstein.

"What's in them?" asked Maggie.

"That's my mystery," said Mrs. Marmelstein. "But you may eat as many as you want."

Maggie tasted a muffin. "You put cinnamon and cloves in these, didn't you?"

"Among other things," said Mrs. Marmelstein. "Remember what I said about real flavor? Now what kind of real flavor are you putting in your first column?"

"I'm stuck," said Maggie. She smiled. "Maybe I'll write about cloves and cinnamon."

"As your invaluable consultant, I think you should skip cloves and cinnamon in your column," said Mrs. Marmelstein. "They're exciting in muffins and boring in columns."

"So what's exciting besides cloves and cinnamon?" asked Maggie. She took another bite. "Wait! Movie stars are exciting."

"Like Cary Grant?" said Mrs. Marmelstein.

"Right," said Maggie. "And I could tell the kids everything I know about him. Well, maybe not," said Maggie. "Besides, then everyone would know that Maggie Marmelstein wrote about Cary Grant. I would give away that I'm the Mystery Person. Still, it would be fun to write about an exciting person," said Maggie. "But maybe they don't have to be famous. Maybe they could be regular people."

Mrs. Marmelstein handed Maggie another muffin. "What kind of regular people?" she asked.

"I only know one kind," said Maggie. "Regular people like me and like you."

"Like you sounds good," said Mrs. Marmelstein.

"Hey, I could write a column about *kids* I know," said Maggie. "Or maybe one kid at a time. A personality profile. I see them in magazines."

"I see them, too," said Mrs. Marmelstein. "They tell you all sorts of things you don't want to know about people you don't want to know."

"This would be different," said Maggie. "It would be about kids you'd like to know better. I could start with someone really super."

"Like super who?" asked Mrs. Marmelstein.

"Like . . ." Maggie was thinking. "Like Ellen. Everybody should know Ellen better because it's hard to know Ellen at all."

"Everyone will know that Ellen isn't the Mystery Person if you write about her," said Mrs. Marmelstein. "In fact, everyone you write about will be eliminated as a possibility. You'll narrow the field."

"No," said Maggie. "Because I'll say that anybody I write about in the column could or could not be the Mystery Person writing about the Mystery Person."

"Now *there's* your cinnamon and cloves," said Mrs. Marmelstein. "*That* gives your column the best flavor of all. The flavor of total confusion. I love it, Maggie!"

"So do I," said Maggie. "Thanks for your help, invaluable consultant." Maggie grabbed another muffin and went to her room.

She sat down at her desk and started to write.

## Thinking and Writing About the Selection

1. What did Noah discover as a result of his survey?

2. Why would the Mystery Person have to be a good keeper of secrets?

3. Do you think Maggie's idea of writing personality profiles for the column was a good one? Do you think students would want to read about others in their class? Explain your answers.

4. If you were a newspaper columnist, what kind of column would you like to write?

## Applying the Key Skill
### Context Clues

Read the sentences below. Use context clues to choose the correct meaning of the underlined words. Write the words and their meanings.

1. When Maggie was in school, she tried to concentrate on her classes. During her leisure time, she concentrated on ideas for the newspaper column.
   a. time that is spent at home
   b. time that is spent thinking
   c. time that can be used any way a person chooses
   d. time that is not important

2. Noah's phone call confirmed Maggie's belief that she had been chosen to be the Mystery Person.
   a. destroyed
   b. announced
   c. satisfied
   d. proved

3. Noah was adamant about deadlines. Maggie had to turn in every column on time, even her very first one.
   a. nervous
   b. adventurous
   c. firm
   d. sensible

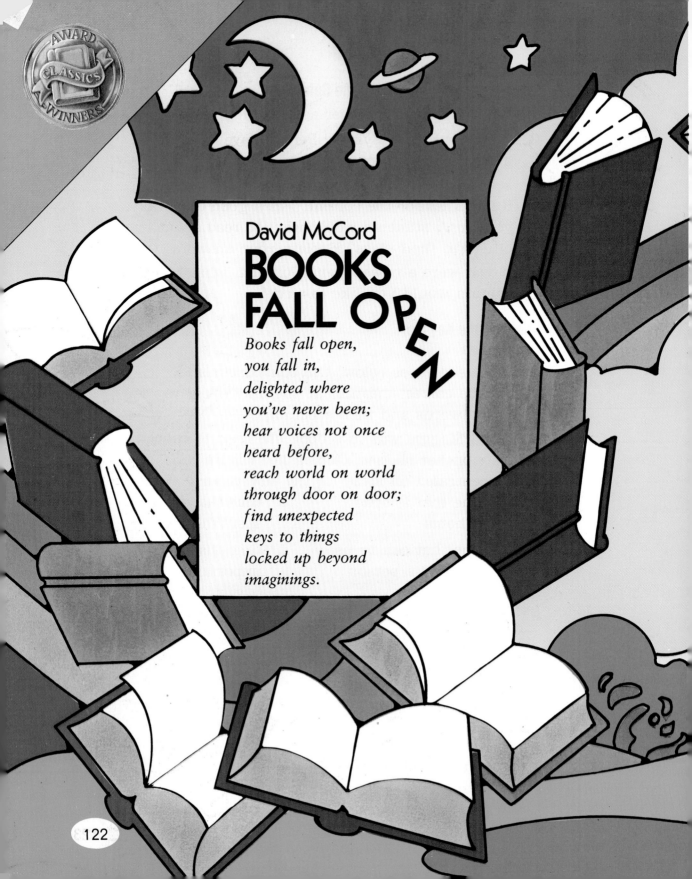

## David McCord

# BOOKS
# FALL OPEN

Books fall open,
you fall in,
delighted where
you've never been;
hear voices not once
heard before,
reach world on world
through door on door;
find unexpected
keys to things
locked up beyond
imaginings.

AWARD
CLASSICS
WINNERS

What might *you* be,
*perhaps* become,
*because one book*
*is somewhere? Some*
*wise delver into*
*wisdom, wit,*
*and wherewithal*
*has written it.*

*True books will venture,*
*dare you out,*
*whisper secrets,*
*maybe shout*
*across the gloom*
*to you in need,*
*who hanker for*
*a book to read.*

# The
# BEST
## *Kind of*
# BOOK

Edward Eager

*What is the best kind of book? John, Barnaby,*
*Susan, Fredericka, and Abbie think they know.*
*But they are in for quite a surprise. It all*
*begins one Saturday morning in their library.*

 # FINDING IT

"The best kind of book," said Barnaby, "is
a magic book."

"Naturally," said John.

There was a silence, as they all thought
about this and how true it was.

"The best kind of magic book," said Barnaby, leaning against the library table and
surveying the crowded bookshelves, "is when
it's about ordinary people like us, and then
something happens and it's magic."

"Like when you find a nickel, except it
isn't a nickel—it's a half-magic talisman," said
Susan.

"Or you're playing in the front yard and
somebody asks is this the road to Butterfield,"
said Abbie.

"Only it isn't at all—it's the road to Oz!"
shrilled Fredericka.

"If you could have a brand-new magic
book, specially made for you," said John,
"what would you choose?"

"One about a lot of children," said Abbie.

"One about five children just like us," said
Fredericka.

"They're walking home from somewhere and the magic starts suddenly before they know it," said Susan.

Miss Dowitcher, the librarian, came skimming across the room. "Have you found enough books to take?" she murmured.

Of course they had not, for who has ever found enough books?

They scrabbled together the ones they had chosen and lined up at the desk to have the date stamped in them. It was then that Susan looked back and saw the book sitting all by itself at one end of the bottom shelf.

It was a red book, smallish but plump, comfortable and shabby. There had once been gilt letters on the back, but these had rubbed away, and Susan couldn't read the name of what it was. Still, it looked odd enough to be interesting and worn enough to have been enjoyed by countless generations. On a sudden impulse she added it to the pile in her arms and took her place at the end of the line.

Miss Dowitcher stamped the book and a minute later Susan and the others emerged from the library into the bright, new-washed June morning.

Susan looked at the little old shabby-looking book on the top of her pile. She opened the worn red cover and began to read.

These are the words that Susan read:

"'The best kind of book,' said Barnaby, 'is a magic book.'

'Naturally,' said John.

126

There was a silence, as they all thought about this and how true it was.

'The best kind of magic book,' said Barnaby, leaning against the library table and surveying the crowded bookshelves, 'is when it's about ordinary people like us, and then something happens and it's magic.'

'Like when you find a nickel, except it isn't a nickel—it's a half-magic talisman,' said Susan.

'Or you're playing in the front yard and somebody asks is this the road to Butterfield,' said Abbie.

'Only it isn't at all—it's the road to Oz!' shrilled Fredericka."

Susan's voice trailed off. She looked at the others.

"It can't be," said Barnaby.

"It is," said Susan. "It's about us! All of us and every single thing we said!"

Barnaby reached for the book. "You're right," he muttered as he read. "We're all in it."

"What's happening?" said Abbie. "Do you suppose we're magic, suddenly?"

"Either we are," said John, "or that book is."

"Do you suppose," said Susan, "we're not really real at all but just characters in this book somebody wrote?"

"Suppose we *are* book characters?" Barnaby said. "Characters have all kinds of interesting things happen to them. There's a whole bookful of adventures and we're just at the beginning!"

128

"What happens next?" said Fredericka.

"What happens at the end?" said Abbie.

Barnaby tried to turn to the back of the book. "It's stuck or something," he told them. "The whole rest of the book's shut solid tight."

"I'm beginning to see it all," continued Barnaby. "Don't you remember? We said we wanted a special magic book of our own."

"About five children just like us," said Abbie.

Barnaby turned to Susan. "Where'd you find it in the first place?"

"On the bottom of the fairy-tale section," she said, remembering.

Barnaby nodded excitedly. "It all adds up. Think of it sitting there all those years, with the magic from all those other books dripping down into it! It's probably been sitting there waiting for somebody to come along and make a wish in front of it. We came and wanted a magic story; so that's what it turned into."

"What kind of wish is that?" asked Fredericka. "What good is a book about us? We know about us."

"We don't know what's coming next," said Barnaby. "All we've had is the beginning. What else did we wish for? Think back."

"I said the people in the book would be walking home from somewhere and the magic would start suddenly before they knew it," said Susan.

"That part came true," said Barnaby.

"You mean," said Susan, "there's a whole book still going to happen to us?"

"That's what I think," said Barnaby.

"If it's all there in the book," said John, "why not use the magic and wish the book open? Then we can read the next chapter and know what to expect."

"I don't think it works like that," said Barnaby. "If we could pry open the rest of the pages, they'd probably be blank. I think it's probably up to us to make more wishes and have them come true, to fill the pages up!"

"Sort of make up the book as we go along?" said Abbie.

"You mean it's ours to use?" said Susan. "Like a wishing ring?"

"That's the idea," said Barnaby. "More or less."

Everyone thought about this.

"That book," said John, "had better be handled with care from now on."

"Don't anybody dare even think about wishing," said Susan, "till we've talked it out and decided what kind of adventure we want."

"You ought to do the deciding," said Barnaby. "You're the one who found the book in the first place."

"No, you go first. You'll do it better."

"No, you ought to be the one."

"No, honestly, I'd rather."

"Oh, for heaven's sake," said Fredericka. "If everybody else is too polite around here, let me!" She laid hold of the book.

131

"Stop her, somebody!" cried Abbie. But it was too late.

"I wish we'd have a magic adventure, with wizards and magic things in it, and I wish it'd start right now, this minute, so we'll know for certain it's really our wish coming true and not just a coincidence!"

But nothing happened. They kept on walking. Round a bend in the road they saw a house. It had an interesting sign by the driveway.

"Slow," warned the sign, "Cats, et cetera."

In the past the five children had often stopped and waited by the driveway, in hope that something other than a cat would come out. Up until this second nothing had.

At this second something did. What came out was a dragon.

 # USING IT

The dragon was bright red all over, except for its eyes, which were green. It was flying low over the driveway, puffing purple smoke as it came.

Abbie stopped short and clutched the others. But Fredericka pressed forward curiously. The dragon seemed just as curious as Fredericka.

It hovered over her in hawk-like circles, peering down. Then it scooped her up and flew away with her, over the trees.

"Stop!" cried John.

"Do something!" cried Abbie.

"Look!" said Susan, pointing.

A ground-floor window of the house was open and a face was staring out.

Abbie ran up to the face, and the others followed.

"Was that your dragon?" she demanded.

"Oh dear," said the face. "Is *that* what it was? I was *afraid* that was what it was! I don't know what could have gone wrong," he went on. "I was practicing my tricks the way I always do, and I reached into my hat to pull out a rabbit, and something came out, only it was something else!"

Barnaby looked at him. He remembered the rest of Fredericka's wish. "You must be a wizard," he said.

The round gentleman looked pleased. "How did you guess? That is my profession, though 'magician' is the proper term."

"You'll help us won't you?" said Abbie. "You'll find my sister for us?"

The round gentleman looked uncertain. "Well, I'll try," he said. "Won't you come in?"

When the round gentleman opened the door of the house, the four children hesitated. Cats wreathed about the round gentleman's feet. The children knew now what the "et cetera" on the sign had stood for. The "et cetera" was kittens.

A woman appeared from the back of the house. "Who are all these?" she said.

"It's all right, Mrs. Funkhouser," said the round gentleman. "These visitors are for me.

Mrs. Funkhouser is my landlady," he went on. "Now if you'll step this way."

When they saw the room beyond the door, Abbie's eyes grew wide with wonder, and John said, "Whew!" Bottles of colored liquid and jars of colored powder were on every table.

"I'm afraid I may be a bit rusty," the gentleman said. "It's years now since my farewell appearance. I never found a lost girl, even in the old days. I'm not certain how it's done."

"Where's my box of tricks?" said the gentleman. He found a card index and riffled through it. "Transformations," he muttered.

His eyes roamed the room. "There's this," he said, picking up a bottle of purple liquid.

"It's supposed to make a red flare," said the round gentleman, "but the way things have been going, *anything* might happen!" He emptied the bottle into a bowl.

As he did so, Susan had an idea. She wasn't sure yet just how the magic of the book worked. It had already proved it could get them into adventures, but after that, did it just sit back and watch or would it help?

Still, there was no harm in trying. So she held the book firmly and wished with all her might that this time the magic would prove successful.

The round gentleman struck a match and lit the fluid in the bowl. It made a red flare, all right. But other things happened too. There was a whooshing noise, followed by a whirring one.

135

"We're moving," said Barnaby. "Flying, I think."

John ran to the window. "That's right, we're off the ground. We're heading the same way the dragon did!"

The other children ran to the window and looked down. It wasn't modern Connecticut any more. The country below had a long-ago, fairy-tale look.

"What country *is* it, do you suppose?" Susan asked.

"I don't care for the look of it," said Mrs. Funkhouser, joining her at the window.

"We're landing," said Barnaby.

Meadows and caves were suddenly rushing nearer, and a crowd of people could be seen below, staring upwards.

There was a slight jar. Then all was still. "Come on," said John. He and Barnaby and Susan and Abbie and the round gentleman made their way out of the house.

A crowd of people stood nearby. "Hooray, hooray!" they said. "Have you come to kill the dragon and save us all?"

"Why, yes," said Barnaby, trying to sound more courageous than he felt. "Lead us to your dragon."

Beyond the house was a cave in the rock. A huffing sound of breathing came from within, and with each huff a puff of purple smoke issued from the cave's mouth.

Abbie ran to the mouth of the cave. "Fredericka!" she called.

137

Within the lair Fredericka heard her sister's voice and struggled in the dragon's grip. "Help!" she called back.

"We've got to do something fast," said Barnaby, turning to the round gentleman.

"Oh dear," said the round gentleman.

"You save that little girl," said Mrs. Funkhouser.

"Well, I'll try," said the round gentleman.

At that moment the steeple bells in the nearby village chimed noon, and the dragon emerged from its lair.

"Don't just stand there. Do something!" Fredericka called from the dragon's grasp.

Susan roused herself. "I will," she said. She handed the book to the round gentleman.

If you have understood about the book so far, you will know that for each person its power was different, because to each person it was the particular book that person had always longed to find.

So that while for the five children it was a magic story with them in it, for the round gentleman it was something else again.

"'*Wishful Ways for Wizards*!'" he read, from the title page. "Why, this is wonderful!" He turned the pages, sampling the contents.

"Don't just skim! Find the right place!" called the captive Fredericka.

"To be sure," said the round gentleman shamefacedly. "I was forgetting. 'How to Shrink a Dragon.' I'm sure I saw it here somewhere."

138

"Oh, for pity's sake let me!" said Mrs. Funkhouser, taking the book from him. But of course once in her hands, the book was a book of another color.

"'*Helpful Hints for Homemakers*,'" she read. "'To put out an oven fire, use salt.' That ought to do it," said Mrs. Funkhouser. "Fetch the salt, somebody."

John came running out of the house with the salt box, and Mrs. Funkhouser shook it full in the dragon's face.

There was a hissing sound, and the dragon's fire went out.

The crowd cheered.

The dragon trembled with rage and frustration and snapped at Mrs. Funkhouser.

"Bite me, would you?" said Mrs. Funkhouser, dodging it easily. She consulted the book again. "'For bites, stings, et cetera, use household ammonia,'" she read.

Barnaby did not wait to be asked but went rushing into the house.

"This is undignified," said the dragon. "Either get a sword and fight me properly, or withdraw from the combat!"

Mrs. Funkhouser did not answer. Barnaby was back by now with the bottle from under the sink, and she took it from him and emptied it in the general direction of the dragon.

The dragon sneezed and sputtered and coughed. To be salted and ammoniated is humiliating to a dragon and makes it feel small.

When a dragon feels small, it *is*.

139

"This is monstrous," said the dragon, looking over its shoulder to see how much it had shrunk.

You may have heard that an elephant is afraid of a mouse. With dragons and cats it is very much the same. The dragon saw the magician's cats coming out of the house and shrank in fear. Once it started shrinking, it couldn't seem to stop.

It shrank from the size of a large collie to the size of a medium-sized poodle. The cats stood around it in a circle. The dragon took one look at them and shrank in fear again.

"This is unendurable," said the dragon.

It shrank until it was the size of a mouse, and the cats played with it, batting it to and fro. Then it shrank until it was the size of a small lizard.

As the five children watched in horrified fascination, the smallest kitten pounced on the dragon and gobbled it down as easily as it might have swallowed a fly.

"Three cheers for the wonderful wizard!" shouted the villagers. "May he reign over us and rule the land forever! Three cheers for the woman, too!" they cried.

"That wizard didn't do a thing, really," muttered Abbie to the others. "Mrs. Funkhouser and the cats did it all!"

"I guess that's the way with wizards," said Barnaby. "They let others do the work and then take the credit. Now it's time to go."

"How do we *do* that?" said John.

141

"I'm not sure," said Barnaby. He went up to Mrs. Funkhouser and the round gentleman, and the other four followed.

"Could we have our book now?" said Susan. "We'll be taking it home with us."

"What method of travel were you planning to use?" the round gentleman asked the five children.

"That's just it," said Susan. "We're not quite sure."

"Vanishing cream," said Mrs. Funkhouser promptly, without so much as a glance in the book's direction. "There's some in my bureau drawer." Fredericka ran to fetch it.

"Shall we let her?" whispered Abbie. "What if we just *vanish*?"

"Trust the book," counseled Barnaby. "It's done pretty well so far."

Then Fredericka returned with the jar of vanishing cream, and Mrs. Funkhouser rubbed a little on the foreheads of each. Susan clasped the book tight and wished, too, just in case.

The next second they found themselves sitting on the front steps of Barnaby and Abbie and Fredericka's house in Connecticut.

**The five children were returned home safely from their first magical adventure. It would not be their last, however. On each of the next six days, they would wish on the book for a new adventure and write another chapter with them in it. You can read about these adventures in Seven-Day Magic by Edward Eager.**

143

# *Enterprises*

Communication is an important part of successful projects. In *Enterprises*, you read about people who used a variety of ways to communicate information. You discovered how advertising helped students start their own businesses and even played a part in turning a calamity into an opportunity. You also found out how enterprising people your own age became writers and reporters to communicate their views. As you undertake your own enterprises, you will learn even more about the importance of communicating through reading, writing, speaking, and listening.

## Thinking and Writing About *Enterprises*

1. If Janie from "Kid Power" were interviewed by a reporter from *Penny Power*, what advice do you think she would offer about how to get a job?
2. How did advertising help Homer Price from "The Doughnut Machine" turn a disaster into a success?
3. How might the television interview on the Joe Smiley Show help Rufus Mayflower from "The Toothpaste Millionaire" expand his enterprise?
4. What might Henry and Midge from "Henry Reed's Journal" learn about starting a business if they talked with Janie from "Kid Power" and Rufus from "The Toothpaste Millionaire"?
5. Do you think Maggie Marmelstein would make a good reporter for Children's Express? Why or why not?
6.  Write a letter to the editor of your local newspaper about a topic that interests or concerns you. Express your point of view so that readers will understand why you feel the way you do.

Introducing Level 11

# FRONTIERS

*Go west, young man,*
*and grow up with the country.*

**Horace Greeley**

UNIT

# 2

In the 1800s, many Americans were inspired to start new lives in the lands west of the Mississippi River. The stories in this unit are about the pioneers who made this westward journey. You will travel with them by covered wagon, and visit their homes, towns, and schools. You will see the pictures they painted, and follow them to gold mines. What do you think motivated people to go west?

# DIABLO BLANCO

## THOMAS FALL

8/1/04

*T*he Spanish explorers who came to the Americas in the early 1500s brought the first horses to Mexico. The wild horses that roamed throughout the southwestern part of our country in the 1800s probably were the descendants of these Spanish horses.

*This story is about a wild mustang named Diablo Blanco (dē ä′ blō blän′ kō) who lived on the Texas prairie in the 1870s. For years, this proud and clever white stallion had avoided capture. Some who had tried to take him had lost their lives. Roberto's father was one of them. Now Roberto is determined to find the horse and take his revenge. To carry out his plan, Roberto must first become an expert horseman.*

Roberto knew that there was much about wild horses he must learn. The Comanches were the finest horsemen in America, and many of their best horses were mustangs that had once run wild.

I will go into the mountains and find Chief Leaning Rock. He will help me, Roberto said to himself.

The mountain up which he rode was rough and steep. After several days of hard riding, Roberto spied a lookout from an Indian camp and approached him cautiously.

"I am searching for Chief Leaning Rock," Roberto said to the lookout, who seemed surprised to hear the Comanche

147

tongue. "I am the boy who helped your chief when he was wounded. My grandfather and I were coming out of New Mexico when we found him."

The lookout eyed Roberto solemnly. "Follow me. I will take you to Chief Leaning Rock."

Roberto entered the chief's tepee. At his invitation, Roberto sat beside the ashes in the ring of fire stones at the center of the tepee. "My grandfather died a few weeks ago," he said to the chief. "I came to ask a great favor of you."

The chief shook his head sadly. "Your grandfather was my friend. What do you want me to do, Roberto?"

"Send me to Conas with the young braves from your clan."

"That is a special training camp for teaching young men the arts of warfare."

"That is why I want to go."

"Do you want to become a Comanche?" the chief asked.

"No," said Roberto. "I will always be the Comanche's friend, but I will not become one myself."

"Then why do you want to go to Conas?"

"To learn riding and mustang-catching. I was too young to

learn enough from my father before he died. I am going to catch Diablo Blanco."

"Many men have tried to capture Diablo Blanco," said the chief. "Some of them have been killed, including your father."

"I know," Roberto said.

"The war instructor at Conas this year is Yellow Cloud," said the chief. "I will send you out of gratitude to your grandfather."

Roberto's pulses pounded at the thought of going to Conas, the principal town of all the Comanche tribes. It was there that they kept their eternal fire burning—*conas* meant "fire" in the Comanche language. It was there that they held their largest and most important training for future warriors.

Roberto set out for Yellow Cloud's training camp. The stream near Conas flowed across a level area nestled among some rolling grassy hills above the Colorado River in central Texas.

*       *       *

That winter, Roberto learned which cacti would provide water and which roots and herbs would keep him alive when no other food was available. He went into the hills and over the prairies and onto the desert for days at a time. He learned to track others who had gone ahead of him.

Yellow Cloud drew Roberto aside one day and said, "I think you could become a Comanche if you wanted to. You are the best student in the camp."

"Thank you," said Roberto, "but I am going to hunt for a white stallion called Diablo Blanco as soon as our training here is completed. Then, I am going to become a professional mustanger."

Several days later, Yellow Cloud called together all the boys who were ready for the special horsemanship instruction. At last Roberto would begin the part of the training that he had been waiting for.

"First you must learn to braid buckskin arm loops into your horse's mane," said Yellow Cloud. "Your life may depend on the strength of your braids."

As the young men watched, Yellow Cloud demonstrated with heavy buckskin thongs the method of braiding loops into the long mane of a training horse. He then placed a rawhide belt, with short loops of buffalo sinews for stirrups, over the horse's back and cinched it tight.

"Now you will see how important the braids are," Yellow Cloud told them. He put a foot into one stirrup and an arm through a loop in the mane. He drew himself instantly off the ground into a hanging position at the horse's side. "Notice that both my hands are free."

Yellow Cloud then showed them how he could drop from a normal position astride the horse to a hanging position. He threw one foot over into the stirrup on the opposite side and let his arm slide through a mane loop. He did it at a trot and then at full gallop.

"Roberto can try first," he said.

Roberto had probably spent more time on a horse during his

life than the Comanche boys. They were not allowed horses of their own until they completed training. He sprang astride the horse, threw his leg over and let himself dangle off the ground at the horse's side. He performed as Yellow Cloud had shown them.

Not too bad,'' Yellow Cloud admitted.

After days of practicing, Roberto could swing himself from side to side, picking up objects from the ground at full gallop. He beat all the other boys in his class at this difficult task.

He excelled at the trick of riding on the side of his horse into a mustang herd, to single out the lead stallion, drive him from the herd, and rope him. He learned to throw the mustang, leap down, and tie its forelegs before it could get up. He learned to gentle the wild ones by talking to them blindfolded. He would rub their backs and pat them, quietly placing a rawhide belt on them. Then he would ride them, letting them run themselves into exhaustion if they wanted to.

Roberto felt that he was ready. He had learned well what he had to know. Now that his training was completed, he took his Comanche horse and headed for the prairie.

At dusk he looked for a place to spend the night. The spring air was chilly when he finally hobbled his horse and lay in a bed of oak leaves at the edge of some low scrubby hills. He burrowed under the leaves to keep warm, thinking of the day he would capture Diablo Blanco.

In the morning he selected a temporary campsite on a small mesa (mā′ sə). He knew that, until he had caught a mustang and gentled it for trading, he must work from this camp.

The next day he found a mustang herd shortly after sunup. He prepared a coil of rope and slipped down alongside his horse. He circled the mustangs casually for half an hour and then gradually went closer. Already he had singled out a young stallion. With a gentle tug on his horse's mane, he cut the stallion off from the herd.

He swung his loop quickly. By the time it landed over the stallion's head, the entire herd had thundered toward the horizon. But he had his stallion.

The young stallion reached the end of the rope in a burst of power. The tame horse, an old hand at roping, drew back at exactly the right time. The stallion tumbled in a heap and Roberto was on top of him, tying his forelegs.

The stallion got up and reared wildly, but he could not run. While the trained horse held him, Roberto circled him on foot. He finally swung another loop that caught the hind legs, once more throwing him to the ground. The young horse struggled on his side, kicking the dirt. Roberto stood by and let him wear himself out.

After three hours the exhausted horse lay still. Roberto tied a cloth over the horse's face for blinders. All the while he talked gently to the terrified animal.

"I will not hurt you," he said in a soft voice. "I wonder what name I should give you. You are very tough, I think I will call you Cactus. Please, please do not run away."

He picketed his own horse, then spoke softly to Cactus, patting him gently. With the long rope still tied to his tame horse's neck, he released Cactus's legs at last and let him up. Blindfolded, the horse stood still until Roberto approached. Then, despite the blinders, he screamed and ran in a circle.

Roberto let him run. Leading his own horse, he maneuvered Cactus to the edge of the hills. He tied him to a tree where he could graze and sleep during the night.

Roberto rode him on the fourth morning.

He had somewhat soothed Cactus's nerves by now. He walked up to him and placed the halter over his head. "Thank you for not biting me," he said. "You see, I am not a bad fellow." He rubbed the horse's back gently. When he decided the time had come, he casually untied the long rope and sprang suddenly onto the wild horse's back. Startled, Cactus reared for a moment, and then shot across the prairie. Roberto held a slack rein, prepared to stay with him until he ran it out of his system.

They were a good fifteen miles from Roberto's camp on the mesa when the horse finally gave in and slowed down to a walk.

"Cactus, I like you," Roberto said to the horse, patting the animal's steaming neck. "I wish I did not have to sell you. But I need a knife very badly. And I will need some clothes, especially boots, when I go after your big white cousin called Diablo Blanco. Someday, somehow, I will capture him, Cactus. But for now, old boy, we have a long walk back to my camp. You put up a very good fight, I am proud of you."

Roberto sold Cactus to a traveling peddler he met while on his way to the trading post. With the money, he bought a secondhand army blanket, matches in a waterproof box, flour, a skillet with a folding handle, a canteen, a spade, a skinning knife, an ax, and a sheepskin pad for a saddle.

His heart and spirits soared as he headed northwest toward the tall-grass waterhole on the far side of the prairie where he had first seen Diablo Blanco. For many weeks he had been working out a plan for capturing the great white stallion. He would need at least two more fast horses as well as luck.

He worked until he captured and gentled two more mustangs. Then he made a small corral by fencing across the opening to a narrow box canyon. There he set up his permanent camp, where he would return to continue mustanging after he sold Diablo and had enough money to outfit himself in a real way.

Roberto got his first glimpse of Diablo on the rim of a river canyon. His long mane flowed out and glowed white against the sky. With his ears back, he snorted angrily, wheeled, and fled the canyon. His herd followed, sending dust clouds high into the sky.

Roberto began the pursuit. He knew that none of his horses could possibly catch Diablo Blanco in a race. His plan was to use them in relays, keeping the white stallion on the move for days until he was exhausted.

Roberto had learned that wild horses were creatures of habit. Even though they sometimes roamed for many miles, or ran for hours if they were being chased, they always moved in great circles back to the grass-land they considered home. By following the dust trails raised by the herd, Roberto knew that in time he would be back in this part of the prairie.

He kept Diablo moving all day. Toward nightfall, when he passed near his camp, he changed to a fresh mount. Then he followed by moonlight. He feared he had lost Diablo before daybreak, for his only clue to direction was the sound of pounding hoofbeats. But the early sunlight showed him dust on the horizon again.

The herd became smaller as the mares and younger stallions fell behind and scattered out alone. During the third day he caught several glimpses of the big white horse.

Diablo was now visibly tired. He would stop on a knoll or at the top of a hill, staring at his pursuer with flared nostrils, breathing heavily. He would paw and stamp the ground the moment Roberto came into sight. Then he would be off again for a five- or six-mile run.

On the fourth day, Diablo traveled completely alone. To-morrow, Roberto decided, would be the day to attempt the catch.

He slept an hour at daybreak again. He had rested his Co-manche horse well for this final pursuit. When he passed near his camp on the mesa that morning, he changed to the Comanche horse. He carried three good ropes and set out after Diablo at the most leisurely pace possible.

He soon saw the horse on the rim of an arroyo (ə roi′ ō), glaring back at him pitifully.

"I am sorry to treat you this way, Diablo," he said. "But you

are going to be mine today. My father died trying to leap onto your back."

Diablo seemed to wait longer than usual before he broke into a run toward the horizon this time. Roberto dug his heels into his Comanche horse and flew in swift pursuit.

The stallion was taken by surprise, for this had not been the pattern of the past few days. He ran for a mile, then looked back. Roberto was close, urging the Comanche horse on.

Diablo snorted and squealed in a mixture of fright and bitter anger. He thundered ahead, skimming across the prairie for five miles before pausing to look back. Still Roberto was right on him.

Away he went again, but Roberto closed in rapidly, for his Comanche horse still had plenty of reserve strength. Leaning forward, he let out a loop in his lariat and swung it swiftly over his head. He threw the lariat and watched it settle around Diablo's neck. His heart pounded furiously. This was the moment he had worked toward for more than a year.

Diablo reached the end of the rope, lunged against it, and tumbled head over heels into the grass.

Roberto leaped down and ran to tie the killer horse's forelegs. But Diablo was too quick, despite his weary condition, and still much too strong. With a wild squeal, he righted himself and nipped Roberto painfully on the leg as he came up. Then he reared, ready to strike at his enemy with his front hoofs.

But the Comanche horse backed away expertly, tightening the rope and veering Diablo's blow to one side.

Diablo snorted and wheeled, then went at the Comanche horse. He walked on his hind legs, pawed and bit.

Roberto caught hold of a ring in the mane of his Comanche horse, leaped astride, and quickly untied the rope, setting Diablo free. Then he reined away from the stallion.

"I am going to capture you today, Diablo!" he shouted in

anguish. "You are only free for a little while!"

The gigantic horse watched him for an instant. He snorted and squealed wildly, then broke into a furious run toward the horizon.

Roberto immediately dug his heels into the Comanche horse and went after him. "I will not let you rest, Diablo!" he vowed.

They ran four miles before Diablo slowed up. Roberto drew alongside Diablo and leaned over as far as he could. Then, springing mightily, he leaped onto the horse's back. It was the broadest, strongest back he had ever sat astride. The power still churning in the tired muscles as the animal pounded the prairie was simply astonishing.

Roberto let the horse run for half an hour, then tossed a loop of rope over his nose. Diablo's head rose high in resentment, and he burst into a faster and more frenzied pace.

Roberto leaned low on the neck, clutching deep handfuls of the heavy white mane, rolling with the animal's thundering gait.

Within an hour Diablo stopped. He stood perfectly still in a shallow arroyo, as though getting himself out of sight of any other mustangs before admitting that he had been captured.

"*Buenos dias*, Señor Diablo Blanco," Roberto said softly, patting the horse on his sweat-foamed neck. "You are a brave horse. Believe me, I am very tired myself. . . ."

## Thinking and Writing About the Selection

1. Why did Chief Leaning Rock agree to let Roberto attend the Comanche training camp?
2. How did Roberto capture Diablo Blanco? What were the important steps in his plan?
3. Do you think Roberto had great respect and love for horses? Give reasons to support your answer.
4. Imagine you are Roberto. What would you do if you had captured Diablo Blanco?

## Applying the Key Skill
### Cause and Effect

Copy the chart below on your paper. Fill in the missing information about cause-and-effect relationships from "Diablo Blanco."

| CAUSE | EFFECT |
|---|---|
| | Roberto wanted to go to Conas. |
| | Chief Leaning Rock agreed to send Roberto to Conas. |
| Roberto needed money to buy supplies. | |
| Roberto knew that none of his horses could outrun Diablo Blanco. | |
| | By the third day, Diablo Blanco was visibly tired. |

AWARD CLASSICS WINNERS

# GOING WEST

**BY**

**Russell**

**Freedman**

*Imagine traveling west along the Oregon Trail in the 1800s. Your house would be a covered wagon. Your playground would be a dusty prairie, a hot desert, or a rocky mountain pass. For six to eight months, you would be on the trail. Spring, summer, and fall would pass before you reached California or Oregon. You and your family would make the difficult journey to claim free land for farming or ranching. In this selection, you will read about a typical journey across the continent. Photographs taken at the time will show you what life was like on the frontier.*

It was a typical wagon train of the 1840s. The swaying wagons, plodding animals, and walking people stretched out along the trail for almost a mile.

Near the end of the train, a boy holding a stick moved slowly through the dust. He used the stick to poke and prod the cows that walked beside him.

"Get along!" he shouted. "Hey! Hey! Get along!"

Dust floated in the air. It clogged the boy's nose, parched his throat, and coated his face. His cheeks were smeared where he had brushed away the big mosquitoes that buzzed about everywhere.

161

Up ahead, his family's wagon bounced down the trail. He could hear the *crack* of his father's whip above the heads of the oxen that pulled the wagon. The chains on their yokes rattled with every step they took.

His mother sat in the front seat of the wagon, holding the baby on her lap. His sisters had gone off to hunt for wild herbs.

The family was traveling west along the Oregon Trail in what someday would be the state of Wyoming. They followed the sandy banks of the North Platte River past rocky hills dotted with sagebrush and greasewood. This was Indian country, the land of the Oglala Sioux.

Back in Missouri, their wagon had been a brand-new prairie schooner with red wheels, a blue body, and a white canvas top. Now the top was stained and patched. The paint was faded and crusted with mud. The wagon creaked and groaned, but it was still sturdy.

The wagon was crammed with the family's possessions—with food, clothing, and furniture; with tools, bedding, kitchenware, and tent supplies. Tied to its side were a plow and a hoe. Hanging from a rope was a sealed pail of milk. The pail bounced steadily as the wagon jolted along. By evening, the milk would be churned into butter.

There were forty wagons in the party, and nearly two hundred men, women, and children. A few of the pioneers rode saddle horses, but most of them walked. The only ones riding inside the wagons were little children with their mothers and people who were sick or injured. Following the wagons were herds of milk cows and beef cattle. Extra oxen, mules, and horses also trailed behind.

The pioneers had been up since four that morning, when the sentries started the day by firing their rifles.

In the darkness, they had kindled fires, put on kettles of water, milked cows, pulled down tents, loaded wagons, and fixed breakfast. By seven, they were ready to roll. The train captain gave the signal to move out. Slowly the lead wagons rolled forward. The others fell into line behind them.

At noon they stopped for an hour's rest. The teams of oxen and mules were turned loose from the wagons. Blankets and buffalo robes were spread out beside the trail. The pioneers ate a cold lunch. They relaxed a bit, and then rolled down the trail again.

As they moved along, they passed the wreck of an abandoned wagon. Every two or three miles, they saw wooden grave markers where pioneers had been laid to rest beside the trail. As the day wore on, children began to climb aboard the wagons to curl up and nap.

Late that afternoon, the train captain gave the signal to stop for the night. One after another, the wagons pulled off the trail and began to form a large circle, or corral. The wagons were locked together, front to rear, with chains. A gateway was left open to admit the live-stock. Then the last wagon was rolled into place, sealing the corral.

Safely inside, the pioneers tended their cattle, pitched tents, and started campfires for the evening meal. Families sat together eating beans, dried buffalo meat, and camp-baked bread from tin plates.

By eight o'clock, sentries had taken their posts around the corral. Children ran past playing tag. Some girls sat in a circle, sharing secrets and laughing. A boy lay beside a campfire, studying a copy of the *Emigrants Guide to Oregon and California*. Grown-ups stood in small groups, chatting and planning the day ahead.

Gradually the pioneers drifted off to their tents and wagons. They had traveled perhaps 15 miles (24 km) that day, nearly 700 miles (1,120 km) since leaving Missouri in May. They still had more than twice that distance to go.

The first pioneers to travel west by wagon train had set out from Missouri in the spring of 1841. Each year after that, emigrants streamed westward in ever-increasing numbers. By the spring of 1869, when the first transcontinental railroad was completed, more than 350,000 pioneers had followed the Oregon Trail across the continent.

At the beginning, most of them headed for the Pacific Coast. They went west to claim free land in the Oregon and California territories, or to strike it rich by mining gold and silver.

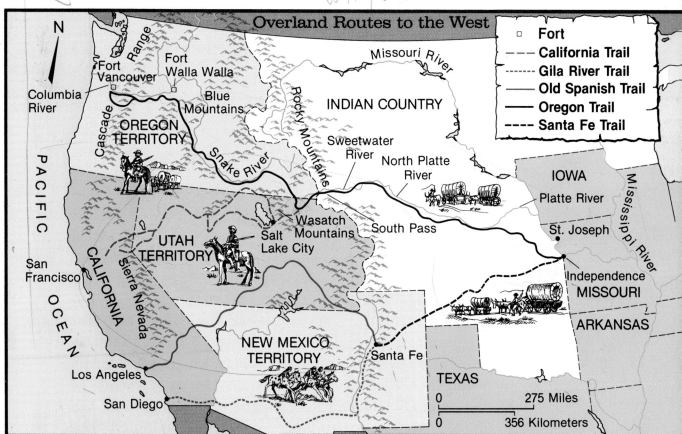

**Overland Routes to the West**

Legend:
- □ Fort
- ----- California Trail
- ········· Gila River Trail
- ——— Old Spanish Trail
- ——— Oregon Trail
- - - - Santa Fe Trail

N

Cascade Range
Columbia River
Fort Vancouver
Fort Walla Walla
Blue Mountains
OREGON TERRITORY
Snake River
Rocky Mountains
Missouri River
INDIAN COUNTRY
Sweetwater River
North Platte River
South Pass
IOWA
Platte River
Mississippi River
St. Joseph
Wasatch Mountains
Salt Lake City
UTAH TERRITORY
PACIFIC OCEAN
San Francisco
Sierra Nevada
CALIFORNIA
Independence
MISSOURI
ARKANSAS
Los Angeles
San Diego
NEW MEXICO TERRITORY
Santa Fe
TEXAS

0 ___ 275 Miles
0 ___ 356 Kilometers

They called themselves "emigrants" because they were actually leaving America. During the early 1840s, the United States ended at the banks of the Missouri River. The region that later would be Kansas and Nebraska had been set aside by the United States government as Indian Territory. California was still a part of Mexico. The wilderness of the Oregon country was claimed jointly by the United States and Great Britain. Gradually these western territories would become part of the United States. But when the first emigrants set out, they were entering a foreign land.

Their journey started in one of the frontier towns along the Missouri River. These towns were known as the "jumping-off places." Wagons rumbled through the muddy streets. Fur trappers and Indians mingled with westbound emigrants on sagging wooden sidewalks. Each year the wagon trains started rolling in late April or early May. Timing was important. If the emigrants started too early, they might not find enough spring grass on the prairie to graze their livestock. If they started too late, they might be stranded in the western mountains by early winter blizzards.

Several trails led west. The best-known and most popular by far was the Oregon Trail. It led across the Great Plains. It climbed over the Rockies, and then branched off toward Oregon in one direction and California in the other.

For most of its route, the Oregon Trail was little more than a pair of wheel ruts. It cut across 2,400 miles (3,840 km) of prairie sod, mountain rocks, and desert sand. When the trail came to a river, the ruts stopped at the water's edge. If the river was not too deep, the emigrants could ford it with their wagons. Otherwise they had to lift the wagons off their wheels and float them across on rafts. Horses and cattle swam alongside.

The first weeks on the trail were always the easiest. Their wagons were packed with fresh supplies. Their animals were sleek and healthy. The land was flat. The weather was often mild.

As the emigrants entered the foothills of the Rockies, the trail began to climb uphill. Oxen and mules struggled against their loads. Teamsters shouted and lashed their whips to urge on their tired teams. To lighten the load, the emigrants began to dump household possessions. Bureaus and tables were left beside the road to crack and scorch under the western sun.

By now, hardship and fatigue showed in the emigrants' faces. At times it seemed that almost half of them were ill.

Gradually the trail climbed the Rockies. It crossed the continental divide at South Pass, a valley that cut through the mountains. Beyond the Rockies, the trail branched off. One branch led northwest toward the coast of Oregon. The other led southwest toward California. At this point the emigrants were only about halfway there.

Emigrants bound for California had to cross the deserts of Utah and Nevada. Then they had to pull their wagons over the Sierra Nevada Mountains. If they kept on schedule, they could make it across the mountains before the first snowfall. The road to Oregon followed the twisting Snake River along steep, rocky ledges. It passed through a plateau. Then it climbed west over the Blue Mountains and the Cascades.

As the emigrants pressed forward, oxen and mules were overcome by heat and exhaustion. Animals stumbled in their tracks and died. Once past the deserts, wagons had to be hoisted up mountain slopes with chains and ropes, then eased down with their wheels locked. Sometimes chains snapped, and wagons tumbled down hills and toppled over mountain ledges.

If food supplies ran low, the emigrants had to kill their oxen and mules and eat them. Some pioneers were forced to abandon their wagons altogether and cross the mountains on horseback or on foot.

Babies were born during the westward journey, and many emigrants died. One out of every seventeen emigrants who started the trip was buried beside the Oregon Trail.

Many emigrants spent six to eight months on the trail. Often it was November or December before they finally came down from the mountains into the fertile valleys of Oregon and California.

## Thinking and Writing About the Selection

1. Why did the pioneers call themselves "emigrants"?
2. What can photographs of the pioneers tell us about the past?
3. What kind of people were the pioneers?

 4. Imagine that you are a pioneer going west in the 1840s. Write a letter to a friend who lives in the East. Describe a day on the trail or an adventure you might have had.

## Applying the Key Skill
### Maps

Use the map in "Going West" to answer the following questions.

1. What symbol represents the Oregon Trail?
2. What mountains are directly east of San Francisco?
3. What is the easternmost river shown on the map?
4. What forts were located in the Oregon Territory?
5. In what territory was Santa Fe located?
6. About how many miles is it from Santa Fe to Los Angeles?
7. About how many kilometers is it from Fort Vancouver to San Francisco?
8. What is the southernmost trail shown on the map?

# Western Wagons

They went with axe and rifle, when the trail was still to blaze.
They went with wife and children, in the prairie-schooner days.
With banjo and with frying pan—Susanna don't you cry!
For I'm off to California to get rich out there or die!

We've broken land and cleared it, but we're tired of where we are.
They say that wild Nebraska is a better place by far.
There's gold in far Wyoming, there's black earth in Ioway,
So pack up the kids and blankets, for we're moving out today!

The cowards never started and the weak died on the road,
And all across the continent the endless campfires glowed.
We'd taken land and settled—but a traveler passed by—
And we're going West tomorrow—Lordy, never ask us why!

We're going West tomorrow, where the promises can't fail.
O'er the hills in legions, boys, and crowd the dusty trail!
We shall starve and freeze and suffer. We shall die, and tame the lands.
But we're going West tomorrow, with our fortune in our hands.

*Rosemary and Stephen Vincent Benét*

# MAPS

Maps often help you better understand stories and articles you read. A **map** is a drawing of the earth's surface as seen from above. It shows the location of important places and gives information about direction and distances.

All maps are smaller than the areas they represent. A **scale bar** shows you how many miles or kilometers on the earth's surface are represented by a certain distance on the map. Find the scale bar on the map on the next page. It shows how many miles are represented by one inch, and how many kilometers are represented by two centimeters. How many miles on the earth are represented by one inch on the map?

There is not room on maps to show things exactly as they are. Much of the information is given by symbols. A **symbol** is anything that stands for something else. Symbols can be drawings or lines. Color is a special symbol used on maps. Map symbols are explained in the **key**. What does the symbol ♛ represent on the map? How is water shown?

Most maps are drawn so that north is toward the top. In addition, many maps have a **north arrow** indicating which way north is. If you know which way north is, you can easily figure out the other directions. When you face north, east is to your right, west is to your left, and south is behind you. In what direction from Fort Union is Sutter's Fort?

**ACTIVITY** Number your paper from 1 to 8. Use the map to answer the questions. Write the answers on your paper.

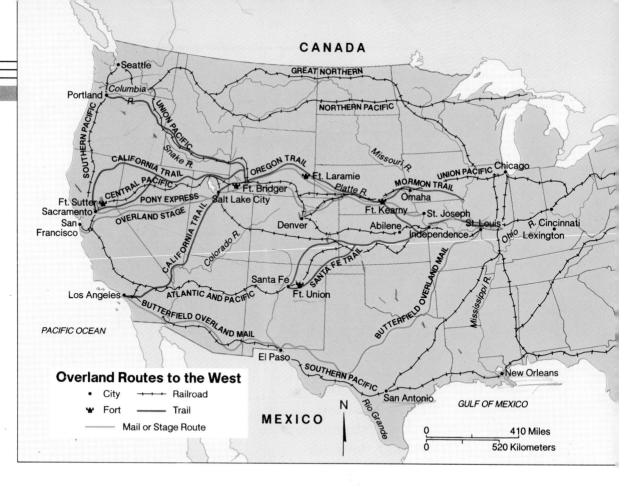

Overland Routes to the West

Legend:
- • City
- ⚑ Fort
- ┼─┼─┼ Railroad
- ──── Trail
- ──── Mail or Stage Route

0    410 Miles
0    520 Kilometers

1. What does this map show?
2. In what city did the Butterfield Overland Mail route begin? In what city did it end?
3. On what railroad line was Santa Fe located?
4. How many miles was it between San Antonio and New Orleans on the Southern Pacific route?
5. How many kilometers was it between Portland and Sacramento on the Southern Pacific route?
6. Was there an overland stage route between St. Louis and St. Joseph? Between St. Joseph and Denver?
7. One branch of the California Trail went to Sacramento. Where did the other branch go?
8. What city was at the westernmost point on the Oregon Trail?

# BY THE SHORES OF

*Laura Ingalls Wilder's books include nine "Little House" novels. The books describe her experiences and those of her family as pioneers during the late 1800s.*

*By the Shores of Silver Lake is the fifth book in the series. The Ingalls family has moved to the Dakota Territory, where Pa has a job working for the railroad. In this excerpt from the novel, settlers are streaming into the territory and the rush is on to claim land. Mr. Ingalls has already found a homestead. In order to keep it however, he must file a claim on the land before anyone else.*

"No music tonight," Pa said that evening at the supper table. "Early to bed and early to rise, and day after tomorrow our claim's filed on the homestead."

"I'll be glad, Charles," said Ma. After all the bustle of last night and this morning, the house was quiet and composed again. The supper work was done, Grace slept in the trundle

# SILVER LAKE

### Laura Ingalls Wilder

bed, and Ma was packing the lunch that Pa would eat on the way to Brookins.

"Listen," Mary said. "I hear somebody talking."

Laura pressed her face to a windowpane and shut out the lamplight with her hands. Against the snow she saw a dark team and a wagon full of men. One of them shouted again, then another jumped to the ground. Pa went to meet him and they stood talking. Then Pa came in and shut the door behind him.

"There's five of them, Caroline," he said. "Strangers, on their way to Huron."

"There isn't room for them here," said Ma.

"Caroline, we've got to put them up for the night. There isn't any other place they can stay or get a bite to eat. Their team is tired out and they're greenhorns. If they try to get to Huron tonight, they'll lose themselves on the prairie and maybe freeze to death."

Ma sighed, "Well, you know best Charles."

So Ma cooked supper for the five strange men. They filled the place with their loud boots and loud voices, and their bedding piled in heaps, ready to make their beds on the floor by the stove. Even before the supper dishes were finished, Ma took her hands from the dishwater and said quietly, "It's bedtime, girls."

It was not bedtime, but they knew that she meant they were not allowed to stay downstairs among those strange men. Carrie followed Mary through the stair door, but Ma held Laura back to slip into her hand a strong sliver of wood. "Push this into the wood above the latch," Ma said. "Push it well in and leave it there. Then no one can lift the latch and open the door. I want the door to be locked. Don't come down until I call you tomorrow morning."

In the morning, Laura and Mary and Carrie lay in bed after the sun was up. Downstairs they heard the strangers talking, and the breakfast dishes clattering.

"Ma said not to come until she called us," Laura insisted.

"I wish they'd go away," said Carrie. "I don't like strangers."

"I don't either, and neither does Ma," Laura said. "It takes them a long time to get started, because they're greenhorns."

At last they were gone, and at dinner Pa said he would go to Brookins tomorrow. "No use starting unless I start early," he said. "It's a long day's trip, and there's no sense in starting after sun-up and having to camp out overnight in this cold."

That night more strangers came. The next night there were more. Ma said, "Mercy on us, aren't we to have one night in peace by ourselves?"

"I can't help it Caroline," said Pa. "We can't refuse folks shelter, when there's nowhere else they can stay."

"We can charge them for it, Charles," Ma said firmly. Pa did not like to charge folks for shelter and a meal, but he knew that Ma was right. So he charged twenty-five cents a meal, and twenty-five cents for shelter overnight, for man or horse.

There was no more singing, no more comfortable suppers or cozy evenings. Every day more strangers crowded around the supper table, and every night as soon as all the dishes were washed, Laura and Mary and Carrie had to go up to the attic and fasten the door behind them.

The strangers came from Iowa, from Ohio, from Illinois and Michigan, from Wisconsin and Minnesota and even from faraway New York and Vermont. They were going to Huron or to Fort Pierre or even farther West, looking for homesteads.

One morning Laura sat up in bed, listening. "Where's Pa, I wonder?" she said. "I don't hear Pa's voice. That's Mr. Boast talking."

"Maybe he's gone to get the homestead," Mary guessed.

When at last the loaded wagons went away to the West and Ma called the girls downstairs, she said that Pa had started before sunup.

"He didn't really want to go and leave us in this rush," she said, "but he had to. Someone else will get the homestead if he doesn't hurry. We had no idea that people would rush in here like this, and March hardly begun."

This was the first week in March. The door was open, and the air felt like spring.

"When March comes in like a lamb, it goes out like a lion," said Ma. "Come, girls, there's work to be done. Let's get this house in order before more travelers come."

"I wish nobody'd come till Pa gets back," Laura said while she and Carrie washed the stacks of dishes.

"Maybe nobody will," Carrie hoped.

"Mr. Boast is going to look after things while your Pa's gone," Ma said. "He asked Mr. and Mrs. Boast to stay here. They'll sleep in the bedroom, and Grace and I'll go upstairs with you girls."

Mrs. Boast came to help. That day they cleaned the whole house and moved the beds. They were all very tired, when in the last of the sunset they saw a wagon coming from the East. There were five men in it.

Mr. Boast helped them put their horses in the stable. Mrs.

Boast helped Ma cook their suppers. They had not finished eating, when another wagon brought four men. Laura cleared the table, washed the dishes, and helped put the supper on the table for them. While they were eating, a third wagon brought six men.

Mary had gone upstairs to be away from the crowd. Carrie sang Grace to sleep in the bedroom with the door shut. Laura cleared the table again and washed the dishes again.

"This is the worst yet," Ma said to Mrs. Boast when they met in the pantry. "There isn't room for fifteen on the floor, we'll have to put some beds in the lean-to. And they'll have to use their robes and blankets and coats for bedding."

"Rob will tend to it, I'll speak to him," said Mrs. Boast. "Mercy me, that's not another wagon?"

Laura had to wash the dishes again and reset the table again. The house was so full of strange men, strange eyes and strange voices and bulky coats and muddy boots, that she could hardly get through the crowd.

At last they were all fed and for the last time the last dish was washed. Ma with Grace in her arms followed Laura and Carrie to the stairs and carefully fastened the door behind them.

There was loud talking and walking. Ma sat up to listen. The downstairs bedroom was still, so Mr. Boast must think that the noise was all right. Ma lay down again. The noise grew louder. Sometimes it almost stopped, then suddenly it burst out. A crash shook the house, and Laura sat straight up, crying out, "Ma! What's that?"

Ma's voice was so low that it seemed louder than all the shouting downstairs. "Be quiet, Laura," she said. "Lie down."

Laura thought that she could not sleep. She was so tired that the noise tormented her. But another crash woke her out of a sound sleep. Ma said, "It's all right, Laura. Mr. Boast is there." Laura slept again.

In the morning Ma gently shook her awake, and whispered, "Come Laura, it's time to get breakfast. Let the others sleep."

They went downstairs together. Mr. Boast had taken up the beds. Tousled, sleepy and red-eyed, the men were getting into their boots and coats. Ma and Mrs. Boast hurried breakfast. The table was small and

Mary was sleeping in bed, and Laura could not keep her eyes open while she undressed. But as soon as she lay down, she was awakened by the noise downstairs.

there were not dishes enough, so that Laura set the table and washed the dishes three times.

At last the men were gone, and Ma called Mary, while she and Mrs. Boast cooked more breakfast and Laura washed dishes and set the table once more.

"My, such a night!" Mrs. Boast exclaimed.

"What was the matter?" Mary wondered.

"I think they were drunk," Ma said, tight-lipped.

"I should say they were!" Mr. Boast told her. "They brought bottles and a jug of whisky. I thought once I would have to interfere, but what could I do against a crowd of fifteen drunks? I decided to let them fight it out, unless they set the house afire."

"I'm thankful they didn't," said Ma.

That day a young man drove up to the house with a load of lumber. He had hauled the boards from Brookins, to build a store on the townsite. Pleasantly he urged Ma to board him while he was building, and Ma could not refuse because there

was no other place where he could eat.

Next came a man and his son from Sioux Falls. They had brought lumber to build a grocery store. They begged Ma to board them, and after she had agreed she said to Laura, "Might as well be hung for a sheep as a lamb."

"If Ingalls doesn't hurry back, we'll have a town here before he comes," said Mr. Boast.

"I only hope he's not too late to file on the homestead," Ma replied anxiously.

That day did not seem real. Laura's eyelids felt sandy and she yawned all the time, yet she did not feel sleepy. At noon young Mr. Hinz and the two Mr. Harthorns came to dinner. In the afternoon their hammers could be heard pounding on the framework of the new buildings. It seemed a long time since Pa had gone.

He did not come that night. All the next day he did not come. That night he did not come. And now Laura was sure that he was having a hard time getting the homestead. If he did not get it, perhaps they would go west to Oregon.

Ma would not let any more strangers sleep in the house. Only Mr. Hinz and the two Harthorns bunked down on the floor by the stove. The weather was not so cold that men would freeze, sleeping in their wagons. Ma charged twenty-five cents just for supper, and far into the night she and Mrs. Boast cooked and Laura washed dishes. So many men came to eat that she did not try to count them.

Late in the afternoon of the fourth day Pa came home. He waved as he drove by to put the tired team in the stable, and he walked smiling into the house. "Well, Caroline! Girls!" he said. "We've got the claim."

"You got it!" Ma exclaimed joyfully.

"I went after it, didn't I?" Pa laughed. "Brr! It's chilly, riding. Let me get to the stove and warm myself."

Ma shook down the fire and set the kettle boiling for tea. "Did you have any trouble, Charles?" she asked.

"You wouldn't believe it," said Pa. "I never saw such a jam. It looks like the whole country's trying to file on land. I got to Brookins all right the first night, and next morning when I showed up at the Land Office I couldn't get anywheres near the door. Every man had to stand in line and wait his turn. So many were ahead of me that my turn didn't come that day."

"You didn't stand there all day, Pa?" Laura cried.

"Yes, Flutterbudget. All day."

"Without anything to eat? Oh no, Pa," said Carrie.

"Pshaw, that didn't worry me. What worried me was the crowd. I kept thinking maybe somebody ahead of me is getting my quarter section. Caroline, you never saw such crowds. But my worry then wasn't a patch to what came later."

"What, Pa?" Laura asked.

"Let a fellow get his breath, Flutterbudget! Well, when the Land Office closed I went along in the jam to get supper at the hotel, and I heard a couple of men talking. One had filed on a claim near Huron. The other said De Smet was going to be a better town than Huron, and then he mentioned the very piece I picked out last winter.

He told the numbers. He was going to file on it first thing next morning. He said it was the only piece left vacant any-where near this townsite. So he was going to have it, though he'd never seen it.

"Well, that was enough for me. I had to beat him to that claim. At first I thought I'd be up bright and early next morn-ing, and then I figured I wouldn't take any chances. So as soon as I got some supper, I made tracks for the Land Office."

"I thought it was closed," said Carrie.

"It was. I settled right down on the doorstep to spend the night."

"Surely you didn't need to do that, Charles?" said Ma.

"Need to do that?" Pa re-peated. "I wasn't the only man who had that idea. Lucky I got there first. Must have been forty men waiting there all night, and right next to me were those two fellows that I'd heard talking."

He blew on the tea to cool it, and Laura said, "But did they know you wanted that piece?"

"They didn't know me from Adam," said Pa, drinking the

tea, "till a fellow came along and sang out, 'Hello, Ingalls! So you weathered the winter on Silver Lake. Settling down at De Smet, uh?'"

"Oh, Pa!" Mary wailed.

"Yes, the fat was in the fire then," said Pa. "I knew I wouldn't have a chance if I budged from that door. So I didn't. By sun-up the crowd was doubled, and a couple of hun-

"Just as it opened," said Pa, "the Huron man crowded me back. 'Get in! I'll hold him!' he said to the other fellow. It meant a fight, and while I fought him, the other'd get my homestead. Right then, quick as a wink, somebody landed like a ton of bricks on the Huron man. Go in, Ingalls!' he yelled. 'I'll fix'im! Yow-ee-ee!'"

Pa's long catamount screech curled against the walls, and Ma gasped, "Mercy! Charles!"

"And you'll never guess who it was," said Pa.

"Mr. Edwards!" Laura shouted.

Pa was astounded. "How did you guess it, Laura?"

"He yelled like that in Indian territory. He's a wildcat from Tennessee," Laura remembered. "Pa, where is he? Did you bring him?"

"I couldn't get him to come home with me," said Pa. "I tried every persuasion I could think of, but he's filed on a claim south of here and must stay with it to keep off claim jumpers. He told me to remember him to you, Caroline, and to Mary and Laura. I'd never have

dred men must have been pushing and shoving against me before the Land Office opened. There wasn't any standing in line that day, I tell you! It was each fellow for himself, and devil take the hindmost.

"Well, girls, finally the door opened. How about some more tea, Caroline?"

"Oh, Pa, go *on!*" Laura cried. "Please."

got the claim if it hadn't been for him. Golly, what a fight he started!"

"Was he hurt?" Mary asked anxiously.

"Not a scratch. He just started that fight. He got out of it as quick as I ducked inside and started filing my claim. But it was some time before the crowd quieted down. They—"

"All's well that ends well, Charles." Ma interrupted.

"I guess so, Caroline," Pa said. "Yes, I guess that's right. Well, girls, I've bet Uncle Sam fourteen dollars against a hundred and sixty acres of land, that we can make out to live on the claim for five years. Going to help me win the bet?"

"Oh, yes, Pa!" Carrie said eagerly, and Mary said "Yes, Pa!" gladly, and Laura promised soberly, "Yes, Pa."

"I don't like to think of it as gambling," Ma said in her gentle way.

"Everything's more or less a gamble, Caroline," said Pa. "Nothing is certain except death and taxes."

There was no time for a good talk with Pa. Already the sun-shine from the western window slanted far across the floor, and Ma said, "We must be getting supper. The men will be here soon."

"What men?" Pa asked.

"Oh, wait, Ma, please, I want to show him," Laura begged. "It's a surprise, Pa!" She hurried into the pantry and from the almost empty sack of beans where it was hidden, she pulled out the little sack full of money. "Look, Pa, look."

Pa felt the little sack in amazement. He looked at their faces, all shining with smiles. "Caroline! What have you girls been up to?"

"Look inside, Pa!" Laura cried. She could not wait while he untied the little sack. "Fifteen dollars and twenty-five cents!"

"I'll be jiggered!" Pa said.

Then while Laura and Ma started to get supper, they told him all that had happened while he was away. Before they had finished talking, another wagon pulled up at the door. There were seven strangers at supper that night; another dollar and seventy-five cents. And now that Pa was home, the strangers could sleep on the floor around the stove. Laura did not care how many dishes she washed, nor how sleepy and tired she was. Pa and Ma were getting rich, and she was helping.

In the morning she was surprised. There was hardly time to talk; so many men were there for breakfast, she could hardly wash the dishes fast enough, and when at last she could empty the dishpan and hang it up there was hardly time to sweep and scrub the muddy floor before she must begin peeling potatoes for dinner. She had only a glimpse of the sunny, cold, blue-and-white-and-brown March day outdoors, while she emptied the dishpan. And she saw Pa driving a load of lumber toward the townsite.

"What on earth is Pa doing?" she asked Ma.

"He's putting up a building on the townsite," said Ma.

"Who for?" Laura asked, beginning to sweep. Her fingers were shrunken in ridges, from being so long in the dishwater.

"'For whom', Laura," Ma corrected her. "For himself," and

she tugged through the doorway an armful of bedding that she was taking outdoors to air.

"I thought we were going to move to the claim," Laura said, when Ma came in.

"We have six months before we must build on the homestead," said Ma. "Lots in town are going so fast your Pa thinks he can make money by building on one. He's using the lumber from the railroad shanties and putting up a store building to sell."

"Oh, Ma, isn't it wonderful, all the money we're making!" Laura said, sweeping vigorously while Ma gathered another armful of bedding.

"Draw the broom, Laura; don't flip it, that raises the dust," said Ma. "Yes, but we mustn't count chickens before they're hatched."

That week the house filled with steady boarders, men who were building houses on the townsite or on their homestead claims. From dawn until far into the night, Ma and Laura hardly had time to catch their breaths. All day long there was a racket of wagons passing. Teamsters were hauling lumber from Brookins as fast as they could, and yellow skeletons of buildings rose every day. Already you could see Main Street growing up from the muddy ground along the railroad grade.

Every night beds covered the floor of the big room and the lean-to. Pa slept on the floor with the boarders so that Mary and Laura and Carrie could move into the bedroom with Ma and Grace, and more boarders' beds covered the whole floor of the attic.

The supplies were all gone, and now Ma had to buy flour and salt and beans and meat and corn meal, so she did not make so much money. Supplies cost three and four times as much as they cost in Minnesota, she said, because the railroad and the teamsters charged so much for the hauling. The roads were so muddy that the teamsters could not haul large loads. Anyway, she made a few cents' profit on every meal, and any little bit they could earn was better than nothing.

Laura did wish she could get time to see the building that Pa

was putting up. She wished she could talk to him about the building, but he ate with the boarders and hurried away with them. There was no time for talking now.

Suddenly, there on the brown prairie where nothing had been before, was the town. In two weeks, all along Main Street the unpainted, new buildings pushed up their thin false fronts, two stories high and square on top. Behind the false fronts the buildings squatted under their partly shingled sloping roofs. Strangers were already living there; smoke blew gray from the stovepipes, and glass windows glinted in the sunshine.

One day Laura heard a man say, through the clattering at the dinner table, that he was putting up a hotel. He had got in the night before with a load of lumber hauled from Brookins. His wife was coming out on the next load. "We'll be doing business within a week," he said.

"Glad to hear it, sir," Pa said. "What this town needs is a hotel. You'll be doing a land-office business, as quick as you can get started."

As suddenly as the hurry had begun, it ended. One evening Pa and Ma and Laura and Mary and Carrie and Grace sat down to supper. No one else was there. Around them was their own house again, no one else was in it. A beautiful quiet was there, peaceful and cool, like the silence when a blizzard stops, or the restfulness of rain after a long fever of drought.

## Thinking and Writing About the Selection

1. How much land did Mr. Ingalls file his claim for?

2. Why might other homesteaders think that the location of Mr. Ingalls' claim made it especially valuable?

3. What kinds of things do you think were sold in the new stores along Main Street? What buildings besides stores would be important in the new town?

4. If you had been a pioneer, would you have chosen to live in or near a town? Or would you have preferred to live far away from settled areas? Explain your answer.

## Applying the Key Skill
### Cause and Effect

The questions below are about cause-and-effect relationships in "By the Shores of Silver Lake."
Use complete sentences to answer them.

1. Why did Pa change his plans about the day he would go to Brookins to file his claim on the homestead?

2. Why couldn't Pa file his claim the first day he went to the Land Office?

3. Why didn't the Ingalls family move to their homestead right away?

4. What caused the prices of supplies in the Dakota Territory to be higher than the prices in Minnesota?

5. Why did travelers no longer ask to stay at the Ingalls home?

# EVERY CLOUD HAS A SILVER LINING

A **proverb** is a short statement that tells a truth, expresses a bit of useful wisdom, or gives practical advice. When Ma Ingalls said, "Early to bed and early to rise," she was giving only the first part of a proverb that ends "makes a man healthy, wealthy, and wise." Like many proverbs, this one is easy to remember because it rhymes.

"When March comes in like a lamb, it goes out like a lion" states a folk belief that if the weather is nice at the beginning of March, it will be bad at the end of the month. The other part of the proverb is, "When March comes in like a lion, it goes out like a lamb."

When Ma Ingalls said, "We musn't count chickens before they're hatched," she was really telling Laura not to plan on the money before they actually had it.

How many of the proverbs below have you heard? Do you know what they mean?

Every cloud has a silver lining.　　Look before you leap.
A stitch in time saves nine.　　Out of sight, out of mind.
Little pitchers have big ears.　　Haste makes waste.
A penny saved is a penny earned.　　Waste not, want not.

## AUTHOR'S PURPOSE
## AND POINT OF VIEW

Authors write for many different reasons. Laura Ingalls Wilder's purpose in writing "By the Shores of Silver Lake" was to entertain. Of course, you probably learned a lot about pioneer life as you read the story, but it was meant primarily as a story to be enjoyed.

Sometimes an **author's purpose** is to persuade, or convince, readers. An author might want to persuade people to vote a certain way or to write to their representatives in government. Editorials in newspapers are often written to persuade readers to support an idea or plan of action.

Authors who write articles in encyclopedias want to inform their readers. They present facts and other information about topics.

When we talk about an **author's point of view**, we are talking about the way the author feels about his or her subject. To figure out an author's point of view, you must carefully read what is said and pay attention to the way in which it is said. Read the passage below.

> If you want to improve your life, don't stay in the East—go West! There you will find rich farmlands, valuable mineral deposits, and a need for businesses of all kinds.

If you read the passage carefully, you probably know that it was written to convince people to move West. The author felt that the West had many opportunities for people to improve their lives.

**ACTIVITY**  Read the passages below. Then write one of the following phrases to describe the author's purpose.

to entertain      to inform      to persuade

1.  When was the last time you visited the Pioneer Museum? It's just the place to spend an exciting afternoon. Adults and children will enjoy the exhibits. There's so much to see—a real prairie schooner, a sod house, and a collection of unique photographs.

2.  The wagon trains that traveled on the Oregon Trail covered a distance of about 15 to 20 miles (24–32 km) per day. The boat-shaped wagons carried about a ton and a half of goods, including plows, tools, stoves, and furniture. There was little room in the loaded wagon, so the family cooked, ate, and slept outdoors.

3.  Elizabeth tried to fall asleep, but she just couldn't. The stars never looked so bright or the sky so big. The campfire glowed. Elizabeth didn't want to miss a moment of this first day on the trail. It had been such an exciting day. Up before dawn to help with the final packing, the last-minute good-byes, the final look at the house and yard that had been home ever since she was born. Yes, there was much to look forward to and much to remember.

# *The* ART *of the* OLD WEST

## *Shirley Glubok*

**The United States was a very young country when Americans began exploring the vast lands west of the Mississippi River. The first expeditions crossed into the West in the early 1800s. With them went pioneer artists who brought back sketches of the people, the scenery, and the wildlife.**

One of the earliest pioneer artists was Titian R. Peale, who went west at nineteen. He was the first American to make drawings of the buffalo, the prairie chicken, the black-tailed deer, and other animals native to the West.

Peale's father, artist Charles Willson Peale, founded the first American museum, in Philadelphia. Peale's Museum exhibited the earliest portraits of Western Indians.

The Thomas Gilcrease Institute of American History and Art, Tulsa, Oklahoma.

A self-taught painter named George Catlin admired the Indian portraits in Peale's Museum. Then one day he saw a group of Western Indians on their way to Washington. Catlin decided to paint the Indians in their homelands before settlers reached them and changed their ways.

In 1832 Catlin traveled up the Missouri River on the first steamboat to make the trip. He went into Indian villages and painted portraits of the chiefs and other members of the tribes.

Man-Mah-To-He-Ha, known as Old Bear, was a medicine man of the Mandan Indians. In his portrait, he wears a bearskin around his waist and foxtails attached to his heels. In each hand he holds a ceremonial pipestem, decorated with eagle feathers. His headdress and face paint are different from those of Chief Tchan-Dee, known as Tobacco, of the Oglala Sioux Indians.

Spectacular landscapes of the West were painted on huge canvases by Albert Bierstadt (bir′ shtädt). He was a member of an expedition that traveled the Oregon Trail. This trail had been used by fur traders for many years and had become a popular route for pioneer families heading west.

When Bierstadt traveled this rugged route, he made many sketches of the landscape and of the early travelers with their covered wagons. In his painting *The Oregon Trail*, the sky and mountains seem to go on forever. Each figure in the foreground is painted with great care, even the grazing cattle and sheep. The tiny figures in the distance help to emphasize the large height of the mountains.

The best-known artist of the old West is probably Frederic Remington. He was born in New York State, the son of a Civil War cavalry officer. Remington studied art for a short time. Then he went west, working as a cowboy and prospecting for gold in Arizona. He roamed cattle trails from Canada to the Mexican border, and became an expert in handling a lariat.

Remington's paintings reflect the hardships of the Old West, where settlers fought to establish new homes while Indians tried to protect their lands. Even his quiet scenes are filled with a sense of danger. The Indian scout in the empty night scene below seems alert to possible danger. He has just halted his horse and now leans forward to sense whether the people in the distance

*The Scout: Friends or Enemies?* c. 1890 by Frederic Remington. Sterling and Francine Clark Art Institute, Williamstown, Massachusetts.

are friends or enemies. In another painting, a pioneer stands in the moonlight with his rifle ready, guarding a sleeping wagon train. The lone, upright figure and the large round wheels on either side create a strong design.

Remington first became well known as a magazine illustrator. As time went on, he wrote his own articles and books on Western subjects. In later years he devoted himself to oil painting.

C.M. Russell, "Cowboy Camp During the Roundup," o/c, c. 1887. Courtesy Amon Carter Museum, Fort Worth.

Charles Marion Russell, sometimes called "Kid" Russell, became known as the "cowboy artist." Born in St. Louis, he went to Montana at age sixteen, where he worked as a sheepherder, horse wrangler, and cowhand.

Russell loved the open ranges, the Indian ways, the great sky, the wildlife, and the freedom of the West. In this scene, cowboys are preparing for spring roundup, when they gather the cattle which have wintered on the open range. The men are breaking in wild horses.

Frederic Remington, "The Bronco Buster," bronze. Courtesy Amon Carter Museum, Fort Worth.

Sculpture of the Old West ranges from reliefs on coins to larger-than-life-size monuments in parks and other public places.

The painter Frederic Remington turned to sculpture late in his life. He made small statues in order to give fuller expression to action than was possible on a flat surface. In *Bronco Buster* there is a wonderful feeling of movement and balance.

A leading American sculptor, James Earle Fraser, who was brought up in South Dakota, designed the famous five-cent coin known as the "Buffalo Nickel." Three different Indians posed for the profile head.

What is known as the Old West lasted for little more than a hundred years. In that short time the herds of buffalo and the unfenced cattle ranges vanished forever. The rough-riding cavalrymen, the sun-hardened cowboys, the pioneers, and the prospectors have disappeared. The earliest inhabitants—the Indian tribes of the Great Plains, the Southwest, and the Pacific Coast—no longer roam the land. But the Old West lives on in the paintings and sculptures of the pioneer artists who have preserved its memory.

## Thinking and Writing About the Selection

1. What is the "Buffalo Nickel"?

2. Look at the paintings of Indians once again. What do the clothes and ornaments tell you about the Indian way of life?

3. The artists in the story did not paint in studios. They went west and painted what they saw. In what ways were they pioneers?

4. Reread the last sentence in the selection. Then list several other ways the Old West has been kept alive in our minds.

## Applying the Key Skill
### Author's Purpose and Point of View

Read the incomplete sentences below. Then choose the best ending or endings for each. Write the complete sentences.

1. The author probably wrote "The Art of the Old West" to ___.
   a. explain how to paint a landscape
   b. describe some of the artists, paintings, and sculptures of an earlier time in the history of our country
   c. compare painting and sculpture
   d. show how much can be learned by looking closely at paintings and sculpture

2. The author would probably agree that ___.
   a. much can be learned about history by studying paintings and sculptures
   b. the only way to find out about the past is by looking at art
   c. Frederic Remington's paintings are better than his sculptures
   d. what is past should still be remembered

11/10/04

# Caddie Woodlawn

Carol Ryrie Brink

*O*n the Wisconsin frontier in the 1860s, there were plenty of opportunities for adventure, and Caddie Woodlawn took advantage of them. One wintry Saturday, Caddie spent a typical morning at school. But the afternoon was anything but usual.

*Spelling Bee*

After the first few weeks, school had settled into a quiet routine. For Caddie, the chief delight of school was the Saturday morning spelling bee. On that day there was a review of the week's work, and, after that, they could choose sides for a spelldown. Each week the two best spellers, who stood out from the rest, were allowed to choose their teams for the next week. Caddie and her brother Tom both had the sportsman's love of any test of skill. But Caddie was the better speller. She pored over the tattered spelling book with excited concentration, and she was usually the first to toss back her curls and fling up her hand to let Teacher know that she was ready to spell. She and Jane Flusher or Jane's brother Sam were usually the last ones standing at the end of the match, and then it was a fierce struggle to see which of them would go down first. The teacher had to turn to the back of the speller to "piccalilli" or "soliloquize" before either Caddie or the Flushers would be "spelled down" and have to take a seat in laughing confusion and defeat.

Saturday afternoons were free. Sometimes the young Woodlawns went coasting or sleigh riding. Sometimes they all went with Tom to set traps for muskrats on the ice. Sometimes, and that was best of all, Father took Tom and Caddie and Warren with him to the mill, and let them skate on the millpond. The ice froze there in a smooth sheet over the quiet pond, and only a little clearing of snow was needed to make good skating.

It was one Saturday late in December that Caddie came near drowning for the second time that year.

Father had brought them to the mill for the first skating of the season, and, while he was busy, Caddie and the two boys strapped on their skates and tried the ice. Tom was an expert skater, cutting figure-eights and scrolls and spirals over the new ice. Caddie and Warren were eager to do as well as Tom, but they could only follow along in awkward imitation of his skill. What they lacked in skill, they tried to make up in daring.

"You better be careful of that black ice," called Tom. "It's kinda thin looking."

"Who's afraid," laughed Caddie. "You can't scare *me*!" and away she went. The black ice began to creak and then to crack. Crash! Smash! Caddie was in

over her head again! But what is only an adventure in a summer lake may be no joke in an ice-covered pond. Warren shrieked his alarm, but there was no time to fetch Father from the mill. Tom saw that only instant action on his part could save Caddie. With cool presence of mind, he made Warren lie down on the ice, and, catching hold of Warren's feet, he pushed him out over the thin ice until he could reach Caddie's groping hands.

"Hold tight, Warren," he shouted. "I'll pull you both in!" And he did. Nobody made much fuss over it. Pioneer children were always having mishaps, but they were expected to know how to use their heads in emergencies.

But it changed a large part of the winter for Caddie. Father dried her off as best he could in the engine room of the mill, wrapped her in buffalo robes, and drove her home. Mother put her into a steaming washtub before the kitchen fire, and then to bed with hot stones wrapped in flannel, and hot tea made of the dried leaves of wild strawberry plants. But Caddie had caught a bad cold, which kept her in bed for a week and home from school for several weeks.

Her mother sat on the foot of Caddie's bed the night of the accident, with a cup in one hand and a spoon in the other, and shook her head in despair. Exasperation and fond concern struggled on her face.

"Caddie, why can't you behave like a young lady? Only a few weeks ago you were fighting with that awful Obediah Jones. And now you've nearly killed yourself skating on thin ice. If it isn't one thing, it's another!"

"I'm sorry, Mother," croaked Caddie hoarsely from the depths of a red-flannel bandage.

"Well, well," sighed Mrs. Woodlawn. "It seems to be your nature. What will you have for supper? A little turkey broth?"

Caddie sighed. "Isn't there any bean soup, Mother?"

"No, it's turkey, dear."

"Well, turkey then."

"That's a good girl. Go to sleep now."

Christmas came and went while Caddie was still recovering. She had intended to spend some of her silver dollar for presents, but it still lay snug and safe in

the wooden trinket box, because she was not able to take it to the store.

Tom and Warren and Hetty went back to school, and the house seemed very empty. Caddie was not allowed to play with Minnie and baby Joe because of her cold, and when other household tasks were done, Mother and Clara were busy sewing. Father was at the mill and Mrs. Conroy did not want to be bothered in her kitchen. Caddie looked at the family Bible and read Tom's dog-eared book of Andersen's *Fairy Tales*. Then her wandering feet took her upstairs to the attic. Here were old boxes from their home in Boston, and a beautiful round-topped trunk, lined with colored paper, with pictures of smiling children decorating the various compartments. And on a low shelf was a row of clocks, waiting for Father's expert hand to mend them. The attic was drafty, but, near the head of the stairs, a big stone chimney came up from the kitchen, and there it was warm. Caddie drew some of the boxes over to the chimney and sat with her back against it, while she looked through them.

Then she turned her attention to the clocks. They had been at the back of her mind all the time. She had been reserving them as a sort of final treat, as she often did with the things she liked best. She picked them up, one by one, and shook them to see if they would start ticking. Among the others stood Mr. Tanner's clock. Caddie remembered what he had said—it was the "face of a dead friend." Surely he would soon return, and Father had not yet started work upon the clock. How dreadful it would be, if Mr. Tanner should return and find his clock unmended! Caddie turned

the clock thoughtfully in her hands. She had seen Father mend so many of them! Of course, they were not all alike inside, but she knew how the little screws came out and how the back came off, and then inside you saw all of the fascinating wheels and gimcracks. Why shouldn't she mend it herself? She sat down with her back against the chimney and began to loosen the screws.

It was more of a task than she had supposed. But Father's tools were there on the shelf, and she found a screwdriver of just the size she needed. The back came off, revealing the wheels and springs. Caddie knew enough about clocks to see what was the matter. Mr. Tanner had wound his clock too tightly, and in some way the spring had caught so that it could not unwind as it should have done. Caddie looked it over carefully. Then she began to loosen the screws which held it in place. She had to loosen several before she found the right ones. Time slipped away unheeded, she was so deeply absorbed in the clock. Her cheeks were flushed and her face, bent low over her work, was curtained by her dangling curls.

At last she loosened the right screw! Whizz! Bang! The spring flew out with a whirr and hit the low ceiling. Screws and cog wheels flew in every direction. It was like an explosion. Mr. Tanner's clock had suddenly flown to pieces! Caddie uttered a cry of despair and looked wildly about her. What would Father say?

There was a low chuckle from the stairway. Caddie followed the sound with startled eyes. Standing on one of the lower steps, so that his eyes were just above the level of the attic floor, stood her father. How long he had been watching her, she had no idea.

"Father," she wailed, "it went to pieces!" Her father leaned against the wall of the staircase and laughed. Caddie had almost never seen him laugh so hard. She, herself, did not know whether to laugh or to cry.

"Father," she repeated, "it went to pieces!"

Still laughing, Mr. Woodlawn came up the stairs.

"Let's pick up the pieces," he said. "We're going to put that clock together, Caddie. I've been needing a partner in my clock business for a long time. I don't know why I never thought of you before!"

"A partner!" gasped Caddie. She began to race about the attic, picking up screws and springs. "A real partner?"

"If you do well," said her father. "Clara is too busy, and Tom hasn't the patience nor the inclination. Yes, Caddie, I believe you'll be my partner."

Together they sat on the attic floor and put the clock in order. Mr. Woodlawn explained and demonstrated, while Caddie's eager fingers did the work. Together they cleaned and oiled the parts and made the nice adjustments that were required. By the time the work was finished, it was growing dark in the attic.

"Now take that down and show your mother, Caddie," said Mr. Woodlawn. Together they marched downstairs, one as proud as the other, and Caddie set the clock in the middle of the dining-room table.

"So you mended Mr. Tanner's clock, did you, Johnny?" said Mrs. Woodlawn carelessly.

"No, not this time," said her husband, with a twinkle in his eye. "Caddie did it."

"*Caddie did it?*" Mrs. Woodlawn and Clara and the children, who had just come in from school, crowded around to see.

"It runs," marveled Tom, and Warren uttered an admiring "Golly!"

Mr. Tanner's clock no longer looked like the "face of a dead friend." It appeared to be very much alive and spoke up with a cheerful tick.

Caddie never forgot the lesson she had learned that day in the attic. Wherever she was, all through her long and busy life, clocks ticked about her pleasantly, and, if they didn't, she knew the reason why.

## Thinking and Writing About the Selection

1. What school activity did Caddie enjoy most?

2. What did Tom do to show that he knew how to use his head in an emergency?

3. Mr. Woodlawn asked Caddie to be a partner in his clock repair business. Do you think Caddie would make a good partner? Explain your answer.

 4. Caddie's curiosity often got her into difficult situations. Think of another mishap Caddie might have. Write about another adventure in the life of Caddie Woodlawn.

## Applying the Key Skill
### Synonyms and Antonyms

The sentences below are from "Caddie Woodlawn." The underlined word is a synonym or antonym for a word in the story. Find the sentence in the story. Write the underlined word and the word it replaced in the sentence. Then tell if the two words are synonyms or antonyms.

1. Pioneer children were always having <u>accidents</u>, but they were expected to use their heads in emergencies.

2. And on a low shelf was a row of clocks, waiting for Father's <u>unskilled</u> hand to mend them.

3. Caddie turned the clock <u>carelessly</u> in her hands.

4. Caddie uttered a cry of <u>hopelessness</u> and looked wildly about her.

# Carol Ryrie Brink

Carol Ryrie Brink was raised by her grandmother. It was from her grandmother that she first heard the true stories of pioneer life on which *Caddie Woodlawn* was based. "Gram's house was large and pleasant," the author recalls. "I had pet dogs, cats, chickens, and best of all, a fat sorrel pony who carried me all over the Blue Idaho hills. On these long rambles with my pony I used to make up stories to tell myself. The pony, the mountains, my own stories, made me very happy. I said to myself, 'When I grow up I am going to write books!'"

It was not until she was married and the mother of two children that Carol Ryrie Brink thought seriously of writing for a wider audience. As she read the stories her children brought home from Sunday school, she thought she could do better. So she sent her first stories to religious publishers. These stories soon led to several plays and eventually to full-length novels.

When writing, this author has said, "I like to start with something I know—a place, a person, an experience—something from which I have had an emotional reaction. Then I try to re-create my feelings for my readers. I write in the mornings and usually I can put things down in fairly final shape at the first writing. That is because much of the preliminary work had been done in my head as I did other tasks."

**More to Read** *Magical Melons: More Stories About Caddie Woodlawn, Winter Cottage, Two Are Better Than One*

# REFERENCE SOURCES:
# ENCYCLOPEDIA, ALMANAC, ATLAS

Where would you look if you wanted to know more about the Western Indians and artists you read about in "The Art of the Old West"? A good place to start would be in an encyclopedia. An encyclopedia is just one of the several reference sources that can be helpful to you in finding answers to questions.

An **encyclopedia** contains articles about important people, places, things, events, and ideas. An encyclopedia is usually a set of books, like the one shown below. Each book in the set is called a volume.

The articles in an encyclopedia are arranged in alphabetical order. The guide letters on the back edge of each volume are the first letter or letters of the first and last article in that volume. For example, if you were looking for an article on art, you would look in Volume 1 of the sample set.

212

When you look for information in an encyclopedia, it is important to decide what **key word** or words to use to find the article that will provide the answer. Suppose you wanted to find the answer to this question: *What states border the Missouri River?* The key words here are *Missouri River*, not *states* or *border*. You would find an article on the Missouri River in Volume 8 of the sample encyclopedia set.

**ACTIVITY A**  Decide which key word or words you would use to find an encyclopedia article to answer each question below. Write the word on your paper.

1. In what state is the city of Philadelphia?

   a.  state          b.  city                    c.  Philadelphia

2. What kind of food did the buffalo of the Great Plains eat?

   a.  food           b.  buffalo                 c.  Great Plains

3. When did Congress pass the first Homestead Act providing land for pioneers?

   a.  Congress       b.  Homestead Act      c.  pioneers

**ACTIVITY B**  Use the sample encyclopedia set to answer the questions. Write the answers on your paper.

1. In which volume would you look to find an article about the Sioux Indians?

   a.  Vol. 5     b.  Vol. 6     c.  Vol. 10     d.  Vol. 11

2. In which volume would you look to find an article about the Oregon Trail?

   a.  Vol. 8     b.  Vol. 9     c.  Vol. 10     d.  Vol. 11

Another useful reference source is an almanac. An **almanac** is a single volume that is usually published every year. It has information on current events, and gives facts and figures on many subjects. An almanac has many charts and tables. It is a good place to look for such things as sports records, population figures, names of government officials, and winners of important prizes or awards.

You must use the index or table of contents to find information in an almanac. Choosing the right key word to answer a question is as important in finding information in an almanac as it is in an encyclopedia.

**ACTIVITY C** Number your paper from 1 to 8. Read each question below. If the best place to look for the answer would be in an encyclopedia, write **encyclopedia**. If the best place to look is in an almanac, write **almanac**.

1. Who won the Academy Award for best actress last year?
2. What kinds of materials do sculptors use?
3. What recognition did Frederic Remington receive in his lifetime?
4. How did the Indians of the Great Plains live before settlers came?
5. What is the present-day population of South Dakota?
6. What is the name of the current governor of California?
7. What states were carved out of the region once known as the Dakota Territory?
8. What country led the world in the production of wheat last year?

Another useful reference source is an atlas. An **atlas** is a book of maps. A world atlas has maps of the entire world, as well as maps of smaller parts of the world, such as continents and countries. The maps may show both physical features (rivers, lakes, deserts, swamps, mountains) and political features (countries, states, cities). You can use an atlas to find the location of places and to determine directions and distances. Most atlases have an index listing place names. The index will tell you where to look to find the place you want to know about.

**ACTIVITY D**  Number your paper from 1 to 10. Decide which reference source would be the best place to look to find the information listed below. Write **E** for encyclopedia, **AL** for almanac, and **AT** for atlas.

1. How Albuquerque, New Mexico, got its name
2. The population of Albuquerque
3. The distance from Albuquerque to Denver
4. The winner of the Nobel Prize for peace last year
5. The important events in the life of Alfred B. Nobel
6. The direction of Stockholm, Sweden, from London, England
7. The countries that in part lie north of the Arctic Circle
8. Why we see rainbows
9. The zip code for Texarkana, Texas
10. The name of the islands that lie 550 miles west of Casablanca

# FRONTIER SCHOOLS

## RICHARD UHLICH

Frontier schools were every bit as rugged as the rest of frontier life. But the pioneers believed in education. Of all the possessions packed into their covered wagons, books were among those they valued most. As you read this article about the schools of more than a hundred years ago, think about what it must have been like to be a student in a frontier school.

# THE SCHOOLHOUSE

When the first pioneer families settled in a new area, there were no schools of any kind. Young children were sometimes taught at home in spare moments by an older brother or sister. Or they would meet in a neighbor's home for lessons in reading, writing, and arithmetic. Their teacher was usually a pioneer woman with her own home and family to care for. Often her blackboard was the dirt floor, and her chalk was a long stick.

A school was put up when enough children lived in an area. Families worked together to gather the materials and build the school. Most schools were built of wood, but on the plains where wood was scarce, schools were built of sod. Both kinds of schoolhouses had dirt floors, unplastered walls, and few windows.

The schoolroom had no desks. Children sat in rows on hard, flat wooden benches without backs. Roxanna Rice, a pioneer girl in Kansas, described her early schooldays: "I remember the first school I attended, a room crowded full of big boys and girls. . . . I and my brother, with another boy, occupied a bench with no back, near the stove. When the stove became too warm, we whirled around and faced the other side. The boy with us wore a paddle fastened around his neck. On the paddle were posted several letters of the alphabet and these were changed (by his parents) every day. How I envied that boy because his parents were making such pains with him."

Frontier schools, like frontier homes, had no electricity, no plumbing, and no running water. The schoolrooms were poorly lighted. The "restroom" was an outhouse, one for the boys and one for the girls. The "drinking fountain" was a bucket and dipper kept in a corner of the room.

"There wasn't any drinking water," one student explained, "so usually two kids went after it. You'd go to the nearest house with the bucket. It was quite a thing to do that. It was during classes, you see, and you got out of class. But you had to be good or she (the teacher) wouldn't send you. Then everybody who wanted a drink would line up and use the same bucket and the same dipper."

Pioneer children started their day long before school began. By four o'clock in the morning, many were already up doing their daily chores. One pioneer remembered what it was like. "I'd get up and get the cows in and milk them and get the horses and the hogs fed. Then we'd get ourselves fed. Then I'd stick my books and my lunch in a pail and go to school. Across the fields it was two miles, and I'd run all the way."

Each morning the teacher would ring the iron bell that hung outside the schoolhouse to announce the start of school. Some children came on foot or on horseback. Others came in wagons. stop here!

# SCHOOL SUBJECTS

Classroom time was spent mostly on the three R's, reading, writing, and arithmetic. Students also studied some history and geography. A single teacher taught all the grades from one to eight. The teacher worked with only a few children at a time. The others studied by themselves. One pioneer remembered: "The first thing in the morning the teacher would read to us. Usually it was a story or something like that. Then she would work with one grade at a time. She'd say: 'Fourth grade, turn, rise, and pass.' Then everybody in that grade—there might have been four or five or just one— would go up to the recitation bench in front and sit there and recite their lesson. While they were reciting, you were supposed to be working on your lesson. But you'd also be kind of listening."

Few schools had textbooks. Children brought what-ever books they could find at home. They came with

dictionaries, spellers, storybooks, the family Bible, and old almanacs. A group of children might learn to read from twenty different books.

A part of each schoolday was given to spelling. Children used several ways to learn difficult words. One was to break a word into syllables, spell one syllable at a time, then repeat each syllable before going on to the next one. Another way was memorizing a sentence in which the first letter of each word would give you the spelling. Here's one of the sentences that children used for a difficult word.

**"A rat in the house may eat the ice cream."**
**(Arithmetic)**

The daily spelling bee was a popular school activity. The students had to line up, and the teacher would ask each one to spell a word. If someone misspelled a word, he or she had to sit down. As the words got harder, only the very best spellers remained standing.

Children also studied arithmetic each day. Paper was scarce, so students often did their figuring in their heads. Classes would often have "ciphering matches" or "figure-downs." In these challenging contests, a student would have to think fast to solve a problem without writing it down.

Geography was taught by group singing since few schools had maps or globes. One of the most popular songs gave the name of each state, the name of the capital city, and the river on which it was found. The lines for the first two states went like this:

"Maine, Augusta, on the Kennebec.
New Hampshire, Concord, on the Merrimac."

Students enjoyed learning geography this way. Many also found it a good way to memorize facts.

Recitation was another important school subject. One pioneer remembered: "Every Friday afternoon we had speakin'. Everybody had some piece to recite,

some famous poem or speech they had learned or just some funny stuff, whatever we wanted. This was to help us speak properly, not to be ashamed in front of the public." These pieces were meant to be "acted out." Pronunciation, rhythm, and gestures were important.

Another pioneer recalled his brother's speakin' piece. "'Lincoln was a great man. Washington was a great man, but here, my friends, is a greater.' Then my brother would hold up a cheese grater. His friends thought that was a riot."

# TEACHERS

In parts of the frontier, teachers were hard to find and even harder to keep. One reason for this was the low pay. Some teachers earned as little as $10 or $15 a month. They were paid only during those months that school was open. Often it was only three or four months out of the year. To make up for the low pay, many

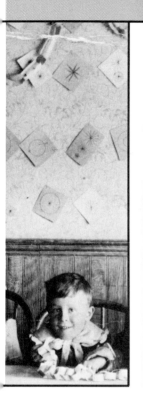

teachers "boarded around" at the homes of their students. In return for free room and board, they helped with the chores.

". . . I will tell you how I earned my board," recalled Belle McNair Logan, a teacher in Kansas in 1872. "I arose early each morning and got breakfast; we always had biscuits for breakfast, and beans and corn bread for dinner. . . . After breakfast I washed the dishes and Hattie wiped them. I put the beans on before going to school and ran down at recess to make the corn bread. At noon I finished dinner, ate and ran back to school, after school made beds, washed the dinner dishes, then mopped, ironed or patched as was necessary, while on Saturday I did our washing."

Many frontier teachers had little training for the job, but schools were glad to accept anyone who was willing to try. One such school was in a small mining town in California. Prentice Mulford, an unsuccessful gold-seeker, once applied for a teaching job there. He

was interviewed by the school trustees—in this case, a doctor, a miner, and a saloonkeeper.

"I expected a searching examination, and trembled," Mulford recalled. "It was years since I had seen a schoolbook. I knew that in geography I was rusty and in mathematics musty. Before the doctor lay one thin book. It turned out to be a spelling book."

The examination was short and simple. Mulford was asked to spell the following words: *cat*, *hat*, *rat*, and *mat*. When he did this without stumbling, the doctor said: "Young man, you're hired."

# LOOKING BACK

The frontier schoolroom is now a thing of the past. But the idea that it stood for—the idea of a basic education for all—is one which Americans still believe in today. Vera Pearson, a pioneer girl in Kansas, recalled, "The miracle was that a love of learning ever survived the rigors of schooldays then. But it did. . . ."

## Thinking and Writing About the Selection

1. What subjects were usually taught in frontier schools?

2. How was a ciphering match like a spelling bee?

3. If a teacher of frontier times could visit a classroom of today, what do you think he or she would be most surprised to see?

4. What is your favorite subject in school? What makes it interesting to you? If you had gone to a frontier school, what subject would have been your favorite? Why?

## Applying the Key Skill
### Main Idea and Supporting Details

Find the paragraphs from "Frontier Schools" listed below. Then copy the diagrams and complete them by writing the main idea and/or supporting details.

1. second paragraph under "School Subjects"

| Few schools had textbooks. | MAIN IDEA |
|---|---|
|  | SUPPORTING DETAILS |
|  |  |
|  |  |

2. third paragraph under "School Subjects"

| | MAIN IDEA |
|---|---|
| Some children broke words into syllables. | SUPPORTING DETAILS |
|  |  |

# MAIN IDEA AND SUPPORTING DETAILS

Writers organize paragraphs around the important points they want to make. The most important point in a paragraph is called the **main idea**. The other information in the paragraph makes up the **supporting details**. These details support or explain the main idea.

When looking for the main idea of a paragraph, ask yourself, "What point is the writer trying to make?"

Read this paragraph from "Frontier Schools." See if you can decide which of the sentences below is the main idea and which are supporting details.

> Pioneer children started their day long before school began. By four o'clock in the morning, many were already up doing their daily chores. One pioneer remembered what it was like. "I'd get up and get the cows and milk them and get the horses and the hogs fed. Then I'd stick my books and my lunch in a pail and go to school. Across the fields it was two miles, and I'd run all the way."

a. Pioneer children started their day long before school began.
b. By four o'clock, many children were up doing chores.
c. One pioneer child milked cows and fed livestock before going to school.

Did you choose sentence **a** as the main idea? Did you realize that sentences **b** and **c** were supporting details?

The main idea is sometimes found in the first sentence, as it is in the paragraph above. But it can also be found in a sentence in the middle or at the end of a paragraph.

**ACTIVITY A**  Read the paragraph below. Then write the sentence that states the main idea on your paper.

Early schools on the Great Plains were usually built of sod. In areas where trees were plentiful, the schools were built of wood. Sturdy schools of stone were put up in places where rock was easily quarried. The materials used in pioneer schools depended on the natural resources close at hand.

a.  Early schools on the Great Plains were usually built of sod.
b.  Schools were built of wood where trees were plentiful.
c.  Stone schools were put up in places where rock was easily quarried.
d.  The materials used in pioneer schools depended on the natural resources close at hand.

**ACTIVITY B**  Read each paragraph below. On your paper, write a sentence stating the main idea of each. Write two sentences giving supporting details.

1.  At first there were no real schools or teachers in pioneer communities. Children were sometimes taught at home by an older brother or sister. Often a small group of children would meet in one family's house for lessons. Their teacher was usually a pioneer woman with her own home and family to care for. Often the teacher had little or no training.

2.  When schools were built, pioneer children had a place to meet for classes. The buildings often served not only as schools but also as community meeting places. Sometimes they were used as voting places. Women might gather there for quilting bees. Community social events, such as harvest suppers and picnics, might be held there.

Cassie Tomer Hill

# WOMEN OF

LISA YOUNT

## CLARA BROWN:
## Finding Her Family

For most of the nineteenth century, the land west of the Mississippi River was wild and unknown. Yet many women gave up their homes in the East and made the difficult journey to the new land.

Many made the journey simply because their husbands or parents did. Others, however, came for themselves. The West offered determined women a chance to do things that few of them could do in the East. Out West, women could own their own farms or businesses, and make their own fortunes.

Clara Brown and Cassie Hill were two such women. As you read, think about the qualities that helped them to become women of the West.

Like the "forty-niners" who came to California seeking gold at the end of the 1840s, the "fifty-niners" who came to Colorado ten years later had many plans for the wealth they hoped to find. Some wanted to buy mansions and never work again. Some simply hoped for enough money to buy their own farm.

# THE WEST

Clara Brown

Clara Brown had a different dream. Clara was the first black woman, and one of the first women of any race, to come to the Pikes Peak region of Colorado. Like the other people who went there, Clara hoped to become rich. She didn't want money for herself, though. She wanted it for just one thing: to locate her family and bring them to her.

Clara had been born a slave in Virginia around 1800. She grew up in Kentucky, married there at age eighteen, and had several daughters and a son. When Clara was thirty-five, her master died, and Clara and her family were sold. Clara, her husband, and her children all went to different owners.

After twenty more years as a slave, Clara was freed. She still, however, had to leave Kentucky or risk being made a slave again. She went to St. Louis, Missouri, where she began working as a cook.

The fabulous gold fields of Colorado were the main subject of table talk at many a meal where Clara Brown set down the plates. "Pikes Peak or Bust!" was the slogan on everyone's lips. The speakers seldom noticed the tall, sturdy black woman who listened so eagerly to their conversation. Still less did they know the plan that was forming in her mind.

One day Clara heard that a large wagon train was getting ready to go to Colorado. She went to see one of the men who was organizing it. "I want to go with you," she said. "I can't pay you, but I can do cooking and washing in exchange for my passage."

The man agreed, and soon Clara and her laundry tubs were bundled into the back of a covered wagon ready for the long trip. She, like others in the train, hoped that the "promised land" of her dreams would lie at the end of the journey.

Clara arrived in Denver in June of 1859. She had no plan—and no need—to mine gold herself. She simply set up her stove, boilers, and washtubs, and began doing a brisk business. Soon she moved to the new mining camp of Central City, where her services were even more in demand.

Above: Central City, Colorado, as it looked during the late 1870s. The town was little more than a mining camp when Clara Brown moved there in 1860.

Laundry prices, like the prices of everything else in the mining camps, were high—as much as 50¢ a shirt. The miners were glad to pay Clara for her work, however. She provided a service they needed badly. Furthermore, they knew that she helped people in many ways for which she charged nothing.

No sick or homeless person was ever turned away from her house. It became a hospital and a hotel for all who needed it, whether they could pay or not. A church group and Central City's first Sunday school met there, too. It was no wonder that people in Central City soon called Clara Brown "Aunt Clara."

But Clara's own plans were just beginning. She worked long hours and saved her money carefully. She invested some of it in property. By the end of the Civil War she had saved about $10,000, a good-sized sum.

Now Clara could begin doing what she had dreamed about during all those hours of boiling and scrubbing shirts: reuniting her family. In 1866 she set out for Kentucky and Virginia to start her search. In the following years she brought twenty or thirty black people, most of them close relatives, to Colorado. She paid for their journey and helped them find work in the new land. One of the people she helped was her daughter, Eliza Jane.

Unfortunately, poor management by others as well as her own generosity used up most of Clara's money. When she died in 1885, Clara Brown owned only the small house in which she lived. But "Aunt Clara" was rich in the love and respect of the many people she had helped— the citizens of Central City and the black people to whom she had given a new life.

## CASSIE HILL:
## A Life on the Railroad

Cassie Tomer had come west from Iowa, traveling in a covered wagon with her parents and five brothers and sisters, when she was just two years old. The Tomers had lived in the Nevada Territory for several years and then moved to a ranch in California. The ranch was at Woodland, not far from Roseville.

When Cassie first saw the town of Roseville, in northern California, it was simply a group of five or six frame houses—"hardly more than shacks," as Cassie wrote later—a train station, and a general store. The year of that first visit was 1866. Cassie herself was only twelve at the time.

Cassie, Roseville, and the Central Pacific Railroad grew up together. Roseville was a railroad town from its beginning. Only a few years before Cassie first visited it, it was known simply as "Junction," because two tracks of the newly completed Central Pacific met there. The first building in the town was the railroad's freight station or depot.

Below: This 1906 photo shows Cassie (seventh from right) near the Roseville depot that was her home.

Roseville grew quickly as more and more farmers and ranchers came there to ship their goods.

The railroad became part of Cassie's life when she married George Hill in 1876. Her husband was given the job of station agent and telegraph operator for the town of Hanford, California, and he and Cassie went there to live.

Cassie and George were happy in Hanford, and their family grew quickly. Busy as she was with her young children, Cassie still found time to take an interest in George's job. She often helped him in his work as a station agent. She also learned how to read Morse code and operate the telegraph. The telegraph was a very important part

of an agent's job. It was the only way to send messages over long distances quickly.

George Hill became the station agent at Roseville in 1881. A big new depot had been built there in 1874 to replace the one that had started the town. Cassie must have been surprised to learn that she and her family were expected to live in one end of it—especially since the other end contained a saloon! The station itself was in the middle.

Cassie soon made a real home of her part of the station, however. She loved the clatter and bustle of the depot, with people and trains going and coming constantly. It was to remain her home for more than twenty-five years.

Tragedy struck in 1885. George Hill died, leaving Cassie with five small children to feed. But Cassie knew what work she could do—if the railroad would let her do it.

"Let me take over George's job," Cassie asked the Central Pacific officials. She explained how she had helped him over the years. "I can use the telegraph, too," she pointed out.

The post of station agent was a demanding one. Some of the railroad officials wondered how Cassie could handle it and raise her family, too. But they gave her a chance—and Cassie soon showed what she could do.

Cassie's workdays as a station agent began early in the morning and ended long after sunset. She had to sweep out the station and build a fire there. As trains came and went, she greeted passengers and sold them tickets. She also took care of freight shipments. She was the agent for the shipping and banking firm of Wells Fargo as well as for the railroad. She kept records of all the station's business. Green visor cap shielding her eyes, she tapped out messages with her telegraph key and wrote down the coded answers as they came in. Cassie Hill was one of the first women to work as a telegrapher.

Cassie lived and worked in the Roseville depot until 1907. At that time, the Central Pacific—by then the Southern Pacific—built a new depot and decided to tear the old one down. Forced to leave her home, Cassie retired from her job as well.

Cassie lived quietly in Roseville for most of the rest of her life. She died in 1955, soon after celebrating her 100th birthday. During all those years Cassie never forgot her beloved depot home. When it was torn down in 1907, she wrote a poem about her unusual "railroad life." Here is part of what she wrote:

My *children, from their infancy,*
*No other home they knew;*
*And now how sad for them to*
    *see*
*The old go for the new. . . .*

*No more will I the clatter hear*
*Of instruments at my door;*
*And wonder why the trains*
*Don't stop as they did in days*
    *of yore.*

*Goodbye Espee,* I'll not forget*
    *you*
*Nor all the kindness you have*
    *shown;*
*You have sheltered me from*
    *girlhood.*
*I for you, with age have*
    *grown.*

_____

*Espee: S.P., the Southern Pacific Railroad.

## Thinking and Writing About the Selection

1. What did Clara Brown plan to do once she reached Colorado?

2. Why was Cassie Hill well suited for the job of station agent?

3. In what ways were Clara Brown and Cassie Hill alike? What qualities did they share?

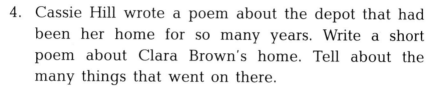 4. Cassie Hill wrote a poem about the depot that had been her home for so many years. Write a short poem about Clara Brown's home. Tell about the many things that went on there.

## Applying the Key Skill
### Main Idea and Supporting Details

Use complete sentences to answer the following questions about "Women of the West."

1. Reread the paragraph about Clara Brown that begins, "No sick or homeless person was ever turned away from Clara's house."
   What is the main idea of the paragraph?
   What are two details that support the main idea?

2. Reread the paragraph about Cassie Hill that begins, "Cassie's workdays as a station agent began early in the morning and ended long after sunset."
   What is the main idea of the paragraph?
   What are two details that support the main idea?

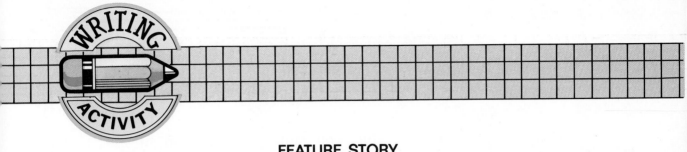

## FEATURE STORY

### Prewrite

Many of the stories in this unit tell about the emigrants who went west in the early days of our history. Horace Greeley, the editor and founder of the *New York Tribune* during those times, gave some advice in an editorial. "Go West, young man, go West," he said. And go they did, men, women, and children.

Imagine you are a writer on Mr. Greeley's newspaper. You have been told to write a feature story about the reasons people are going west. A feature story focuses on a particular topic. A feature story differs from a news article in that it often includes opinions and anecdotes, or little stories, as well as facts.

This is the topic for your feature story:

People are going west for many reasons.

Before you begin to write, discuss with other students some reasons people had for going west. Look back over the stories in this unit for reasons. For example, what were Clara Brown's and Frederic Remington's reasons? Check other books, magazines, and your social studies book for ideas. Then make a list.

Next, list some examples that support every reason. One reason people had for going west was to get land. An anecdote about Charles Ingalls and his family would support that reason. Make notes of your examples and possible anecdotes.

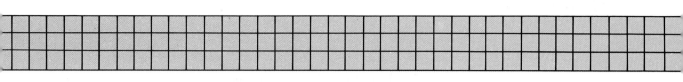

**Write**

1. Look at your notes and choose three or four reasons you are going to use.
2. The first paragraph of your feature story should explain your topic: why people are going west. Then introduce the reasons you have chosen. Remember, you are writing as if you lived in those pioneer days.
3. The next paragraphs should talk about the reasons you have chosen with examples or anecdotes to support them.
4. Try to use Vocabulary Treasures in your story.
5. Now write the first draft of your feature story.

| **VOCABULARY TREASURES** | |
| --- | --- |
| frontier | opportunities |
| emigrant | rigors |

**Revise**

Read your feature story. Have a friend read it, too. Think about this checklist as you revise.

1. Did you state your topic in the first paragraph of your feature story?
2. Did you give an example or anecdote to support each of your reasons? If not, add them where needed.
3. Are your anecdotes really interesting? What verbs, adverbs, or adjectives could you add to keep your reader's interest?
4. Did you use too many choppy sentences? Are too many sentences connected by *and*? Try to use such words as *when, however,* and *because* to combine some sentences.
5. Now rewrite your feature story to share.

# SAVED
## BY A
# WHISKER
### SID FLEISCHMAN

*In 1849, the California Gold Rush was on. Thousands of forty-niners rushed to California hoping to strike it rich. Many traveled by wagon train along the Oregon Trail. Others traveled by ship. Twelve-year-old Jack Flagg and his aunt's loyal butler Praiseworthy set out from Boston for San Francisco on the side-wheeler Lady Wilma. They were determined to strike it rich in the gold fields. If they didn't, Aunt Arabella would be forced to sell the family mansion.*

*After five months at sea, Jack and Praise-worthy arrived in San Francisco. But their journey wasn't over yet. They still had to get to Sacramento City, and from there to the diggings.*

In his pea jacket and stocking cap Jack felt fourteen years old at least. Maybe fifteen. He stood in the bow of the whale boat and watched the Long Wharf come closer. They bumped against the boatstairs and Jack was the first out. His heart raced with the excitement of the moment. They had arrived, and he was ready to start digging.

"Not so fast, Master Jack," said Praiseworthy. "Don't forget your pick and shovel."

A hilltop telegraph had signaled the arrival of a sidewheeler and now it seemed as if all of San Francisco had turned out. The wharf was alive with men, women, and children—not to mention dogs, mules, and chickens. Seagulls flocked in the air like confetti.

Weighted down with their belongings, Praiseworthy and Jack started along the wharf. There were barrels and boxes piled everywhere. Peddlers and hawkers and hotel runners mixed with the crowd and shouted at the newcomers.

"Welcome, boys! Welcome to the fastest growing city in the world!"

"Flannel shirts for sale! Red flannel shirts, gents! They don't show the dirt!"

"Try the Niantic Hotel. Cleanest beds in town."

"Horn spoons! You'll need 'em at the diggin's. Carved from genuine ox horn!"

"Stay at the Parker House. None better!"

Praiseworthy and Jack continued along the boardwalk, which was hammered together mostly out of barrel staves, and reached the United States Hotel. Captain Swain had recommended it.

"A fine room, if you please," Praiseworthy said to the hotel clerk. "And I think a tub bath would be in order."

"Very good, sir," replied the clerk. "That'll be ten dollars extra—each."

"What's that?" Praiseworthy scowled.

"Water's a dollar a bucket," said the hotel clerk, "unless you want to wait until next November. Prices come down when it rains."

"We'll wait," said Praiseworthy with decision. In this part of the world, he thought, a man had to strike it rich just to keep his neck clean. He signed the register and Jack gazed at a bearded miner pacing back and forth across the lobby floor. He wore a floppy hat and chestnut hair tumbled out on all sides like mattress stuffing coming loose. He kept glancing at the wall clock as if every second might be his last.

Jack couldn't take his eyes off the man. Tucked in his wide leather belt were a revolver, a horn spoon, and a soft buckskin bag. Gold dust! Jack thought. He must have just got in from the mines!

"Ruination!" the miner began to mutter. "Ruination!"

Praiseworthy blotted the register. "How," he asked the clerk, "does one get to the mines?"

"Riverboat leaves every afternoon at four o'clock from the Long Wharf. Fare to Sacramento City is twenty-five dollars. From there you make your way to the diggings by stage, muleback, or foot."

Jack shot a glance at Praiseworthy. Twenty-five dollars—each! Why, they didn't *have* that much money! But the butler didn't so much as raise an eyebrow. "We'll be taking the boat tomorrow," he told the clerk.

"Ruination!" said the miner.

"Come along, Master Jack," said Praiseworthy.

The walls of their room were lined with calico, and there was matting on the plank floor. The window looked out on the shipping in the bay, the masts as thick as a pine forest. There were not only gold ships, but Navy frigates and Chinese junks and the going and coming of longboats. But Jack wasn't interested in the view.

"*Fifty* dollars just to get to Sacramento City!" he said. "We'll have to walk."

"Good exercise, no doubt, but we haven't time for it." Praiseworthy gazed out at the distant hills across the bay. Sacramento City was more than a hundred miles up river, he had heard, and the diggings in the foothills beyond that. "Let me see. It took us five months to get this far, and it will take us another five months to get home. If we are to keep your Aunt Arabella from being sold out—we have two months left. Two months to fill our pockets with enough nuggets."

Jack found himself pacing back and forth like the miner in the lobby below. "Ruination!" Jack said. "We've come all this way and now— we're no closer."

"Nonsense," said Praiseworthy. There was a pitcher half filled with water on the chest, and he poured a small amount into the washpan. "We'll be on tomorrow's riverboat, I promise

you. Now then, I suggest we wash up as best we can, Master Jack."

Wash! Jack thought. There wasn't time to wash! "How will we pay the fare?"

"Let me see. We have thirty-eight dollars left. That's a start, isn't it? Of course, we'll have our room and meals to pay. But if I detect one thing in the air—it's opportunity. The sooner you wash, Master Jack, the sooner we can tend to our financial dilemma. Your Aunt Arabella wouldn't allow you abroad on the streets with dirty ears and sea salt in your eyebrows. And don't forget the soap."

"Ruination," Jack muttered again. He might as well be home in Boston.

They washed and changed into fresh clothes. Then they returned to the lobby. The shaggy miner was still there, pacing and muttering in his dusty beard. He glanced at Jack, and then the butler and the boy went out on the street.

But as they ambled along the boardwalk, Jack began to realize that the miner was following them. He was still at their heels when the butler and the boy crossed the street. Now Jack was beginning to feel anxious. Even a little scared. finally he looked up at Praiseworthy.

"He's following us."

"Who's following us?" asked the butler.

"That miner from the hotel."

"Stuff and nonsense. The streets are free to everyone."

"But he's following us, Praiseworthy."

"Nothing to fear in broad daylight, Master Jack."

They continued along the sandy plaza, still looking for opportunity, and the miner marched right behind them. Praiseworthy stopped and the miner stopped, and they stood face to face. "Sir," said the butler. "Are you following us?"

"Ruination. I sure am!"

"I'll thank you to go your way, sir!"

"No offense, gents," the miner said. "Been on the verge of breakin' in on your conversation, but it didn't seem courteous." It was hard to see his mouth for the fullness of his beard. "They call me Quartz Jackson, and I've just come in from the diggin's. My fiancée's due in on the stage any minute. Comin' up from the capital at Monterey. We've never met, but we have written a lot of letters. And that's just it."

"And that's just what?" said Praiseworthy.

"We're supposed to be gettin' married. But *ruination*—when she takes one look at me, she's goin' to think I'm part grizzly bear." He whipped off his floppy hat and his dusty hair fell out on all sides. "She'll get right back on the stage for Monterey. But shucks, I'm not such a bad-lookin' gent—leastways, I wasn't when I went to the diggin's. I'm just a mite growed over, you might say. Well, I've been trampin' every street in town lookin' for a barber, but they all left for the mines. That's why I couldn't help starin' at the lad here."

"Me?" said Jack.

"Why, that hair of yours looks fresh from the barber shop. All cut and trimmed. I figured you must have flushed out a barber, and maybe you'd do Quartz Jackson the favor of leadin' me to him."

If Jack had feared the miner for a moment, he couldn't help smiling at him now. He liked the man. "No, sir," he said. "I haven't been to a barber. Unless you mean Praiseworthy."

"Praiseworthy?"

"At your service," said the butler. "It's true, I've been cutting Master Jack's hair, but only out of necessity."

The miner's face—what could be seen of it—broke into a sunny smile. "I'd be much obliged if you'd barber me up, Mr. Praiseworthy. Name your price."

"But I'm not a barber, sir. I'm a butler."

"A what?"

"I couldn't accept any money for merely—"

"Well, now, that's mighty good of you. Tell you what I'll do. I'll let you have all the hair you cut off."

Praiseworthy and Jack exchanged fresh glances. What earthly use did they have for the man's shorn locks? But it seemed wise to humor him, and Praiseworthy said, "I'll be glad to help you in your hour of need, sir. Consider it a modest wedding present."

Twenty minutes later the miner was seated on a nail keg in a corner of the hotel porch, and Praiseworthy was snipping away with the shears. Quartz Jackson insisted that every lock be caught as it fell. Jack was kept busy holding a washpan under Praiseworthy's busy scissors.

"My, hasn't the town grown, though," said the miner. "Must be all of four or five thousand folks in the place. You gents figure on goin' to the diggin's?"

"We do indeed," said Praiseworthy.

"I come from Hangtown. The boys have been locatin' a good lot of color up that way."

"Color?"

"The yellow stuff. Gold. If you get up Hangtown way, tell'em you're a friend of Quartz Jackson. Tell'em I'll be comin' home with my bride in a couple of weeks. Sure is nice of you to shear me this way."

Quartz Jackson's face began to appear, snip by snip, like a statue being chipped out of stone. When Praiseworthy had finished, the miner turned to look at himself in the hotel windowpane, and he almost jumped out of his jackboots.

"By the Great Horn Spoon!" he said. "Is that *me*?" Quartz Jackson was obviously pleased. "Why, I'd forgot I was so young!"

Quartz Jackson was a fine-looking gent at that, Jack thought. He had good teeth and an easy smile. Except for his revolver, his horn spoon, and his red flannel shirt, he hardly seemed the same man. But what did he expect them to do with the hair cuttings? Stuff a mattress?

"Your fiancée will be very pleased," smiled Praiseworthy. "Our congratulations on your forthcoming marriage, sir."

"Much obliged, Praiseworthy. You saved me from certain ruination. The least I can do is teach you how to work a gold pan. Water boy! You there! Fetch us a bucket of dew over here."

The miner paid for the water by taking a pinch of fine gold dust from his buckskin pouch.

Jack was eager to get the hang of mining and Quartz Jackson, peculiar or not, was clearly an expert.

"Give me the washpan, Jack, young Jack."

Jack handed over the tin pan, piled high with chestnut whiskers and trimmings. The miner wet them down with fresh water and began to swish the pan around.

"Gold's heavy," he explained. "Nothin' heavier. Even the yellow dust sinks to the bottom if you keep workin' the pan. Like this."

Then he handed the washpan to Jack and taught him the motion. The water turned brown from the dirt and mud that had gathered in Quartz Jackson's whiskers and hair. Finally he poured off everything—everything but a thin residue at the bottom of the pan. Jack's eyes opened like blossoms.

*Gold dust!*

"Why, look there!" the miner roared with laughter. "The boy's panned himself some color. I figured I scratched enough pay dirt into my beard to assay out at about $14 an ounce. Since I gave you the whiskers and all—the gold is all yours!"

Jack had never known a more exciting moment in his life. The grains of gold dust sparkled like yellow fire—and there was even a flake or two.

Half an hour later, while Quartz Jackson was having a $10 tub bath, Praiseworthy and Jack were plucking opportunity from the air. They put up a sign that said,

"FREE HAIRCUTS: Miners Only."

## Thinking and Writing About the Selection

1. Why did Praiseworthy and Jack decide not to order a tub bath until they reached the diggings?

2. Why would the price of water go down during the rainy month of November?

3. How do Praiseworthy and Jack intend to earn the boat fare they need to get to Sacramento City? Do you think they will be successful?

 4. Imagine you found some photographs of the gold rush days in an antique shop. Describe the scenes in two of the photographs that you found. Use the details in the story that tell about life during the gold rush to help you.

## Applying the Key Skill
### Author's Purpose and Point of View

Read the incomplete sentences below. Then choose the best ending or endings for each. Write the complete sentences.

1. The author probably wrote "Saved by a Whisker" to ___.
   a. entertain readers with a humorous story
   b. describe a funny but true story that took place in 1849
   c. persuade people to get haircuts
   d. explain why people went to California in 1849

2. The author probably would agree that ___.
   a. San Francisco was an interesting place to be in the mid-1800s
   b. prices at the United States Hotel were reasonable
   c. digging for gold is the best way to get rich quickly
   d. you never know who might help you solve a problem

# GIT-UP-AND-GIT

In "Saved By a Whisker," Jack Flagg and Praiseworthy were trying to reach Sacramento City, then the gateway to California's gold-mining region along the Sierra foothills. In this area, camps and mining towns sprang up, with names such as **You Bet**, **Lousy Ravine**, **Git-Up-And-Git**, and **Volcano**. These "boom towns" and the hundreds like them that grew up as "gold fever" spread throughout the West were often abandoned as suddenly as they appeared. They survive today as "ghost towns," but their names are a reminder of one of the most colorful periods in American history.

Many towns took their names from the minerals that were mined: **Goldfield**, **Gold Hill**, **Silverton**, **Silver Plume**, and **Copperopolis**. It was not unusual for a town to change its name several times. The camp first known as **Dry Diggins** in California later became known as **Hangtown**, and later still as **Placerville**. A placer is a deposit of gravel or sand that contains particles of valuable minerals. What do the changes in name tell you about this town?

**Fiddletown**, California, took its name from the fact that the younger miners were "always fiddling," or wasting time. **Loafer Flat** has a similar origin.

You might want to find out how these other early mining towns got their names: Tin Cup, Colorado; Garnet, Montana; Last Chance, Idaho.

# Oh, Susanna
## Music by Stephen Foster

I __ came from Sa - lem   ci - ty With  a   wash pan on my   knee,

I'm __ goin' to Cal - i - for - nia, The __ gold dust for to   see.

It __ rained all night the  day I  left, The  weath-er  it  was   dry,

The __ sun so hot I  froze to death, O  broth-ers don't you   cry!

*(Chorus)*

Oh,  Su - san - na,   Oh,   don't you  cry  for   me!

I'm __ goin' to Cal - i - for - nia With my __ wash pan on my   knee.

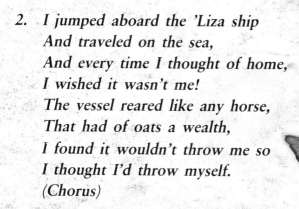

2. I jumped aboard the 'Liza ship
   And traveled on the sea,
   And every time I thought of home,
   I wished it wasn't me!
   The vessel reared like any horse,
   That had of oats a wealth,
   I found it wouldn't throw me so
   I thought I'd throw myself.
   *(Chorus)*

3. I thought of all the pleasant times
   We've had together here,
   I thought I ought to cry a bit,
   But couldn't find a tear.
   The pilot's bread* was in my mouth,
   The gold dust in my eye,
   And though I'm going far away,
   Dear brothers, don't you cry!
   *(Chorus)*

4. I soon shall be in Frisco
   And there I'll look around,
   And when I see the gold lumps there,
   I'll pick them off the ground.
   I'll scrape the mountains clean, my boys,
   I'll drain the rivers dry,
   A pocketful of rocks bring home,
   So brothers, don't you cry!
   *(Chorus)*

*hardtack: a hard biscuit

253

# SAMURAI
## OF GOLD HILL

### YOSHIKO UCHIDA

The Gold Rush brought many people to California. Even after most of the gold had been mined, they continued to come. In the late 1860s, emigrants from Japan began to arrive. Many came to escape the wars that threatened to tear their country apart.

For hundreds of years, Japan had been governed by military leaders called shoguns (shō′ gunz). Throughout this period, the emperor had no power. His lands were controlled by nobles who ruled over clans, or groups of families. The nobles, or lords, hired well-trained soldiers called samurai (sam′ ü rī). The most powerful samurai was known as the shogun.

In 1867, the lords of western Japan united to restore the emperor to power. They forced the shogun to resign. Not all the lords supported this action. Fighting between the supporters of the shogun and the supporters of the emperor began. One of the last supporters of the shogun to be defeated was Lord Matsudaira (mä tsü dī′ rä). In 1868, his castle in the town of Wakamatsu (wäk ə mä′ tsü) was destroyed.

Henry Schnell, an advisor to Lord Matsudaira, suggested that members of the clan of Wakamatsu leave Japan. They could go to Gold Hill in California to start a colony. Later, Lord Matsudaira could join them.

Yoshiko Uchida's *Samurai of Gold Hill* is based on the true accounts of Henry Schnell and Lord Matsudaira. She also made up characters like Koichi (kō ē′ chē). Koichi and his father are among those who decide to go with Schnell to California. They join a group of colonists in Yokohama where they will board a ship that will take them to America. They will leave their familiar life behind to follow a dream.

"Now that we have come safely to Yokohama, I can tell you of our great dream. Listen well, Koichi," his father said. "Tomorrow we board the ship *China* of the Pacific Mail Steamship Lines. Then we sail across the ocean to America and go to Gold Hill in the state of California. Herr Schnell has written many letters to America and believes that Gold Hill would be a fine place to establish a tea and silk farm. Think of it, Koichi," Father continued, his eyes dancing now with excitement, "we shall be the very first colonists from Japan to go to America to farm."

Koichi's head was reeling. They were going to America. They were actually leaving the shores of their own country, when not too many years before, it would have been against the law of the land.

"What of Lord Matsudaira?" Koichi asked now. "What about our castle? Won't we fight once more to get the castle back for our clan?"

"Lord Matsudaira is imprisoned, but at least he lives," Father said quietly. "From now on, there will be no more battles, for Japan must live in peace." Then lowering his voice, he added, "We go to America to establish a safe place for the lord. Perhaps one day he will be free to join us there. Don't you see, Koichi, we are still his loyal subjects, but now we serve him with our labor instead of our swords."

Father touched his chest where he had kept the drawstring bag during the long trip. "The lord gave us two thousand pieces of gold which were not taken by the southern clans," he explained. "With that we can buy land and tools and food and begin a Wakamatsu Colony in America. Herr Schnell has arranged it all. Is it not a magnificent plan?" Father asked. Koichi

256

hadn't seen such brightness in his eyes since before the big battle.

But still Koichi felt confused. He was filled with excitement at the thought of the great new adventure that lay ahead but he also felt a strange disappointment. It simply didn't seem right for Father to be leaving Japan to become a farmer. He was a superb horseman. He could handle any weapon with skill and grace. He was a scholar in Chinese classics and could speak Dutch and a little English and French as well. He would be a perfect teacher, but how could he pick tea leaves, or till the soil, or care for silkworms? A samurai did not do such things. They were tasks for a farmer.

All his life Koichi had dreamed of becoming one day a noble samurai like his father. It was for this that he went to the castle school to study the classics, to learn calligraphy, and to excel in the skills of war and self-defense. He dreamed of one day defending the lord and his castle, just as Father had done. Now, Koichi wondered, what was to become of him? He thought of the samurai sword Grandmother had given to him. Perhaps he would never have a chance to use it, and it would rust in its sheath while he picked mulberry leaves for silkworms.

When they went to the wharf the next day to board the ship, however, Koichi began to feel an overwhelming surge of excitement. He saw the ship's towering masts and the giant side-wheels and thought it seemed like a small floating castle. And when they met the others who had also come from Wakamatsu, he did not feel so much the terrible tug of loneliness at the thought of leaving Japan.

257

Herr Schnell's beautiful Japanese wife was already on the ship with her daughter, Toyoko (tō yō' kō), and her maid, Okei (ō kā' ē).

"Perhaps you will become friends—you and my little Toyoko?" Mrs. Schnell said, speaking softly to Koichi.

Koichi nodded, but he did not say yes. After all, Toyoko was only eight, and worse, she was a girl. Besides, he had Rintaro, one of the colony's carpenters. During the long journey to Yokohama he was strong and reliable and a cheerful companion. He was not much younger than Father, but Father seemed almost to think of him as another son. Koichi began to think of him as a big brother to replace the one he had lost in battle.

Rintaro shared their small crowded cabin with one of the craftsmen. He scratched his head as he examined the narrow shelf-like bunks that jutted from the walls, for he was used to sleeping on the floor.

"I'm going to put my blankets on the floor," Koichi announced. But Father told him that he must get used to sleeping as the foreigners did. So Koichi crept carefully onto his shelf. He clutched the sides so he wouldn't fall out and fell into a restless sleep. He wished that he had his nice smooth wooden pillow instead of the lumpy one for foreign heads.

When he awoke, he heard the slow creaking sounds of the ship all around him. During the night they had slipped out of the harbor. Now Koichi could hear the churning and splashing of the great side-wheels and feel the roll of the ship as it rode the swells of the Pacific. They were on their way.

"*Yah*, we are sailing the ocean now," Koichi shouted. He quickly followed Father and Rintaro outside.

259

He ran to the railing and there it was, the enormous Pacific Ocean, stretching out for endless miles.

The three of them explored the ship from prow to stern like three pioneers in a new and strange land. Then Father turned to Koichi and said a most unexpected thing.

"Now, Koichi," he said very calmly, "let us go see about our treasures."

Treasures! Koichi could scarcely wait to see them. There were probably great scented chests bearing Lord Matsudaira's crest and secured with thick twisted cords of red silk. Inside, there would be gold coins, jade and creamy pearls, precious porcelain bowls, swords glistening sharp and cold, armor, and gold-trimmed spears.

With one of the ship's sailors leading the way, they moved carefully along the ship's slanting creaking corridors. They went down narrow stairways and wobbly stepladders, down, down into the dark dampness of the ship's hold. There, they moved in and out among towering stacks of crates, boxes of tea, and bales of rice. They came at last to a corner that looked like a battered shabby forest of wind-tipped trees.

"Ah," Father said, "here they are, safe and sound."

"Those mulberry trees?" Koichi asked, disappointed. "Those are our treasures?"

"Indeed they are," Father answered, looking pleased to find them intact. "We have several thousand to start our new farm, and here are the tea plants and bamboo, lacquer and wax trees. We have brought thousands of seeds of the tea and sesame plant as well."

Seeing the disappointment that flooded Koichi's face, he explained further. "Don't you see, Koichi, they will help us make a living in California. We will harvest the tea and the oil and the wax, and the craftsmen will make bowls and baskets and boxes and ornaments from the bamboo and lacquer."

"And do not forget our precious cargo of silkworm eggs," one of the farmers reminded him.

"For making the most beautiful silk ever made outside of Japan," Father added.

"We had better pray to the gods that they don't hatch before we get to Gold Hill," Rintaro said with a worried frown.

"We had indeed," the farmers agreed. "This is the fifth month of the year and it is almost time for the eggs to hatch."

With expert hand and eye, the farmers checked their precious cargo and carefully dampened whatever needed water. They also cast an anxious eye on the silkworm eggs, glad for the cool darkness of the hold that would keep them safe until the ship reached port in America.

So they really were going to become farmers, Koichi thought glumly. They did not even own one treasure box of swords or spears or armor.

As if that were not bad enough, Koichi learned that he was to study English each day with Toyoko Schnell.

"Herr Schnell has agreed to instruct you each day," Father explained, "so you will be able to speak some English before we reach America."

By the time the ship stopped at the Hawaiian Islands for fresh water and coal, both Koichi and Rintaro knew many words of English. They did not get off the ship, but they leaned from the ship's railing and

shouted English words down to the men who worked on the dock below.

"*Oi!* I am called Koichi. Table and chairs! Thank you! Good night! I am twelve. Coffee!" Koichi shouted down every English word he had learned. In fact, Koichi tried his English on anyone who would listen.

The morning they were to dock in San Francisco, Koichi was up before dawn. He didn't want to miss a thing and was eager to be on deck to catch the first sight of land. He wore his good silk kimono as Father had instructed, and he saw that Father, too, wore the kimono bearing the family crest. With his two samurai swords at his side, he looked at last as a samurai should. Koichi was glad. He didn't want Father to arrive in the new land looking like a shabby peasant.

The farmers and the craftsmen, Rintaro and the other carpenter too, all wore their finest clothes and assembled near Herr Schnell at the ship's railing, straining eagerly for the first sight of America. The ship passed through a low bank of fog and then suddenly there appeared what seemed a wall of mountains. The captain seemed miraculously to find a small opening through which he steered the *China* into one of America's busiest ports. It was a magnificent sight.

They passed enormous clipper ships and square riggers and giant rafts piled high with lumber and wheat from the California valleys and forests. There were freighters laden with cargo from all over the world, and there were many smaller riverboats. They had reached their destination. They were in America.

"We're here! We've landed! We are in California!" Koichi shouted.

The pier was crowded with people and express wagons and handcarts and coaches. Everywhere, shouting and calling, were voices speaking a strange foreign babble. Koichi listened hard. Was it English they were speaking? Koichi suddenly discovered that he could not utter one word of it now. His tongue, it seemed, had frozen in his mouth.

Koichi, his father, Rintaro, and the Schnell family left the ship together, keeping close to one another.

Now it was they who were the foreigners, in their rustling silk kimonos, their swords, and their black hair done up in strange hairdos. Koichi felt as though he was in a land of fair-skinned, brown-haired giants. And all of them turned to stare. He was relieved when they reached their hotel.

"Keep your sandals on," Herr Schnell reminded them as they walked through the front door. "No one removes shoes in this country."

It was strange, Koichi thought, that everyone brought the dirt and dust of the street into their homes. But Herr Schnell explained that it was because they did not use their floors for sitting and sleeping as they did in Japan. "Here they use chairs, tables, and beds," he explained.

"Let us go up and inspect our first American rooms," urged Rintaro.

The room was big and bare, with two brass beds and a marble-top washstand bearing a basin and pitcher. Koichi had expected more of his first American room.

"I thought . . ." he began and then he stopped. He had been dreaming of the elegant rooms of the castle at Wakamatsu and thinking that America would be even more rich and golden and beautiful.

Their room smelled of stale tobacco and the horses stabled next door.

"Come, Koichi-san, let us go out and inspect this city of the hills," Rintaro said in his loud cheerful voice. "Your father and Herr Schnell have already gone to see about buying supplies and shipping our trees and plants to Gold Hill."

They strode out of the hotel together.

"Look straight ahead," Rintaro told Koichi. "Do not meet their stares and they will leave us alone."

They marched with their eyes straight ahead past a carriage shop and a warehouse heaped with tallow and hides. But Koichi could not keep looking ahead for long, for now they came to buildings of stone and granite, some of them three stories high. There were banks and courthouses and theaters and shops on all sides. Koichi simply had to stop at the windows to gaze at the shawls and jewels and tortoise-shell combs for the ladies and the hats and shirts and collars for men.

The streets were full of people, all rushing about as though they were late for appointments. They all took time, however, to stare at the strange-looking pair.

They walked up and down the streets of San Francisco until they were too hungry to go further. Then they returned to their hotel and had dinner.

Early the next morning, they boarded another side-wheeler, a smaller ship called *The Sitka*. It was to take them up the river to Sacramento.

"From Sacramento we will rent wagons to Placerville," Herr Schnell explained. "And from Placerville, we shall go on to our final destination, Gold Hill."

Koichi liked the name. It sounded as though the hillsides were laden with veins of gold. Even though Herr

Schnell had told them the gold rush was over, perhaps he could find just a little gold that no one had discovered before.

The little *Sitka* crept slowly up the river, passing other riverboats and barges laden with wheat.

"How dry the countryside looks," Father said, for as far as they could see, the low curved hills, dotted with dark clumps of live oak, were the color of golden sand or ripened wheat.

"There has been no rain here," the farmers said anxiously. "The earth is as dry as a bleached bone."

America was not only bigger and noisier, it seemed brighter and sharper. Koichi felt as though he had come from a land of soft gray mist to a land of eternal harsh sun.

"What about the silkworm eggs?" he asked. "Since it is so warm, won't they hatch and die before we can feed them?"

"I have been thinking of them too," Father said, "but there is nothing we can do. I don't even know if they are on this same ship with us."

"How much farther?" Koichi asked Herr Schnell.

"Not far now," he answered reassuringly, but it was almost dusk when they reached Sacramento. It was not until early the next morning that Herr Schnell rented three wagons for the ride to Placerville almost fifty miles away.

The crack of the driver's whip sent the horses dashing down the dusty Green Valley road. It was a long bumpy ride. The road was worn with ruts made by the hundreds of wagons and coaches that had traveled over it during the rush for silver and gold, and by the thundering horses of the pony express.

The horses kicked up a fine spray of red dust. Only Herr Schnell talked with the driver, who was happy to have someone listen to his memories of how it had been during the gold rush years. He pointed out each village they passed, the old pony express stops, and the first farm that owned a mechanical plow.

The wagons rumbled on through the heat of the day and came at last to a busy town where they stopped in front of an old two-storied hotel.

"Well, here we are in Placerville," Herr Schnell called out.

They climbed wearily from the wagons, covered with dust. Mrs. Schnell coughed and fanned herself with a small folding fan. Her beautiful silk kimono was full of wrinkles and her hair grayed with dust.

"Mama, I ache all over," Toyoko groaned.

Koichi felt exactly the same.

"Wait here," Herr Schnell instructed the dreary group. "I must find new wagons to take us to Gold Hill." And he went off down the dusty street.

The terrible searing heat of the afternoon felt like the breath of an angry dragon.

"A nice long soak in a tub would feel good right now," Rintaro sighed, stretching his aching legs.

"And a bowl of rice and pickles," Koichi added.

"I would rather have a sweet bean-paste cake," Toyoko said.

Everyone who went by stopped to glare at them.

"Why do they hate us?" Koichi asked. "What have we done?"

"It is just that they don't know us," Father explained. "When we have built our fine tea and silk farm it will be different. You'll see." Father tried to

268

sound cheerful, but his face was drawn and creased with lines of weariness.

When Herr Schnell came back at last, he had only one wagon and he looked glum. "No one will rent wagons to us," he said darkly.

"Why?" they all wondered.

"Because we arc Japanese."

"Ah. And that is bad?"

"They do not know us, so they do not trust us. It is always bad to be different. I was once different too, in your country." Herr Schnell looked tired and discouraged and Koichi suddenly felt sorry for him.

Koichi looked down on the ground because he didn't know what to say. Presently, he noticed an enormous pair of boots beside him. He looked up at the face that belonged to the boots and saw a tall fair-haired man wearing the working clothes of a farmer. His nose was sprinkled with freckles and his eyes were a friendly blue. He wiped his forehead with a big handkerchief and asked, "Say, aren't you the folks from Japan who're coming up to the Graner place in Gold Hill?"

"We are. We are," Herr Schnell answered eagerly.

"Heard you were coming," the man said. "My name's Thomas Whitlow. I'm ranching close by the Graner place." He held out an enormous hand which Herr Schnell shook vigorously.

"We're in need of two more wagons," Herr Schnell told him.

"I can take some of you," Thomas Whitlow offered. "We could do it in two wagons if you folks don't mind squeezing in some."

The gods had sent this kind man just in time. The sun was low in the sky and the air was growing dusky.

The road to Gold Hill was as bumpy as the Green Valley road, but now the horses jogged along gently for there weren't many miles to go. They passed small villages and farms and dozens of orchards filled with trees bearing apples and plums and peaches and almonds. On the hillsides were vineyards climbing as high as the water could go.

As they bumped along, Koichi's head dropped to his chest, and the rumbling wagon lulled him to an exhausted sleep. The shadowy trees moved by like silent ghosts and the sounds of the buzzing cicadas began to fill the air.

Koichi dreamed he was in Japan, riding to a great battle to win back the castle. The battle was almost won and Koichi was waving the Matsudaira banner in the air when the wagon pulled off the road and came to a stop.

"Here we are," Mr. Whitlow's voice sang out in the warm darkness. "This here's the Graner place."

They had finally come to the end of their journey. This was the Graner house and this was Gold Hill. The Wakamatsu Colony of Japan had arrived at last.

**The Japanese colonists were hopeful that their dream of a successful Wakamatsu Colony would come true. Despite their courage and hard work, however, life in Gold Hill was filled with disappointments. You can read about their life in California in *Samurai of Gold Hill*. Perhaps someday you can also visit the Wakamatsu Tea and Silk Farm, which was named a California Historical Landmark in 1969.**

271

## *Frontiers*

What inspires people to leave their homes and set out for unknown places? What dreams and goals, hopes and purposes help them to endure the hardships and the dangers? In *Frontiers*, you read about people who lived in the early days of our nation's history. You met the men, women, and children who settled the vast lands beyond the Mississippi River. Photographs and paintings, biographies and stories revealed the faces and the voices of those who earned the name *pioneer*. What frontiers exist today to inspire you?

## Thinking and Writing About *Frontiers*

1. What personal qualities did Roberto from "Diablo Blanco" share with the pioneers you read about in "Going West"?
2. How would frontier towns like the one described in "By the Shores of Silver Lake" change over the years as more people came to live there?
3. Are paintings and sculptures as important today as they were in the days when the West was being settled? Why or why not?
4. From what you learned by reading "Frontier Schools," what do you think a typical school day was like for Caddie Woodlawn and her brothers?
5. Would you have gone west with the forty-niners to try to "strike it rich"? Why or why not?

 6. Imagine that you can interview a person or character from one of the selections in *Frontiers*. Whom would you choose? What questions would you ask? Write your questions, and then write the answers you would expect the person or character to give.

## Introducing Level 11

# ENCOUNTERS

# 3

*I am a part of all that I have met.*

**Alfred, Lord Tennyson**

The encounters that we have become part of our personal experience. Such encounters can lead us to discover something new about ourselves, others, or the world around us. They can enrich and change our lives. The stories in this unit are about people who have all kinds of encounters, often unexpected and unusual. What makes an encounter—in life or in books—memorable?

# THE NIGHT OF THE LEONIDS

## E. L. KONIGSBURG

*Lewis and his grandmother know
each other well. They have a special
relationship. One evening, Grandmother
plans to share something very special
with Lewis— something that takes place
only every thirty-three years.*

I arrived at Grandmother's house in a taxi. I had my
usual three suitcases, one for my pillow and my coin
collection. The doorman helped me take the suitcases up,
and I helped him; I held the elevator button so that the
door wouldn't close on him while he loaded them on and
off. Grandmother's new maid let me in. She was younger
and fatter than the new maid was the last time. She told
me that I should unpack and that Grandmother would be
home shortly.

Grandmother doesn't take me everywhere she goes
and I don't take her everywhere I go;

but we get along pretty well, Grandmother and I.

  She doesn't have any pets, and I don't have any
other grandmothers, so I stay with her whenever my
mother and my father go abroad; they send me postcards.
My friend Clarence has the opposite: three Eiffels and two
Coliseums. My mother and my father are very touched
that I save their postcards. I also think that it is very nice
of me.

  I had finished unpacking, and I was wondering why
Grandmother didn't wait for me. After all, I am her only
grandchild, and I am named Lewis. Lewis was the name
of one of her husbands, the one who was my grandfather.
Grandmother came home as I was on my way to the
kitchen to see if the new maid believed in eating between
meals better than the last new maid did.

"Hello, Lewis," Grandmother said.

"Hello, Grandmother," I replied. Sometimes we talk like that, plain talk. Grandmother leaned over for me to kiss her cheek. Neither one of us adores slobbering, or even likes it.

"Are you ready?" I asked.

"Just as soon as I get out of this girdle and these high heels," she answered.

"Take off your hat, too, while you're at it," I suggested. "I'll set things up awhile."

Grandmother joined me in the library. I have taught her double solitaire, fish, cheat, and casino. She has taught me gin rummy; we mostly play gin rummy.

The maid served us supper on trays in the library so that we could watch the news on color TV. Grandmother has only one color TV set, so we watch her programs on Mondays, Wednesday, Fridays, and every other Sunday; we watch mine on Tuesdays, Thursdays, Saturdays, and the leftover Sundays. I thought that she could have given me every Sunday since I am her only grandchild and I am named Lewis, but Grandmother said, "Share and share alike." And we do. And we get along pretty well, Grandmother and I.

After the news and after supper Grandmother decided to read the newspaper; it is delivered before breakfast but she only reads the ads then. Grandmother sat on the sofa, held the newspaper at the end of her arm, then she squinted and then she tilted her head back and farther back so that all you could see were nostrils, and then she called, "Lewis, Lewis, please bring me my glasses."

I knew she would.

I had to look for them. I always have to look for them. They have pale blue frames and are shaped like sideways commas, and they are never where she thinks they are or where I think they should be: on the nose of her head. You should see her trying to dial the telephone without her glasses. She practically stands in the next room and points her finger, and she still gets wrong numbers. I only know that in case of fire, I'll make the call.

I found her glasses. Grandmother began reading messages from the paper as if she were sending telegrams. It is one of her habits I wonder about; I wonder if she does it even when I'm not there. "Commissioner of Parks invites everyone to Central Park tonight," she read.

"What for?" I asked. "A mass mugging?"

"No. Something else."

"What else?"

"Something special."

I waited for what was a good pause before I asked, "What special?"

Grandmother waited for a good pause before she answered, "Something spectacular," not even bothering to look up from the newspaper.

I paused. Grandmother paused. I paused. Grandmother paused. I paused, I paused, I paused, and I won. Grandmother spoke first. "A spectacular show of stars," she said.

"Movie stars or rock and roll?" I inquired politely.

"Star stars," she answered.

"You mean like the sky is full of?"

"Yes, I mean like the sky is full of."

"You mean that the Commissioner of Parks has invited everyone out just to enjoy the night environment?" We were studying environment in our school.

"Not any night environment. Tonight there will be a shower of stars."

"Like a rain shower?" I asked.

"More like a thunderstorm."

"Stars falling like rain can be very dangerous and pollute our environment besides." We were also studying pollution of the environment in our school.

"No, they won't pollute our environment," Grandmother said.

"How do you know?" I asked.

"Because they will burn up before they fall all the way down. Surely you must realize that," she added.

I didn't answer.

"You must realize that they always protect astronauts from burning up on their reentry into the earth's atmosphere."

I didn't answer.

"They give the astronauts a heat shield. Otherwise they'd burn up."

I didn't answer.

"The stars don't have one. A heat shield, that is."

I didn't answer.

"That's why the stars burn up. They don't have a shield. Of course, they aren't really stars, either. They are Leonids."

Then I answered.

"Why don't you tell me about the shower of stars that isn't really a shower and isn't really stars?" She wanted to explain about them. I could tell. That's why I asked.

Grandmother likes to be listened to. That's one reason why she explains things. She prefers being listened to when she *tells* things: like get my elbow off the table and pick up my feet when I walk. She would tell me things like that all day if I would listen all day. When she *explains*, I listen. I sit close and listen close, and that makes her feel like a regular grandmother. She likes that, and sometimes so do I. That's one reason why we get along pretty well.

Grandmother explained about the Leonids.

The Leonids are trash that falls from the comet called Temple-Tuttle. Comets go around the sun just as the planet Earth does. But not quite just like the planet Earth. Comets don't make regular circles around the sun. They loop around the sun, and they leak. Loop and leak. Loop and leak. The parts that leak are called the tail. The path that Earth takes around the sun and the path that Temple-Tuttle takes around the sun were about to cross each other. Parts of the tail would get caught in the earth's atmosphere and light up as they burn up as they fall down. Little bits at a time. A hundred little bits at a time. A thousand little bits at a time. A million bits.

The parts that burn up look like falling stars. That is why Grandmother and the Commissioner of Parks called it a Shower of Stars. The falling stars from Temple-Tuttle are called the Leonids. Leonids happen only once every thirty-three and one-third years. The whole sky over the city would light up with them. The reason that everyone was invited to the park was so that we city people could see a big piece of sky instead of just a hallway of sky between the buildings.

It would be an upside-down Grand Canyon of fireworks.

I decided that we ought to go. Grandmother felt the same way I did. Maybe even more so.

Right after we decided to go, Grandmother made me go to bed. She said that I should be rested and that she would wake me in plenty of time to get dressed and walk to Central Park. She promised to wake me at eleven o'clock.

And I believed her.

I believed her.

I really did believe her.

Grandmother said to me, "Do you think that I want to miss something that happens only three times in one century?"

"Didn't you see it last time?" I asked. After all, there was a Shower of Leonids thirty-three and one-third years ago when she was only thirty, and I'll bet there was no one making her go to bed.

"No, I didn't see it last time," she said.

"What was the matter? Didn't the Commissioner of Parks invite you?"

"No, that was not the matter."

"Why didn't you see it then?"

"Because," she explained.

"Because you forgot your glasses and you didn't have Lewis, Lewis to get them for you?"

"I didn't even wear glasses when I was thirty."

"Then why didn't you see it?"

"Because," she said, "because I didn't bother to find out about it, and I lost my chance."

I said, "Oh." I went to bed. I knew about lost chances.

Grandmother woke me. She made me bundle up. She was bundled, too. She looked sixty-three years lumpy. I knew that she wouldn't like it if I expressed an opinion, so I didn't. Somehow.

We left the apartment.

We found the place in the park. The only part that wasn't crowded was up. Which was all right because that was where the action would be.

The shower of stars was to begin in forty-five minutes.

We waited.

And waited.

And saw:

"What are you crying about?" Grandmother asked. Not kindly.

"I have to wait thirty-three and one-third years before I can see a big spectacular Shower of Stars. I'll be forty-three before I can ever see a Leonid."

"Oh, shut up!" Grandmother said. Not kindly.

"I'll be middle-aged."

"What was that for?" I asked. "What did I do?" I asked. "What did I do?" I asked again. I had always thought that we got along pretty well, my grandmother and I.

"You add it up," Grandmother said. Not kindly.

So I did. I added it up. Sixty-three and thirty-three don't add up to another chance.

I held Grandmother's hand on the way back to her apartment. She let me even though neither one of us adores handholding. I held the hand that hit me.

## Thinking and Writing About the Selection

1. What are the Leonids?
2. How did Lewis and his grandmother show that they "got along pretty well"?
3. Why do you think Lewis held his grandmother's hand on the way home, even though they both didn't much like that sort of thing?
4. Have you ever seen a star shower or a comet? Tell what it was like.

## Applying the Key Skill
### Sequence of Events

The sentences below tell about events in "The Night of the Leonids." Write the sentences in the correct sequence.

Grandmother came home.

Lewis went to bed.

Lewis and Grandmother walked home from the park.

Grandmother announced that there would be a show of stars in the park.

Lewis arrived at his grandmother's house.

Grandmother read the newspaper ads.

Grandmother missed her first chance to see the Leonids.

The star show couldn't be seen.

Lewis and Grandmother watched the news and ate supper.

Grandmother and Lewis bundled up and went to the park.

# Some People I Know

Some people I know like to chatter,
while others speak hardly a word;
some think there is nothing the matter
with being completely absurd;
some are impossibly serious,
while others are absolute fun;
some are reserved and mysterious,
while others shine bright as the sun.

Some people I know appear sour,
but many seem pleasant and sweet;
some have the grace of a flower,
while others trip over their feet;
some are as still as a steeple,
while some need to fidget and fuss;
yet every last one of these people
is somehow exactly like us.

*Jack Prelutsky*

# THE HOUSE OF DIES DREAR

## VIRGINIA HAMILTON

It was a large old house on a hillside, and it held secrets. From 1810 to 1850, it had been a station on the Underground Railroad. The Underground Railroad was a series of hiding places along a route that led from the United States to Canada. Slaves used the Underground Railroad to reach a place of safety and freedom. Hundreds of men, women, and children had hidden in the house Dies Drear (dī'əs drir') had built in Ohio. Many owed their lives to this man who could not accept the idea of slavery.

Now, more than a hundred years later, the Small family was moving into the house of Dies Drear. Mr. Small and his son Thomas had studied the floor plans of the house. They knew that there were hidden tunnels and secret rooms. Thomas was determined to discover them.

As the story begins, Thomas is exploring the house. Over the carvings on the front door, he presses a hidden button without realizing it. The front steps move aside, and Thomas peers into a huge hole.

Lying flat on his stomach, Thomas looked into the hole; his head and shoulders disappeared inside. It was then he lost his grip and fell head first into thin, black air. He landed some five feet down, on damp sod that smelled like a mixture of yellow grass and mildew. All the breath was knocked out of him. He lay there unable to move or think for at least ten seconds, until air seeped back into his lungs. Otherwise he seemed not to have hurt himself.

There was gray light filtering down from the opening of the steps to where Thomas lay, and he could see that he was at the edge of a steep stairway cut out of rock. The stairs were wet; he could hear water dripping down on them from somewhere.

"Move slowly. Think fast," Thomas whispered. "Keep in mind what's behind and look closely at what's in front."

Thomas always carried a pencil-thin flashlight, which he sometimes used for reading in the car. He sat up suddenly and pulled out the flashlight. It wasn't broken from the fall, and he flicked it on. He sat in a kind of circle enclosed by brick walls.

Thomas got to his feet and made his way down the rock stairway into darkness. At the foot of the stairs was a path with walls of dirt and rock on either side of it. The walls were so close, Thomas could touch them by extending his arms a few inches. Above his head was a low ceiling carved out of rock. Such cramped space made him uneasy. The foundation of the house had to be somewhere above the natural rock. The idea of the whole three-story house of Dies Drear pressing down on him caused him to stop a moment on the path. Since he had fallen, he hadn't had time to be afraid. He wasn't now, but he did begin to worry a little about where the path led. He thought of ghosts, and yet he did not seriously believe in them. "No," he told himself, "not with the flashlight. Not when I can turn back . . . when I can run."

Besides, he thought, I'm strong. I can take care of myself.

Thomas continued along the path, flickering his tiny beam of light this way and that. Pools of water stood in some places. His shoes were soon soaked. His socks grew cold and wet, and he thought about taking them off. He could hear water running a long way off. He stopped again to listen, but he couldn't tell from what direction the sound came.

"It's just one of the springs," he said. His voice bounced off the walls strangely.

Better not speak. There could be tunnels leading off this one. You can't tell what might hear you in a place like this.

Thomas felt his feet begin to climb; the path was slanting up. He walked slowly on the slippery rock; then suddenly the path was very wide. The walls were four feet away on either side, and there were long stone slabs against each wall. Thomas sat down on one of the slabs. It was wet, but he didn't even notice.

"Why these slabs?" he asked himself. "For the slaves hiding and running?"

He opened and closed a moist hand around the flashlight. The light beam could not keep back the dark. Thomas had a lonely feeling, the kind of feeling running slaves must have had.

They dared not use light, he thought. How long would they have to hide down here? How could they stand it?

Thomas got up and went on. He placed one foot carefully in front of the other on the path, which had narrowed again. He heard the faint sound of movement somewhere. Maybe it was a voice he heard; he couldn't be sure. He swirled the light around over the damp walls, and fumbled it. The flashlight slid out of his hand. For a long moment, he caught and held it between his knees before finally dropping it. He bent quickly to pick it up and stepped down on it. Then he accidentally kicked it with his heel, and it went rattling somewhere over the path. It hit the wall, but it had gone out before then. Now all was very dark.

"It's not far," Thomas said. "All I have to do is feel around a little."

He felt around with his hands over smooth, moist rock; his hands grew cold. He felt water, and it was icy, slimy. His hands trembled, they ached, feeling in the dark, but he could not find the flashlight.

"I couldn't have kicked it far because I wasn't moving." His voice bounced in a whisper off the walls. He tried crawling backward, hoping to hit the flashlight with his heels.

"I'll go on back," he said. "I'll just walk back as quick as I can. There'll be light coming from the veranda steps. I'll climb up that wall and then I'll be out of this. I'll get Papa and we'll do it together."

He went quickly now, with his hands extended to keep himself from hitting the close walls. Then something happened that caused him to stop in his tracks. He stood still, with his whole body tense and alert, the way he could be when he sensed a storm before there was any sign of it in the air or sky.

Thomas had the queerest notion that he was not alone. In front of him, between him and the steps of the veranda, something waited.

"Papa?" he said. He heard something.

The sound went, "Ahhh, ahhh, ahhh." It was not moaning, nor crying. It wasn't laughter, but something forlorn and lost and old.

Thomas backed away. "No," he said. "Oh, please!"

"Ahhh, ahhh," something said. It was closer to him now. Thomas could hear no footsteps on the path. He could see nothing in the darkness.

He opened his mouth to yell, but his voice wouldn't come. Fear rose in him. He was cold, freezing, as though he had rolled in snow.

"Papa!" he managed to say. His voice was a whisper. "Papa, come get me . . . Papa!"

"Ahhhh." Whatever it was, was quite close now. Thomas still backed away from it, then he turned around, away from the direction of the veranda. He started running up the path, with his arms outstretched in front of him. He ran and ran, his eyes wide in the darkness. At any moment, the thing would grab him and smother his face. At any time, the thing would paralyze him with cold. It would take him away. It would tie him in one of the tunnels, and no one would ever find him.

"Don't let it touch me! Don't let it catch me!"

Thomas ran smack into a wall. His arms and hands hit first; then, his head and chest. The impact jarred him from head to foot. He felt frantically along the wall. The wall was wood. He knew the feel of it right away. It was heavy wood, perhaps oak. Thomas pounded on it.

"Help me! It's going to get me!" he called. "Help!"

Thomas heard a high, clear scream on the other side of the wall. Next came the sound of feet scurrying, and then the wall slid silently up.

"Thomas Small!" his mother said. "What in heaven's name do you think you are doing inside that wall!"

"I see you've found yourself a secret passage," said Mr. Small. "I hadn't thought you'd find that button by the front door so soon."

Mrs. Small stood directly in front of Thomas and then stepped aside so that he could take a few steps into the kitchen. Thomas glanced behind him at the tunnel, a gaping space carved out of the comfortable kitchen. He saw nothing at all on the path.

"You knew about that tunnel, Papa?" Thomas said. He felt discouraged, as though he'd been tricked.

"If anyone came unexpectedly to the front door," said Mr. Small, "the slaves could hide in the tunnel until whoever it was had gone. Or, if and when the callers began a

294

search, the slaves could escape through the kitchen or by way of the veranda steps."

It's not any fun, Thomas thought. Not if he already knows about it.

"Why were you calling for help, Thomas?" asked Mr. Small. "You really made your mama scream."

Thomas bent down to take off his shoes and socks. A pool of water stood dark and brackish on the linoleum. "There was something there," he said. "There was something on that path," Thomas said. "It was coming after me as sure as I'm sitting here." His voice quivered slightly, and the sound of that was enough to tell Mr. Small that Thomas wasn't joking.

"Then what was it?" asked Mr. Small. He watched Thomas closely.

"I don't know," Thomas said. "I didn't see anything."

His father smiled. "It was probably no more than your fear of the dark and strange surroundings getting the best of you."

"I heard something, though," Thomas said. "It went 'ahhh, ahhh' at me and it came closer and closer."

Mrs. Small sucked in her breath. She looked all around the kitchen, at the gaping hole and quickly away from it.

"Thomas, don't make up things!" his father said sternly.

"I'm not, Papa!" There was a lump in Thomas's throat. He had to find just the right words if ever his father was to believe him.

His hands rose in the air. They began to shape the air, carve it. "It was like no other voice," he began. "It wasn't a high voice or a low voice, or even a man's voice. It didn't have anything bad in it or anything. I was just in its way, that's all. It had to get by me and I have a feeling that it would have done anything to get around me along that path."

Mr. Small seemed to be thinking beyond what Thomas had told them. "You say you saw nothing?" he asked.

"I thought I heard somebody moving around," Thomas said, "but that could have been you all in here."

They all fell silent for a moment. Then Mr. Small asked, "And you're sure you heard nothing more than that sighing?"

"That's all," Thomas said. "It just kept coming at me, getting closer."

Mr. Small got up and stood at the tunnel opening. He went into the long hall after a few seconds and came back with a flashlight. "I'll go with you," Thomas said.

"I'd rather you stayed here. I'll only be a minute," said his father.

Mr. Small was gone less than a minute. Thomas and his mother waited, staring into the tunnel opening, flooded with the light from the kitchen. A few feet beyond the opening, the kitchen light ended in a wall of blackness. They could see the light from Mr. Small's flashlight darting here and there along the ceiling of the tunnel until the path descended.

Mr. Small returned by way of the veranda steps. His white shirt was soiled from scaling the brick wall. As he came into the kitchen, muddying the floor as Thomas had, he was thoughtful, but not at all afraid.

He walked over to a high cabinet on the opposite wall from the tunnel. Beneath it, a small panel in the wall slid open at his touch. The panel had been invisible to the eye, but now revealed what seemed to be a jumble of miniature machinery. Mr. Small released a lever. The tunnel door slid silently down, and the patterned wallpaper of the kitchen showed no trace of what lay hidden behind it. Lastly, Mr. Small removed a mechanism of some kind from the panel and put it in his pocket.

"Did you see anything?" Thomas asked him. "Did you find my flashlight?"

"I didn't see anything," Mr. Small said, "and I didn't hear any sighing."

"Well, that's a relief," said Mrs. Small.

"Your flashlight must have fallen in a crack," said Mr. Small. "I couldn't find it. Oh, yes, I removed the control from the panel. Without it, a giant couldn't raise that tunnel door."

"But you said there wasn't anything in the tunnel," said Thomas.

"That's so, but I don't want you wandering around in there," his father said. "The walls and ceiling are dirt and rock. There hasn't been a cave-in that I know of in a century, yet I think it best we don't take chances. I also removed the gears that control the front steps."

Thomas sat at the table. He glanced at his father, who sat across from him filling his pipe.

"Papa, how *do* the tunnels fit together?"

His father explained that they were all of a plan. "Eventually, they lead in the same direction, to the same place," he said.

"But what if an enemy of the slaves knew that?" Thomas said. "He could just wait at that place, because sooner or later he was bound to catch somebody."

"No, Dies Drear knew what he was doing," said Mr. Small. "Let the tunnels meander like a maze, with subpassages and dead ends. Have a sign or symbol marking the main passages, a sign only the slaves would understand. And let the slaves reach that one place where there would be people waiting to take them quickly in

many directions going farther north. No, it wasn't likely that at the time anyone knew for sure what was going on in this house."

"Papa," Thomas said. "It's still light out. I want to see how the house looks all the way around."

His father smiled and said, "What is it you're looking for and why are you in such a hurry?"

"I'm not looking for anything," Thomas said at last. "I just want to figure out which rooms have the passages, after I've seen the outside. Like now, I know this kitchen isn't right. I can tell something's wrong. Please, Papa. When it gets dark, I'll come inside."

Mr. Small took a deep breath. "You have perhaps an hour," he said. "Darkness has a way of falling down on you around here."

Thomas left the kitchen without another word to his father. Outside, he felt ready to explore.

## Thinking and Writing About the Selection

1. How was the hidden tunnel used in the days of Dies Drear?

2. Why do you think Thomas was disappointed that his father already knew about the tunnel?

3. Who or what do you suppose was in the passage?

 4. The author gives a detailed description of the tunnel. She describes the look, feel, sound, and even the smell of the dark passage. Choose a place you know and write a description of it. Describe what your senses would tell you about the place.

## Applying the Key Skill
### Plot, Setting, Mood, Narrative Point of View

Read the following incomplete sentences about "The House of Dies Drear." Choose the best ending for each. Write the complete sentences.

1. The setting for most of the story is ___.
   a. inside the house of Dies Drear
   b. in the underground passages below the house of Dies Drear
   c. on the grounds around the house of Dies Drear

2. The plot of the story involves ___.
   a. a family moving to a new home
   b. a father rescuing his son
   c. Thomas discovering the secrets of the house of Dies Drear

3. The mood of the story when Thomas is in the passage is ___.
   a. mysterious    b. scary    c. sad

4. The story is told from the point of view of ___.
   a. Thomas in the first person
   b. Mr. Small in the third person
   c. Thomas in the third person

# VIRGINIA HAMILTON

*"Being the 'baby' and bright, and odd and sensitive, I was left alone to discover whatever there was to find. No wonder, then, that I started to write things down at an early age. I'm a writer, I think, nearly by birth."*

As the youngest in a family of five, Virginia Hamilton grew up during the Depression on a farm in southern Ohio. Her mother's family, whose ancestor was a runaway slave, had lived in the area since before the Civil War. Her father was a fine storyteller and a talented musician as well.

Her hometown, Yellow Springs, had been a stop on the underground railroad, so it is not surprising that she used that fact in *The House of Dies Drear*. She has called the book her favorite "because it is so full of all the things I love: excitement, mystery, black history, and the strong black family. In it I have tried to pay back all of those wonderful relatives who gave me so much in the past."

Hamilton had some difficulty in becoming a writer. She had tried a number of other jobs, including professional singing, and bookkeeping. Then a friend suggested she turn a short story into a novel. The result was her first book, *Zeely*.

Ideas for her books come to this author from nowhere, usually in the form of book titles. "I'm not really aware of the thinking, for it is lightning swift. I get bits and pieces of conversation, flashes of atmosphere, a location. It's all a jumble at first, until I begin to write it and sort it out."

**More to Read** *Zeely, The Time-Ago Tales of Jadhu, Time-Ago Lost: More Tales of Jadhu*

# ANALOGIES

Comparing is an important thinking skill you use every day. An **analogy** is a way of comparing things. In one kind of analogy, two pairs of words are compared. The two words in the first pair are related to one another in some way. Look at the example of an analogy below.

Ship is to water as plane is to air.

*Ship* and *water* are the first pair of words. A ship is a vehicle that travels through the water. *Plane* and *air* are the second pair of words. Just as a ship is a vehicle that travels through the water, a plane is a vehicle that travels through the air.

An analogy may relate words that have opposite meanings, or antonyms.

Left is to right as north is to south.

Analogies may also relate words that have similar meanings, or synonyms.

Paste is to glue as bowl is to dish.

In fact, the pairs or words or analogies may be related in many different ways. See if you can complete the analogy below by figuring out the relationship and choosing the correct missing word.

Page is to book as card is to ____.

a. library    b. deck    c. number    d. name

A page is part of a book. A book is made up of many pages. The missing word, then, must tell what a card is a part of. The correct answer is *deck*. A deck is made up of many cards.

**ACTIVITY** Number your paper from 1 to 10. Read each incomplete analogy. Decide how the first two words are related. Then on your paper, write the word that correctly completes each analogy.

1. No is to yes as go is to ____.

   a. maybe      b. leave      c. stop      d. answer

2. One is to three as single is to ____.

   a. triple      b. third      c. four      d. first

3. Back is to front as in is to ____.

   a. toward      b. inside      c. come      d. out

4. Hat is to head as sock is to ____.

   a. body      b. foot      c. shoe      d. ankle

5. Story is to tale as end is to ____.

   a. book      b. read      c. finish      d. begin

6. July is to year as Tuesday is to ____.

   a. month      b. Sunday      c. week      d. time

7. Bird is to flock as cow is to ____.

   a. pasture      b. herd      c. farm      d. fly

8. Mother is to woman as father is to ____.

   a. man      b. child      c. boy      d. son

9. Run is to legs as fly is to ____.

   a. planes      b. walk      c. air      d. wings

10. Doctor is to hospital as teacher is to ____.

    a. students      b. school      c. patient      d. job

# A GAME OF CATCH

## HELEN CRESSWELL
### Illustrated by Ati Forberg

*While their parents were making last-minute preparations for the family's move from England to Canada, Kate and Hugh were staying with their aunt. They decided to explore a nearby castle and visit the museum there. The children walked through the halls looking at the old portraits and dusty display cases. They climbed to the battlements and called one another's names, listening to the echoes. It was while they were chasing each other through the halls that Kate heard voices laughing and echoing her name.*

*"Things latch themselves onto names," said Mr. Whittaker, the caretaker. "Names mean more than most people suppose."*

*Then he showed them the painting—two 18th-century children, a girl and a boy about their own ages. The girl, wearing a long green dress, was laughing and stretching out her hands to catch a ball that the boy was holding up. "The Lady Katherine Cottam and her brother Charles," said the inscription.*

*Hugh thinks that Kate has imagined the voices, but Kate is certain they belong to the children in the painting. She is still thinking about it the next day when she and Hugh decide to go skating on the newly frozen lake.*

There was only an hour of daylight left when at last they reached the lake. Hurriedly they pulled up the laces on their boots, delighted to find that no one had been there before them. There was not a scar, not a mark on the whole wide sweep of it, and it beckoned them with the perfection of untrodden snow.

Hugh was the first on, with a few swift, thrusting strokes, and by the time Kate had tied her last lace he was already in the distance, making straight across the middle to the far side.

Kate looked about her at the flawless ice and followed him, her eyes fixed on the furrows left by his blades. But as her fear of the tracklessness vanished, she too was ranging the whole lake, like a bird with the whole vast air of the sky to choose from. Once, years ago, she could remember skating on a frozen canal, sweeping straight up a long white endless road between the stiff sedges until darkness fell. But she had never before been let loose in a freedom like this, with infinite possible paths spoking about her, endless choice. It was almost too much, like a new dimension.

"Kate! Kate!" She heard Hugh calling        urned to see that he too was skating in great arcs, greedily, as if trying to print his signature over the whole blank page of the lake. He beckoned, but she would not go to him, and sped into new distances, staking her own claim.

As the afternoon wore on they hardly met or even came close to each other, spellbound in their private mazes. But the dusk began to gather swiftly, and the sun suddenly appeared at the rim of the meadows, huge and orange in a sky surprisingly tender and tinged with green.

"Kate! Kate!" Hugh was calling again from the far side of the lake. "Catch me! Kate!"

And in that moment the frost released its echoes and she heard her name go folding away across the darkening meadows—*Kate . . . Kate . . . Kate . . . Kate . . .* and on into silence.

"Kate! Kate!" She checked, turned, and drove fast toward him. "Catch me!" *Catch . . . catch . . . .* Then again her name, nearer now, "Kate, Kate!" without echoes, and the sound of steel blades tearing the ice.

Slowing, she looked over to her right, and saw, impossibly, furrows moving across the ice, turning, wheeling, curving like smoke tracks in the sky. Forgetting Hugh, she veered to follow, but always they were beyond her, furling out of the ice ahead, curving mischievously aside, doubling back, elusive as smoke.

"Kate! Kate!" She no longer knew who was calling her, nor cared. Intent on the beckoning tracks she sped and thought she heard laughter beyond the hissing of her own skates and the pounding in her ears.

"Kate!" It *was* Hugh's voice now, close by, and she lifted her eyes to look at him, a stranger for a moment after the spellbound hour when only their paths had crossed.

"You're not even trying to catch me!" he cried. "What are you playing at? Kate!"

But she was away again, panic-stricken now because she had lost track of the unreeling thread and was left with a maze of thin lines, crossing and recrossing endlessly. She stopped and looked about her, listening for the sharp scything of blades that would betray her quarry. There was nothing. She strained her eyes into the dusk and could just make out her brother's figure away again at the far end of the lake. The sun had dropped. It was impossible to unravel the skein on the ice. Everything had gone away into darkness and silence.

She skated to where Hugh was already on the bank changing his boots. He did not look up. If she was ever to tell him what had happened now was the time, with

the frost falling, the cold translating into whiteness and anything possible after the long spell on ice.

But with her first steps onto the bank the world seemed to dip and then steady again, as it did after a day at sea. Her head spun; she sat down fumbling with her laces, and felt the delicious cold of the hoar against her hot legs.

"I forgot my gloves," Hugh said. "I shall get hot-aches when we get in."

"Serves you right," She heard herself say. Served him right for what? She hardly knew. But the moment had passed and she said no more. They went home between the dark hedges of the lane which was all metal now, silver and iron.

"Another frost tonight," said Hugh. Kate smiled.

*     *     *

It did freeze again. It was as if everything were conspiring with the echoes, ground and water turning to stone, the air thin and bitter. Kate woke to see it, and knew that she must spend the day seeking. In particular she knew that she must go to the castle alone.

She waited until Hugh had left for the village and then set out up the lane toward the castle. There was a mist as well as the frost, and at first she could not see even the castle's outline, in a curiously shrunken world, a world with walls now.

All the time she was asking herself questions.

"Is it the picture on the wall that matters? If the picture was taken away, would they go with it?"

She did not know the answer.

"Yesterday, on the lake, whose time was it, theirs or ours? Had they come forward to meet us, or were Hugh and I skating two hundred years ago?"

There was no answer to this either. The frost and the ice and the landscape were all anonymous. Yesterday might have been any day taken from all time. It might have been yesterday or it might have been a thousand years ago.

She looked about her and realized that the same was true today. The mist had swallowed the village behind her. She saw not a single landmark of time, only the fields, the sky and the weather. She hurried her steps toward the castle and Joe Whittaker, who stood with his feet firmly planted in the twentieth century and could anchor her safely there, too.

As she went under the high archway into the center courtyard she could see his light bulb burning through the dusty window. She tiptoed into the hallway, not wanting him to know that she was there yet. She gazed up at the picture, looking for clues. But the children were not even looking at her, they were looking at each other, intent on their game and the ball in the boy's hand. There was only one clue, and even that was hardly more than a hint.

"They're wearing warm clothes—velvet and wool," she thought. "And the girl has a muff hanging from her wrist. It was winter. It could have been this very time of year."

If the girl had been wearing muslin and a straw hat, at least Kate would have known the answer to one of her questions. At least she would have known that yesterday on the frozen lake it had not been Hugh and herself who had stepped out of their time and into that of the picture.

"It's you again, is it, miss?"

She found Joe Whittaker at her elbow, muffler tucked in his jacket, steaming mug of tea in hand.

"Oh! You made me jump. Yes. I wanted to look at the picture again." They stared up at it together.

"It *is* a mystery," remarked the caretaker at last. "No doubt about it. Even to me, and I live with it."

Kate said nothing.

"Have a cup of tea," he invited. "I've only just made some."

She followed him into the office and sat in the rocking chair near the oil stove. She hugged her knees and watched him busy with the crockery, waiting for the right moment to tell her story. The opening came easily, as it happened.

"You put trust in the ice yesterday, then," he said. "I saw you away down there from up top. Good little pair of skaters you are."

310

"Did you watch long?" she asked quickly. "What time was it?"

"Time? I can't say. I don't reckon much by the clock myself. Near dusk, I suppose."

She bent forward.

"Did you—I don't suppose you saw the others, too?"

"Others, miss?" He came over with a cup and saucer and set it down on the table beside her.

"Yes, the other two. There were four of us—in the end, at any rate."

He shook his head.

"I didn't see no four of you. Must've been after."

"Must've been," she agreed. After all, why should he have seen them? Even she had seen only the unfurling of their tracks. But she had half hoped that the caretaker, who lived with echoes and knew that time had nothing to do with clocks, might have taken the centuries in his stride.

"What I suppose is," he went on surprisingly, "that your friends weren't there to *be* seen."

"But they were!" she cried. "I heard them!"

"Oh they were there, right enough," he agreed. "No one knows that better than me. But not to be *seen*."

"I saw their marks on the ice. I heard them. Do you think I'll ever actually see them? Do you?"

"Depends how much you want to, I suppose."

"Oh, I *really* want to, Mr. Whittaker. Just for a moment, even. I want to believe in them."

"Seeing is believing," he said. "We've always to see before we'll believe."

"I don't think Hugh would believe even if he *saw*," she said. "That's really why I want to see them so badly. It always seems to be Hugh that's right and me that's wrong. I'm not saying anything against him, mind, it's just that we're different. Everyone says we are. But I was so sure about this, and at first I thought Hugh was as well. But now he's gone all sensible, as usual, and says I'm imagining things."

"So far as *I* know," said Joe Whittaker slowly, as if airing an opinion to which he had given a great deal of thought, "there's not all that much difference between seeing and imagining. In the end you might say the two was one and the same thing."

"You mean that if a thing *feels* real, it is?"

"Something like that," he said.

Kate drank her tea and stared at him over the top of her cup. There was something she meant to ask him,

something that was at the very tip of her tongue but she couldn't quite remember. He too sat sipping his tea, and just then the electric light suddenly paled as a shaft of sunlight flooded the little room.

"The sun's out!" Kate cried. "I wanted to skate again! We go tomorrow. If I don't see them today, I never shall!"

"Gone for five years you'll be, you say?"

"Yes. But I'll tell you this. If I don't see them, I'll come back. The minute we get back from Canada I'll come straight down here and . . . ."

She broke off. He was shaking his head.

"You'll be five years older," he said.

"What of it?"

"And they won't."

Suddenly she saw what he meant. *Their* time was standing still, but hers was moving. She was not playing an endless game of ball in a gilt frame and waiting for an echo to bring her back to life. She stood up. "I'll have to be going."

He went with her into the hall and suddenly she remembered the question she had been going to ask him.

"What did you mean when you said you knew they were down there, Mr. Whittaker? You said, 'Nobody knows it better than me.' What did you mean, please?"

He looked up at the picture and that, too, was bathed in sunshine now, kindling the dark oils, bringing the two children forward out of their dark background.

"I knew by that," he said.

She stared at him. She half thought she knew what he was going to tell her, but it seemed impossible.

He jerked his head toward the picture.

"They'd gone."

Now that he had actually said it, it was still impossible.

"So you see, miss, you were right. And that brother of yours was wrong."

So they said their good-bys and the caretaker went back to his little room and got out the sweeping brushes, because the sun had lit up the corners and more dust than even he could bear. As for Kate, she walked home with a head full of questions again, because in the puzzle she was trying to solve, every answer brought a new question with it. It was like trying to do a jigsaw puzzle with half the pieces missing.

The sun stayed out for an hour or two and then suddenly went in. The sky filled, a soft, gray snow sky.

"We might be able to skate, if we hurry," Kate said after dinner. "The snow might not come for hours, yet. It might not even come at all."

As they went up the now familiar lane she was filled with unbearable excitement. It seemed certain to her now that today time would finally run free and unfetter all the echoes and the unseen voices. She wanted to make the same patterns as yesterday's all over again, history to repeat itself. She was making toward the moment just before dusk when the invisible blades would come scything out of nowhere and the game of catch would begin again.

But things went wrong. They were not alone on the ice.

"Looks like the Lewises," Hugh said. "I can see their sled. Lucky dogs."

"You go over. They're taking turns on the sled, by the look of it. I want to skate alone for a bit."

Three of them were towing long ropes, harnessed like horses. Deborah, the youngest Lewis, was sitting bolt upright on the sled, waving her arms and shouting.

"Sure you don't mind?" He hesitated.

"Positive."

She watched him skate over to join them, wondering why she didn't go herself now that the lake was crowded and the last hope of a game of catch had gone.

She was gliding dreamily around the circumference of the lake when the snow began to fall. She paused, and stood by the row of trees, scenting the change, feeling the blotting-out of frost that was almost like warmth. The flakes were large and tissue-thin, they floated like white skeleton leaves, and the thicker they fell the faster they seemed to spin. She blinked as they melted on her hot face and ran into her eyes, and when she moved off again she was giddy with their swirling motion.

She realized that she was just by the fence where they had left their things, and stopped again. There was no sign of the others and she listened for their voices, but there was only the enormous blanketing silence of falling snow. They seemed to have gone right away.

She climbed onto the bank and unlaced her skates. Then she hung them on the fence beside Hugh's boots and overcoat and went again to the rim of the lake, straining her ears and eyes into the dizzy mist of white-ness. And as she stared, she did hear voices, and laughter, very faint and muffled. They seemed to be coming not from the ice, but from behind her, and once, quite clearly, she heard her name being called, "Kate! Kate!"

She began to run, stumbling here and there over roots and tussocks because now the snow was falling so thickly that she could see only a yard or two ahead.

"Kate! Catch! Catch!"

"I'm coming! Wait, I'm coming!" she cried, and al-though there were no echoes here, even in the muffling snow, she knew that her voice was ringing, carrying, crossing centuries.

"Catch!" The voice was close by, and as she strained her eyes into the spinning snow something came flying toward her and fell at her feet with a soft thud.

She stared down. It was a ball.

"So *this* is the real game of catch," she thought, and picked it up.

For a moment she stared down at the ball in her hands. It was quite soft and made of dark red leather, sewn together in segments. Then she looked up and they were there, both of them.

Though they were divided from her by the falling snow she saw them clearly, and they were watching her, too, expectantly. Suddenly the girl stretched out her hands and without thinking, Kate tossed the leather ball back straight into her waiting palms. The girl laughed and shook her hair, then darted off.

"Don't go!" she cried. "Kate!" She called the name again. "Kate!"

"Things latch themselves onto names," Joe Whittaker had said.

But the girl had already turned; she threw the ball to the boy, who leaped nimbly forward to catch it before it touched the ground. He straightened up and looked at Kate.

"Catch!" he cried suddenly, and again the ball was in her hands. She threw it back to him and the girl came running from behind the curtain of snow again to catch it in her turn. They tossed it backward and forward, backward and forward, and all the time Kate, watching the ball, watching them, was thinking fast and furiously. And as the ball came to her the next time she held it firmly between both hands and waited. If she kept it, the spell would be broken and they would stay forever. It was the ball in flight that bridged the centuries. Without it they could never return.

They stood waiting, watching her. The girl, puzzled, smiled and held out her hands. Kate shook her head and put the ball behind her back. They waited, all three of them, the game of catch suspended and the snow falling silently all about them.

"Kate! Kate!" Voices were calling in the distance. She saw the girl stiffen, listening. "Where are you? Kate! Kate!"

The voices were nearer; Kate could hear Hugh's among the yells of the Lewises. What would *they* make of the girl in green velvet and the boy with his long hair brushing his shoulders and shirt frilled at his thin wrists? She stared at their white, frightened faces, and hesitated. Then she brought the ball from behind her back and held it up.

The girl's face cleared, she nodded delightedly, and ran forward a few paces from her brother, and Kate, smiling back, threw the ball straight into her cupped hands. For an instant the girl stood there, and then with a swift wave turned and ran, the boy after her. They swam into blurs in the snowstorm and were gone.

"Kate! Kate! Where are you!"

She began to run, playing a new game of catch. Now she was hunter and hunted together. She kept her eyes down at first, looking for footprints, but there was nothing to guide her but laughter ahead and now and again a glimpse of pale green or brown. The farther she ran the fainter the laughter grew, and as it dwindled for the last time she halted, panting for breath, and found herself right on the drawbridge of the castle.

Through the great stone arch she hurried and across the high courtyard with its strange snow-light and muffled echoes. The caretaker's bulb burned behind his long window, but as she ran into the entrance hall and stopped in front of the picture she saw that the room was empty. Joe Whittaker was making the lonely rounds of his castle, battening it against the snow.

She stared up. They were there ahead of her, posed and careless as if nothing had ever happened. They had stepped back into the gilt frame and another time and now they did not even look at her, absorbed in the private game of catch.

And yet, as she stared, Kate felt that there was something different. The children were the same, their clothes, their faces. Impossible to explain—and yet different. Still the girl held up the ball and the boy waited for her throw.

"Perhaps he'll wait another hundred years," Kate thought. She knew that the game was over for her now. Slowly she turned and went out into the snow. It was falling lightly now, the flakes went drifting dreamily with all the time in the world. Over the drawbridge she went and started across the darkening meadows. Down by the lake she could see the outline of a small figure approaching. It was Hugh, alone. The others had gone home, but he had waited. He had seen her, too, because he waved and she heard him call, "Kate! Kate!"

And in those moments as they ran toward each other she suddenly knew what had been different about the picture. *The girl had been holding the ball!* Surely, *surely*, before it had been she who was stretching out her hands to catch it, while the boy held it aloft, teasing her? She, Kate, had been the last to throw it in that strange, triangular game of catch. And she had thrown it not to the boy, but the girl.

"Kate!" Their paths met. "Where have you been? I've been looking everywhere."

"I lost my way in the snowstorm," was all she said, and they went together through the last gate of the fields and into the lane. And still she was trying to remember how the picture had looked yesterday. Surely it had been the boy who held the ball? And the girl had it now, and would have it for who knew how many years to come. Perhaps forever?

"Surely the ball has changed hands," Kate thought again. The snow went on falling.

## Thinking and Writing About the Selection

1. What is the setting of the story?

2. What led Kate to believe that the children in the portrait had been skating with her and Hugh?

3. Why do you think Kate did not share her discovery with Hugh?

4. If you were Kate, what would you have done to try to communicate with the children in the portrait? How might you have convinced them that you could be trusted?

## Applying the Key Skill
### Character's Motives or Feelings

Use complete sentences to answer the following questions about the characters in "A Game of Catch."

1. Why do you think the children in the portrait chose to reveal themselves to Kate instead of Hugh?

2. When Kate was playing the game of catch with the children in the portrait, why did she decide to hold the ball? Why did she change her mind?

3. How do you think Kate felt after skating on the lake for the first time? How did her feelings change after talking to Mr. Whittaker?

4. How would you describe Kate's feelings at the end of the story? What words would you choose to explain how she felt about her experience? What information in the story supports your description?

# The SNOWFLAKE

Before I melt,
Come, look at me!
This lovely icy filigree!
Of a great forest
In one night
I make a wilderness
Of white:
By skyey cold
Of crystals made,
All softly, on
Your finger laid,
I pause, that you
My beauty see:
Breathe, and I vanish
Instantly.

Walter de la Mare

# PLOT, SETTING, MOOD, THEME, NARRATIVE POINT OF VIEW

Sometimes you may want to tell a friend about a story you have read and liked. How do you go about it? A good way to begin is to describe some of the things that make up the story—what we sometimes call story elements. Four important elements in every story are plot, setting, mood, and theme.

The action that takes place in a story is called the **plot.** Everything that the characters do in the story is part of the plot. To understand how important the plot is, just try to imagine a story without one! The series of events that make up the plot of a story takes place in a certain order. In a good story, the order of events helps keep readers interested in the story.

**ACTIVITY A** Read the sentences below and decide which ones describe events in the plot of "A Game of Catch." Then on your paper, write the sentences describing the events in the plot in the order in which they took place in the story.

1. Kate and Hugh always enjoyed visiting their aunt.
2. Kate saw tracks on the ice, but she did not see the skaters who made them.
3. While Hugh was skating with the Lewises, Kate saw the children through the snow.
4. Joe Whittaker talked to Kate about the children in the portrait.
5. Hugh was not interested in make-believe.
6. Kate returned to the castle and looked at the portrait for the last time.

The time and the place of the action in a story are called the **setting.** The place in which the story takes place may be real or imaginary. The author usually tells you where the story takes place. The time in which a story takes place may be the past, the present, or the future. The author does not always tell you when the story takes place. You must figure it out for yourself. Clues that will help you are the way in which the characters talk and dress, and descriptions of the things they use and the things they do in their daily lives.

**ACTIVITY B**  Write the answer to each question below.

1.  Where does the story "A Game of Catch" take place?

    a.  in and near a village in England
    b.  in Canada
    c.  in a museum in England

2.  When does the story "A Game of Catch" take place?

    a.  in the 18th century
    b.  in the 20th century
    c.  in the past and the present

The **mood** of a story is the general feeling we get when we read the story. For example, an adventure story may create a feeling of excitement, a ghost story a scary feeling, or a mystery story a mysterious feeling. A story that turns out well usually gives us a happy feeling, and one that ends unhappily can make us feel sad. Remember that mood refers to the reader's feeling, not to the feelings of the characters.

**ACTIVITY C** Write the answer to the question on your paper. Which word best describes the mood of "A Game of Catch"?

a. thrilling     b. frightening     c. happy     d. mysterious

The **theme** of a story is a general statement of the meaning the story has for us. Sometimes we say the theme is the message of the story. The author does not usually state the theme directly. We must think about the story to decide what its message is.

**ACTIVITY D** Write the answer to the question on your paper. Which sentence best states the theme of "A Game of Catch"?

a. It is always sad to lose old friends.
b. People get to know and appreciate one another by spending time together and sharing experiences.
c. Things can happen that we may believe but cannot explain.
d. Dreams can come true.

**Narrative point of view** refers to the person through whose eyes the reader sees the action. When we read a story, it is important to know who is telling, or narrating, the story. Different people will tell a story from different points of view.

Some stories are narrated in the first person. In a **first-person narrative,** a character in the story describes what happens. The reader learns about the events of the story from that person's point of view. It is easy to tell if a story is narrated in the first person. The storyteller uses such words as *I, me, my, we, our,* and *ours.*

Most stories are narrated in the third person. In a **third-person narrative,** the author acts as the storyteller. Sometimes the author reports how all the characters speak, act, think, and feel. The author is an "outsider" who knows and tells about all the characters. In another kind of third-person narrative, the events that are described are limited to what one person is able to observe. The feelings and thoughts of only that person are made known to us.

Stories are not only told in first or third person. They are also told from a specific **point of view.** The point of view may be the author's. It may also be one of the character's. For example, "The Night of the Leonids" was told in the first person from Lewis's point of view. "The House of Dies Drear" was told from Thomas's point of view in the third person.

**ACTIVITY E** Write the answer to the question on your paper. From which point of view is "A Game of Catch" told?

a. first person, Hugh's point of view
b. first person, Kate's point of view
c. third person, author's point of view
d. third person, Hugh's point of view
e. third person, Kate's point of view

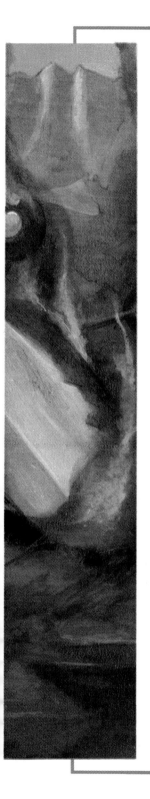

# CANYON WINTER

## WALT MOREY

*Fifteen-year old Peter Grayson was on his way to his father's ranch high in the Cascade Mountains of California. The plane was twenty miles off course when its motor sputtered and died. The plane crashed into the wilderness. The pilot was killed instantly, but Peter was unhurt.*

*Peter knew that if he kept his wits about him, he had a chance to survive. He built a fire at the crash site. For two days he waited, hoping search planes would spot him. But hunger forced him to leave the area and hunt for food. After hiking for several miles, he saw a deer and followed it into a canyon and to a small clearing. A log cabin, the home of Omar Pickett, stood in the open.*

*For nearly fifty years, Pickett had lived alone in the wilderness. His encounter with Peter was an unwelcome change in his peaceful and quiet way of life. He knew that it would be impossible for Peter to leave the canyon until spring, and that was six months away. However, Peter didn't intend to wait that long. He would take any risk, even crossing the wild swollen river that cut through the canyon, to get home.*

Peter was awakened by the old man lighting the fire and getting breakfast. For a few minutes he lay with his eyes shut, reviewing his plan.

They ate breakfast in silence. Afterward, Pickett puttered about the cabin. He took out the ashes and changed his bedding. Finally, he put on his old hat and coat, and went out. Peter watched him head up through the timber.

Peter knew he should wait at least half an hour to make sure the old man had really gone, but he was too keyed up. He got the spare sleeping bag out and stuffed some food into it. Hastily, he made carrying straps with a length of rope and threw the sleeping bag over his shoulder. He slipped out into the nearby brush and ran for the river.

The sleeping bag and canned goods were heavier than he'd expected. They forced him to lean forward for balance. But he was on his way home at last. He began to jog along the shore until he reached the sheer canyon walls where the river plunged into the gorge. For a moment his courage deserted him. Then he stepped into the shallow water and waded to the first narrow, sandy beach.

Peter progressed from beach to beach. He was trying to hurry, and he slipped and fell several times, once going in to his shoulders. He felt the fierce drag of the current reach for him. He grabbed for the jagged edge of a rock and climbed on top. He stood shaking with fright and cold. Slow down, he warned himself, this old river's just waiting.

Peter finally came to a long, straight stretch. He was tired and hungry. He rested a minute, then entered the water and began wading to the next beach. The water continued shallow, the current was not bad. Out in the middle it boomed along, kicking up five-foot waves with foaming tops. At the end of the straight stretch he sat on the extreme tip of the last beach. He rested and studied the gorge ahead.

He was at the head of a bend he could see around. He'd have to wade. There were no more sandy beaches, but the shore was lined with big rocks that he could easily travel over.

Peter slipped his arms through the loops of the sleeping bag, stepped into the swift current, and began wading around the bend. The water grew deeper. It reached his hips, and he held his breath. The current was a solid force that slammed into him. A step at a time he edged around the bend and onto the rocks that lined the river's edge. By choosing his rocks carefully he made good time traveling. But jumping from rock to rock was tiring. He stopped to rest briefly. Ahead loomed another bend. The canyon walls rose sheer, as if sliced by a giant knife.

When he reached the bend, Peter stopped and studied the river. The current slammed into the sheer wall and bounced back toward the center of the channel with breath-catching speed. A half-dozen big boulders rose out of the channel. White water boiled around them.

Peter couldn't see around the bend, but if this current and the sounds up ahead which filled the gorge were any indication, it was not good. He had to get around this shoulder so he could see. From here he could tell the river ran deep at the point and with a speed no one could live through. It looked like his hike was going to end here. He felt discouraged and beat. He should have believed the old man.

He was turning back when his eyes found the small ledge in the face of the rock just above the waterline. It looked about three feet wide and followed the wall around the bend. It was no more than forty feet from where he stood. The water was not too deep to wade to it. The current was fast, but if he was careful . . .

Peter let himself into the river slowly. He edged forward, feeling his way carefully over the rocky bottom. The water crept up his legs. The pressure of the current increased with the depth. When he was halfway to the ledge, it boiled around his hips. He leaned backward against its pull. He stopped and stood looking at the ledge. It was so near. A dozen feet more. Again he moved forward. The water grew no deeper. He was

almost there. Another step. His hand was out reaching for a hand-hold on the ledge when a loose rock turned under his foot. He was thrown off balance, and he lunged for the ledge. His fingers struck, then the current snatched him away.

A giant's strength sucked him deep and tumbled him over and over. His lungs were bursting. He kicked and stroked wildly for the surface. He was tossed upward into sunlight, and he struck something solid. The force of the current pinned him momentarily against one of the huge boulders. Peter scrambled frantically for a hand-hold. His foot found a crevice. He heaved himself upward. The next moment, he sprawled across the flat surface face down, shaking and gagging.

Peter lay there several minutes, afraid to move. Then he carefully raised himself to his hands and knees and looked about. The sleeping bag had been torn from his back. He thought he glimpsed it bobbing through the waves far downriver. He could now see that this would have been as far as he could go. From here the river ran

deep and swift right against the sheer walls of the canyon.

Peter discovered he could sit up safely, but the top of the boulder was wet with spray and moss. He dared not stand. He sat hunched and shivering, thinking about his plight.

A wave of helplessness and fear claimed him. Then it passed, and he began thinking of Omar Pickett. Would the old man come looking for him, or would he figure Peter was good riddance and let him go? If he tried to follow, would he come this far? Or would he figure Peter had such a head start he could never catch him? There was no telling what the old man might do. How could he possibly help anyway?

The boy was ravenously hungry. He wondered how long he could stay on this rock without becoming weak from hunger or falling asleep and rolling off.

The sun finally passed from sight over the gorge. The shadow of the west wall crept over him. He was sitting hunched up, looking at nothing, when he heard the voice above the roar of the water.

"Boy! Boy!" There stood Pickett on the last rock, waving at him. He had a coil of rope looped over his lean shoulders.

Peter yelled at the top of his lungs, "Mr. Pickett! Mr. Pickett!" He started excitedly to his feet.

"Stay down!" the old man shouted. "Stay down!"

Peter sank back on all fours. He watched fearfully as Pickett calmly stepped off the rock into the swift current and edged toward the ledge. Water boiled against his long legs, but he seemed as sturdy as a tree trunk. He pulled himself up on

the ledge, slipped the rope from his shoulders, held one end in his left hand and the coil in his right. "Get ready to catch," he shouted, "but don't stand up."

Pickett swung the coil around his head, then launched it out over the water with all his strength. Peter watched the rope snake out, unrolling as it came. It was nylon and very light. The wind caught it and whipped it downriver. It fell into the water twenty feet short, long enough, but too light to carry all the way.

Pickett stood a moment, undecided, then began searching along the wall. He found a knob of rock, wound the rope about it, and tied it. The opposite end he knotted about his waist. Then he moved slowly back and forth along the ledge, studying the water. Finally, he stopped at a point above Peter.

He took off his hat and coat and laid them on the ledge. Then he shed his old red shirt and boots.

Peter had a sudden suspicion and shouted at the top of his lungs, "You can't! You'll drown! Stay there, Mr. Pickett. Stay there!"

The old man stood tall and lean, long arms hanging at his sides, white hair flying. Peter shouted again, "Don't, Mr. Pickett! You can't make it. Don't try!"

Pickett didn't answer or even look up. He moved along the ledge a few feet, stopped, then moved again. He stood a moment looking at the churning water. Suddenly he launched his lean body straight out into the current in a mighty leap.

He disappeared from sight.

Peter half rose to his feet, felt them slip on the slick surface, and sank back on all fours. His eyes swept the water.

The white head bobbed up and hurtled toward him. Pickett had calculated well. He'd jumped at the very spot where the current could carry him to the rock. A moment later, he struck. Peter grabbed his arm with both hands and began to pull. In seconds, Pickett lay gasping and coughing on the rock alongside him.

Pickett turned his head and grinned at Peter. "Kind of chilly place you've got here. How about goin' ashore where it's warm and dry?"

Peter tried to smile. His throat was thick. He finally managed, "Whenever you say."

"Good!" Pickett sat up, untied the rope from about his middle, and pulled in the slack. He looped the rope around Peter and tied it. He tied the end about himself. "In case the rope slips through our hands, we're tied fast," he explained. "That rock we're anchored to is good and solid."

"What if the rope breaks?" Peter was thinking of both of them tied to this small line.

"It's guaranteed to stand sixteen hundred pounds' pull. The river won't be half that. But if it busts, I'll demand my money back," he grinned. "We'll jump in. When the rope tightens and holds, the current will start workin' for us," he explained. "It'll act as a lever and swing us toward the ledge. But climb the rope hand over hand as much as you can to help. When you reach the ledge, grab hold and climb up. All right. Ready?''

Peter nodded. His mouth was dry.

''When I say 'Jump,' we go together. Jump straight out toward shore as far as you can.''

Peter sucked air into his lungs. His hands, gripping the rope, were clammy.

Pickett said sharply, ''Now! Jump!''

Peter shut his eyes, lunged erect, and leaped as far as he could. Icy water closed over him. The rope tightened with a jerk that almost cut him in two. His lungs screamed for air. The next moment he was tossed to the surface.

''Keep goin'!'' Pickett's voice shouted behind him. ''Pull!''

His arms ached. The rope was slick with water, and his hands slipped. He grabbed the rope again and pulled himself upward with all his strength. Then the current slammed him hard against the rock wall. The ledge was just above his

eyes. He lunged upward, found a handhold. A big hand boosted him from behind, and he sprawled on the ledge. The next moment, Omar Pickett rolled up beside him.

For several minutes they lay side by side, gagging, spitting water, and getting their breath back.

Finally Omar Pickett sat up, leaned his back against the rock wall, and wiped water from his eyes. "We made it," he said. "By golly, we made it! Not many jump into this old river and get out again—and that's a fact. You all right, boy?"

"I'm fine," he said, smiling.

He sat up and looked at the old man beside him. "You saved my life, Mr. Pickett. I'll never forget. But you took an awful chance, jumping into the river. You could have drowned."

Pickett looked at him thoughtfully, "How did you figure to get off that rock, boy?"

Peter shook his head. "I don't know. I couldn't think any more. But because I did a dumb thing is no reason you should risk your life. I'm glad you did though," he smiled.

Omar Pickett squinted his gray eyes at Peter. "You're quite a boy, and that's a fact." He rose stiffly, "Let's get these two old canyon rats out of here before they catch their death of pneumonia." He untied the rope about his middle and put on his boots, shirt, coat, and old floppy hat. He unfastened the rope from the rock and tied the end around himself again. "We'll stay tied together until we pass the jumpin' rocks going back. I'll go first. If I slip and fall, you can hold me with the rope. If you fall, I'll do the same. When the current hits, you lean into it, bend your upstream leg and straighten the downstream one, and push against the water with it. All right, here goes."

Pickett slipped off the ledge almost hip deep into the river. The current boiled against his legs, but he leaned into it and moved ahead. Peter payed out the line, but it wasn't needed. Omar Pickett made the rock, turned, and waved Peter to come on.

Peter lowered himself into the river and did exactly as Pickett had told him. He reached the rock with no trouble. They made their way upstream together. At the first sandy beach, the old man untied the rope and looped it about his shoulders again. They walked back against the rock wall where a cleft at the top let a ray of late sun into the canyon. They sat down in its warmth to rest.

Pickett leaned back, removed his hat, and heaved a sigh, "Sun sure feels mighty good after the river. We'll rest a bit. But we can't sit here long in these wet clothes."

"I lost the sleeping bag and about a dozen cans of food," Peter admitted quietly.

"We've got another sleepin' bag, and you know that the pantry is full of food."

"It was lucky you thought to bring that rope."

"It's the best piece of equipment you can carry here in the canyon."

Peter felt almost drowsy in the warm sun, but his mind could not let go of the amazing afternoon's happening. "You must have started looking for me as soon as you got back to the cabin."

"Just about." Pickett had shut his eyes and lifted his leathery face to let the late sun beat down on it. "I was suspicious right off. You'd never been late for lunch before."

Pickett stretched his long legs luxuriously. "You got further than I figured you would. I thought you'd be scared out where the rock walls begin and the river enters the gorge again. I expected to find you sittin' on the beach waitin' for me. But you made the rock shelf. That's the limit anyone can go on foot. It peters out around that bend. Then you've got a full mile of water, swift as a race horse and a hundred feet deep, with an eighth of a mile of rapids at the end. I wouldn't have believed you could get that far. You did fine. But one bad slip anywhere and you could have drowned."

"I almost did. And I'd still be trapped on that rock but for you. I was a fool to try," Peter confessed.

"You were a boy wantin' to get home mighty bad. I should have thought about that instead of bein' mad because you intruded on my privacy."

"I'm sorry."

"I believe you," the old man smiled. "I had time to do a lotta thinkin' while I was comin' down here lookin' for you." He dug a heel thoughtfully in the sand. "Man can live alone so long as he don't consider anybody or anythin' but himself, and that's a fact. But the important thing before this meetin' is—do you believe me now? Or am I going to chase over this country every few days lookin' for you?"

"I believe you, Mr. Pickett. You won't have to look for me again." Peter thought of the months here if a plane didn't come, and a great loneliness went crying through him.

Pickett said gently, "The time'll go faster if you don't think about it, boy."

Pickett squeezed water from the cuffs of his shirt, then squinted at the sun. He rose abruptly and jammed the old hat down on his wet hair. The sharp, gray eyes regarded Peter. "The name," he said, "is Omar."

"Mine's Peter."

"Then what say we get back, Pete."

## Thinking and Writing About the Selection

1. How did Peter lose his sleeping bag?

2. What did Omar Pickett mean when he said, "You're quite a boy, and that's a fact"?

3. In what ways did Peter and Omar change because of their journey on the river?

 4. If you were lost in the wilderness, what would you need to survive? Describe how you would find or make something you needed.

## Applying the Key Skill
### Character's Motives or Feelings

Read the following incomplete sentences about "Canyon Winter." Choose the best ending for each. Write the complete sentences.

1. When Peter Grayson first came to Omar Pickett's cabin, the old man probably felt ___.
   a. happy to have company
   b. angry, but willing to help
   c. suspicious

2. Peter decided to try to get home even though Omar had told him he would have to wait because he ___.
   a. had no other choice
   b. knew Omar was lying
   c. wanted to get home more than anything else

3. As Omar and Peter set out for the cabin, they probably felt ___.
   a. uncertain about each other
   b. new respect and understanding for each other
   c. that they had to put up with each other no matter what

## CHARACTER'S MOTIVES OR FEELINGS

When you begin to read a story, the characters are like people you have just met. As you continue to read, you learn more and more about each character.

For example, you probably felt you knew and understood both Peter and Mr. Pickett better by the time you finished "Canyon Winter" than you did when you started the story. You learned how they felt and discovered their reasons, or motives, for doing what they did. What characters do, what they say, and what they think help you to learn about them. The way in which they say and do things is also important, as are the author's descriptions of how they look, or their appearance. Read the sentences below.

1. The boy clung fiercely to the slippery rock as the dark waters swirled around him. His voice seemed weak and small as he tried to call, "Help!"

2. The man and the boy pulled themselves slowly through the last few feet of swirling water to the safety of the bank. They lay there for a few minutes, getting their breath back, then turned to one another and shouted, "We did it! We did it!"

What word clues helped you realize that the boy in the first sentence felt frightened? How did you determine that the man and the boy in the second sentence felt tired but jubilant?

In figuring out a character's feelings, it may help to ask yourself how you would feel in the same situation. Putting yourself in a character's place can also help you determine the reasons that a character had for doing what he or she did.

ACTIVITY   Read the story below. Then answer the questions
that follow.

No one had ever made it down the entire course of the
river before. The rapids were too dangerous. In some places,
the river was too narrow. It was crazy to even think about
trying—but Tim and Katy knew they had to. It was the kind
of challenge they thrived on. They had traveled all over the
world in places few had ever seen or even heard about. No
matter how many times they had tried to do the impossible,
each attempt was exciting. There had been failures, but each
unsuccessful expedition had taught them something. Their
well-equipped canoe was in perfect shape. They were prepared for emergencies. Before the sun rose, they were at the
river bank. Working quickly, they got ready to set out.

1.  Why do you think Tim and Katy were prepared for
    emergencies?

    a.  They knew about the possible dangers of the trip.
    b.  They knew about the possible dangers and were
        experienced travelers.
    c.  They had heard about the dangerous rapids.
    d.  They had tried to make the trip before but had been
        unsuccessful.

2.  How do you think Tim and Katy felt when they set out?

    a.  confident
    b.  determined and excited
    c.  anxious and fearful
    d.  determined and excited
        but also anxious

Get ready for a journey into the future. It's a world of computers and robots. Even sports are different. Everyone talks about the latest moonball scores. Things don't always run smoothly, however. While Rodney is thrilled with Clutz, the family's new robot, his parents and Aurora, the family dog, aren't quite sure what to think. It seems that everything Clutz does turns into a disaster. Will Clutz prove himself worthy of Rodney's trust? Is he up to an encounter with Slick, the most advanced robot ever designed?

# G.L.U.T.Z.

Marilyn Z. Wilkes

School didn't start for ten more minutes. As usual everybody was hanging around in front of the EdSec MidSchool, waiting until the last minute to go inside.

"Man, it's the life," Taurus Johnson was saying. "Since we got our robot, nobody at our place does a thing anymore. Old Slick does it all."

"No more chores for us," said his brother Angus. "We spend all our time playing moonball."

"You're so lucky," said Jonni. "I wish our folks would get one."

"Hey, Pentax," said Taurus. "Haven't you got a robot? Or was that a two-legged hat rack I saw you with yesterday?"

Rodney was indignant. "Clutz is a great robot," he said. "He can do anything any other robot can."

"Clutch?" Taurus snorted. "What kind of a name is Clutch?"

"*Clutz*," said Rodney. "Combined Level Unit/Type Z. He was a pioneer in the field."

"I'll bet," said Taurus.

"You'll bet what?" demanded Rodney. Taurus Johnson was such a pain.

"I'll bet my robot is better than your robot," said Taurus. "I'll even prove it."

"How?" asked Rodney.

"My robot can play moonball."

"Well so can Clutz," said Rodney. "I'm teaching him myself."

"In that case," said Taurus, "how about a game? Angus and me and our robot against you and anybody you want and your robot."

"Sure," said Rodney. "Why not?"

"Good," said Taurus. "Tomorrow after school at the court behind Tower 4, 15:00 hours."

"You're on," said Rodney. "Aurora will play goalie, just like always."

"Okay by me," said Taurus. "See you on the court, hotshot."

School that day was endless. Mrs. Wotek had to keep reminding Rodney to pay attention to his computer screen. How could he

concentrate on twentieth-century history when his mind kept wandering to the moonball game?

What had he gotten himself into? Could Clutz do it? The Johnsons must have a Butler robot, from the sound of it. Clutz could go to pieces against competition like that.

A buzzer buzzed. It was 14:00:00 at last, time for classes to end. He waved to his friends and raced for the escalators. Aurora was waiting outside for him, as she did every day. Rodney smiled. Aurora was the best dog on the planet, maybe in the whole galaxy. He ran across the plaza with her and hopped onto the moving walkway that carried them to and from EdSec.

It took eight minutes at walkway speed for Rodney and Aurora to reach the Living Complex. Clutz was in the leisure room, sitting on a float-a-lounge. He was holding a dust cloth tightly in both hands and staring at the telecommunicator. It was projecting a popular show called *Galactic Spy*.

"I just love *Galactic Spy*," Clutz said. "I try never to miss it. It's so wonderful the way the humans always triumph over evil. Especially Captain Stalwart. He's my idea of a real hero."

Rodney sat down on the float-a-lounge and put his arm around the robot. "How would *you* like to be a hero?" he asked.

"Oh, Rodney, me? I'm just a robot." Clutz's ear spring trembled.

"You could be a robot hero," said Rodney. "For service beyond the call of duty."

"There are no limits to a robot's duty," said Clutz. "We serve humanity any and every way we can."

"Then if I asked you to do something you weren't specifically programmed to do," said Rodney, "could you do it anyway, for humanity—I mean, for me?" He studied the robot. "Do you think you could learn to play my favorite sport if it would help me?"

"On that basis—to help a human—my memory banks are programmed to receive new knowledge. However, my exterior

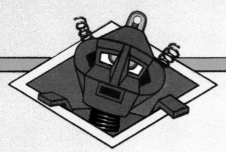

form . . ." He looked embarrassed. "I know I am less than graceful."

Rodney was getting excited. "That won't matter with moonball. You'll see," he said. "Come on." He grabbed the robot by the hand, and they clattered through the front door to the elevator. Aurora ran after them.

A few minutes later they were standing in a special room in a subbasement of the Living Complex. At least they were trying to stand. The artificial one-sixth gravity made it hard to keep from bouncing upward with every movement.

"This is a moonball court, Clutz," Rodney explained. "It has gravity just like the moon's, so players can handle the ball. Otherwise it would be too heavy."

He bent over and picked up a large white plastoid ball, one meter in diameter. In Earth gravity it weighed sixteen kilos, almost half as much as Rodney. In Moon gravity it weighed only about two and a half kilos. Of course, with reduced gravity Rodney's Earth-conditioned muscles had no trouble lifting an object nearly half his own weight.

He tossed the ball to Clutz. Startled, the robot pushed it away— and found himself carried backward and up by the impact. He flailed his feet wildly. But then, as he floated back down to the floor, a delighted grin spread over his face.

"It's like parachute-jumping," he said. "Or bouncing on a trampoline in slow motion. Or freefalling through space."

"Have you really done all those things?" asked Rodney with interest.

"Heaven forbid," said Clutz.

"Well," Rodney said, "do you think you can keep your balance and throw the ball?"

"I'll try," said Clutz.

Rodney tossed him the ball. Clutz spread his arms wide, but the big white ball bounced off his breastplate. The spring in his ear shuddered, and he sailed downcourt, landing on his back.

"It's not as easy as it looks," he said shakily.

"Don't worry, everybody falls at first," Rodney said. "You'll get it," he said. "I know you will. Here's how the game works.

"See the big metal ring fastened to the wall at the edge of the court? It's five meters up from the floor. The idea is to get the moonball away from the other team and put it through the ring for a goal. Meanwhile they're trying to score by getting the ball into the moonring. Got it?"

Clutz nodded.

"There are three players on each team," Rodney continued. "A fullback, a forward, and a goalie, who stays under the moonring and tries to keep the other team from scoring. Aurora is our goalie. She's really good. Show him, girl."

Aurora took up her position under the moonring. She glared at Clutz, daring him to try to score.

Rodney grasped the moonball, faked a pass to Clutz, then bounded down the court toward the moonring. When he had almost reached it, he pretended to throw to the left and tossed the ball to the right.

As Aurora dodged to meet it Rodney bounced up and pushed the ball hard toward the moonring. But Aurora was too quick for him. Leaping high, she intercepted the ball with her shoulders and sent it sailing back toward midcourt. Clutz ducked as it floated past his head.

"Great interception, girl!" called Rodney. "Okay, Clutz. Ready to try a game?" He passed the ball gently to the robot.

\*　　\*　　\*

At 15:00:00 on Tuesday they got to the moonball court. Rodney looked around. Most of the kids in the complex were there. Word sure traveled fast.

Clutz was mumbling nervously to himself. He kept eyeing the tall, sleek, silver-and-black robot at the edge of the court. The robot's red-lit eyes were sharp and penetrating, his white gloves spotless. His elegant body seemed relaxed, yet poised for action. Rodney swallowed hard.

Taurus grinned. "Allow me to make the introductions," he said. He crooked his finger and the Butler robot glided gracefully over.

"Meet Slick," he said, draping an arm over the robot's shoulder. "Best robot in the whole Northeast Sector."

"Delighted," said the robot.

"This is Clutz," said Rodney, giving him a reassuring pat on the back.

"Argle," said Clutz in a strangled voice.

"Do we have a referee?" asked Rodney.

"Here." Terri Khan bounced onto the court. She pulled a whistle out of her pocket and gave a shrill tweet.

"Okay, take your positions and play moonball!"

Aurora trot-floated down to the scoring end of the court. Angus Johnson was already there, under the large metal ring. Clutz and the Butler robot moved to the middle of the court, sizing each other up. Rodney and Taurus Johnson bounced their way to the far end and faced off on opposite sides of the moonball.

In the first few minutes Terri called fouls on both sides. Then Rodney got his arms around the big white ball and sent it arching toward midcourt. Clutz and the Butler robot both leaped toward it.

"Careful, Type Z," hissed the Butler. "At your age one mustn't overdo." He gave Clutz a fierce shove that threw him off-balance and out of the court. "Foul!" yelled Rodney, but Taurus Johnson leaped forward to snatch the ball in midair and continued toward the scoring zone. Rodney turned and galloped after him.

Two meters from the ring, Taurus lobbed the ball back over Rodney's head to the Butler robot, who rushed forward and deposited it in the ring. Aurora leaped to intercept, but was pushed off-balance by Angus. The score was 1–0.

They faced off again and moved downcourt. With the ball in midcourt the Butler robot made a move for it.

"Out of my way, primitive mechanism," he sneered at Clutz.

"PRIMITIVE MECHANISM!" shrieked Clutz. He jumped up and fastened both arms around the robot as the ball sailed by. Rodney caught it and shoved hard. The ball flew toward the ring. Aurora leaped toward Angus Johnson, baring her teeth and growling. Angus backed away in spite of himself, and the score was 1–1.

"Yay!" yelled the crowd.

"End first period," yelled Terri, blowing her whistle.

Rodney huddled in one corner with his teammates. "We've done

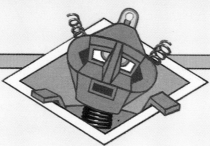

a pretty good job so far," he said. "We just have to keep the pressure on and not let them think we're running scared."

"Terrified is more like it," said Clutz.

"Just pay attention, and don't let that silver smoothie get to you," said Rodney. Clutz nodded and tried to look determined.

They bounced onto the court in a show of confidence. The crowd cheered. The Johnsons came onto the court to an equal chorus of boosters.

With the Butler's help Taurus scored two quick goals. Then everyone gasped as a sleek black-and-silver apparition flew down from midcourt to score single-handed.

It was now 4–1.

Miraculously Rodney and Clutz managed to put together a goal between them. Then, catching Angus off-guard, Aurora deflected a Johnson field shot and nosed the ball in. The score was 4–3.

"Okay, Clutz," yelled Rodney. "Let's even it up."

The ball sailed down the court. Clutz grabbed it just as the Butler robot crashed into him hard from behind.

"H-E-E-L-L-P!" cried Clutz, as he and the ball flew toward the ring together.

"Let go of it!" yelled Rodney. He and Taurus headed for the scoring zone.

There was a free-for-all under the ring. Arms and legs were everywhere. Then Clutz emerged from the heap of bodies, still grasping the ball. He leaped for the ring. The Butler robot leaped with him and pushed. The referee blew her whistle. The ball sailed back out over the players' heads, leaving Clutz draped like a rag doll over the moonball ring. Terri signaled the end of the game.

"Well, Pentax, I guess that proves it," said Taurus. He jumped up to the moonring and pulled Clutz free. The robot dropped to the floor with a metallic clatter.

Rodney helped Clutz to the sidelines and sat him down on a bench.

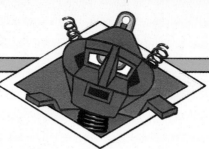

"I feel dizzy," said Clutz.

"The best team won! The best robot won!" Taurus yelled to the spectators. He raised the Butler's arm in victory. "I know a good scrap dealer, if you want to get rid of that thing" was his parting shot to Rodney.

Clutz sat on the bench with his head in his hands.

"I let you down," he moaned. "I embarrassed you in front of all your friends. I brought shame to the names of Pentax and Type Z. The only thing left for me to do is self-destruct."

He clenched his fists and started to heat up his circuits. His ear spring vibrated, and his tarnished brass face turned bronze.

Rodney was alarmed. "Come on, Clutz," he said. "You don't have to go that far. Moonball isn't everything."

"But your honor was at stake," said Clutz, letting his circuits cool down just a notch. "And I defended it by making a fool of myself." He stared dully at the court.

Rodney grinned. "You did look pretty funny hanging up there."

"He sure did," said Terri, swinging her whistle around her finger by its chain. "I never saw anybody get stuck on a moonball ring before. I wouldn't have missed it for anything." She bent down to pet Aurora. "You did a great job, girl. You can outplay Angus Johnson any day." Aurora gave her a large wet kiss.

"You made 'em work for it," said Danno and Jonni. "When's the rematch?"

Clutz looked around at Rodney's friends. His face slowly regained its normal color. "You're not ashamed of me?" he asked.

Rodney put his arm around Clutz. "Anybody would rather win than lose. But you tried your hardest, just for me. Nobody can do more than that for a friend. I appreciate it, and I'm really very proud of you."

Clutz's eyes shone. He stopped trembling and took Rodney's hand. "The wisdom of a human," he said, "is boundless."

353

## Thinking and Writing About the Selection

1. How did the sport moonball get its name?

2. How would you describe Clutz's appearance?

3. At the end of the game, Taurus said that the best robot had won. Do you agree? Why or why not?

 4. Imagine that you are living in the twenty-second century and the Sports Commission has asked you to invent a new team game. Describe the new game and tell how it would be played.

## Applying the Key Skill
### Predict Outcomes

Use complete sentences to answer the following questions about "C.L.U.T.Z."

1. Why did Clutz predict that he would have a hard time learning to play moonball?

2. What made Rodney think that Clutz could learn to play moonball?

3. Why had so many kids come to the game?

4. Why did Clutz think that he had to self-destruct after the game?

5. Do you think Rodney will challenge Taurus to another moonball game? Why or why not?

# IO [INITIALS ONLY]

In the last selection, you read about a robot called Clutz who took his name from the words **C**ombined **L**evel **U**nit/**T**ype **Z**. **Clutz** is an example of the kind of word we call an acronym. An **acronym** is a word formed by combining the initial letters or syllables of a name, title, or group of related words.

Many acronyms are probably familiar to you. For example, an acronym you probably know is **zip**, used in **zip code**. It stands for **Z**oning **I**mprovement **P**lan. **Radar** is an acronym for **r**adio **d**etecting **a**nd **r**anging.

See if you can match the acronyms on the left below with the names, titles, and words on the right.

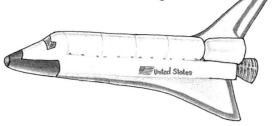

1. SOP    a. National Aeronautics and Space Administration
2. WAVES    b. standard operating procedure
3. laser    c. Cooperative for American Relief Everywhere
4. NOW    d. Women Accepted for Voluntary Emergency Service
5. NASA    e. United Nations International Children's Emergency Fund
6. scuba    f. National Organization for Women
7. UNICEF    g. self-contained underwater breathing apparatus
8. CARE    h. light amplification by stimulated emission of radiation

## ADVENTURE STORY

### Prewrite

Clutz was a fine robot and a great friend for Rodney and Aurora. Imagine that you had your own robot. What adventures would you have together? Maybe you would enter a balloon race and get caught in an electrical storm. Maybe you would hike into a cave and become trapped in the land of the evil Bat King!

You are going to write an adventure story about you and your robot. A story plan will help you organize your thinking. Make notes as you plan.

1. **Characters:** Who will be the characters in your story? How will you describe them?
2. **Plot:** Most plots have a problem the characters must solve. For example, in "C.L.U.T.Z.," the main problem was the moonball game. All the events in the first part of the plot told how the characters got ready for the game. Then the game, the most exciting event in the plot, was described. The last part of the plot told what happened to Rodney and his friends after the game.

   What will be the main problem in your plot? What events will happen before the characters solve the problem? What will happen after they solve the problem?
3. **Setting:** Where and when will your adventure take place? The setting may change several times depending on the events in the plot.

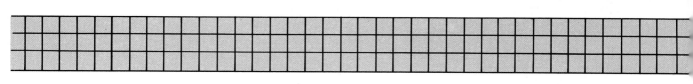

**Write**

1. Reread your notes and review your story plan.
2. Since the story is about you, you will probably write in first person. You will be telling the story from your point of view. Remember that when you write in first person, you use pronouns such as *I, me, mine,* and *we.*
3. Many of the events in the plot will be told by the conversations of the characters. Try to make your conversations sound like those of real people.
4. Don't forget to write a title for your story.
5. Try to use Vocabulary Treasures in your story.
6. Now write the first draft of your story.

---

**VOCABULARY TREASURES**

| | |
|---|---|
| intercepted | plight |
| artificial | resumed |

---

**Revise**

Read your adventure story. Have a friend read it, too. Think about this checklist as you revise.

1. Did each event in the plot connect to the next one so your story makes sense?
2. Do your conversations sound natural? Read them aloud. Would you talk that way to friends?
3. Sometimes the end of the story is the hardest to write. Did you tell what happened to your characters after they solved their problem?
4. Did you use correct punctuation in your conversations?
5. Now rewrite your adventure story to share.

# THE FLIGHT OF ICARUS

A Greek myth retold by Sally Benson

*This story takes place long ago on an island called Crete. Minos, the king of the island, ordered his architect Daedalus (ded' ə ləs) to construct a maze. He wanted the maze to be so complicated that no one could escape. Daedalus followed the king's orders. He built a maze with so many winding passages that escape seemed to be impossible. When someone did manage to escape, the king was furious. He ordered Daedalus and his son, Icarus (ik' ər əs), to remain as prisoners on the island forever. Daedalus was determined to gain his freedom, however. He had a plan and a dream, but it meant doing something no one had ever done before.*

Daedalus was an ingenious artist and was not discouraged. "Minos may control the land and the sea," he said, "but he does not control the air. I will try that way."

He called his son Icarus to him and told the boy to gather up all the feathers he could find on the rocky shore. As thousands of gulls soared over the island, Icarus soon collected a huge pile of feathers. Daedalus then melted some wax and made a skeleton in the shape of a bird's wing. The smallest feathers he pressed into the soft wax and the large ones he tied on with thread. Icarus played about on the beach happily while his father worked, chasing the feathers that blew away in the strong wind that swept the island and sometimes taking bits of the wax and working them into strange shapes with his fingers.

359

**I**t was fun making the wings. The sun shone on the bright feathers, the breezes ruffled them. When they were finished Daedalus fastened them to his shoulders and found himself lifted upwards where he hung poised in the air. Filled with excitement, he made another pair for his son. They were smaller than his own, but strong and beautiful.

Finally, one clear, wind-swept morning, the wings were finished and Daedalus fastened them to Icarus's shoulders and taught him how to fly. He told him to watch the movements of the birds, how they soared and glided overhead. He pointed out the slow graceful sweep of their wings as they beat the air steadily, without fluttering. Soon Icarus was sure that he, too, could fly. Raising his arms up and down, he skirted over the white sand and even out over the waves, letting his feet touch the snowy foam as the water thundered and broke over the sharp rocks. Daedalus watched him proudly but with

misgivings. He called Icarus to his side, and putting his arm round the boy's shoulders, said, "Icarus, my son, we are about to make our flight. No human being has ever traveled through the air before, and I want you to listen carefully to my instructions. Keep at a moderate height, for if you fly too low the fog and the spray will clog your wings, and if you fly too high the heat will melt the wax that holds them together. Keep near me and you will be safe."

He fastened the wings more securely to his son's shoulders. Icarus, standing in the bright sun, the shining wings drooping gracefully from his shoulders, his golden hair wet with spray and his eyes bright and dark with excitement, looked like a lovely bird. Daedalus's eyes filled with tears and turning away he soared into the sky, calling to Icarus to follow. From time to time, he looked back to see that the boy was safe and to note how he managed his wings in his flight. They flew across the land to test their skill before setting out across the wild, dark sea. Plowmen below stopped their work and shepherds gazed upward in wonder.

361

**F**ather and son flew over the islands of Samos (sā′ mäs) and Delos (dē′ läs), which lay to their left, and Lebinthus, which lay on their right. Icarus, beating his wings in joy, felt the thrill of the cool wind on his face and the clear air above and below him. He flew higher and higher up into the blue sky until he reached the clouds. His father saw him and called out in alarm. Daedalus tried to follow Icarus, but he was heavier and his wings would not carry him.

Up and up Icarus soared, through the soft moist clouds and out again toward the glorious sun. He was bewitched by a sense of freedom and beat his wings frantically so that they would carry him higher and higher. The blazing sun beat down on the wings and softened the wax. Small feathers fell from the wings and floated softly down, warning Icarus to stay his flight and glide to earth. But the enchanted boy did not notice them until the sun became so hot that the largest feathers dropped off

and he began to sink. Frantically he fluttered his arms, but no feathers remained to hold the air. He cried out to his father but his voice could not be heard above the roar of the sea.

Daedalus called back to him. "Icarus! Icarus, my son, where are you?" At last he saw the feathers floating from the sky and soon his son plunged through the clouds and into the sea. Daedalus hurried to save him, but it was too late. He gathered the boy in his arms and flew to land, the tips of his wings dragging in the water from the double burden they bore. Weeping bitterly, he buried his small son and called the land Icaria in his memory.

Then, with a flutter of wings, he once more took to the air, but the joy of his flight was gone and his victory over the air was bitter to him. He arrived safely in Sicily where he built a temple to Apollo and hung up his wings as an offering to the god. In the wings he pressed a few bright feathers he had found floating on the water where Icarus fell. He mourned for the bird-like son who had thrown caution to the winds in the thrill of his freedom from earth.

## Thinking and Writing About the Selection

1. How did Daedalus attach the feathers to the wing skeleton?

2. Why did Daedalus have misgivings when Icarus tried his wings for the first time?

3. Daedalus gave Icarus instructions for a safe flight. Why did Icarus not follow them?

4. Daedalus used wax, feathers, and string to construct a kind of flying machine. Throughout history, people have tried everything from kites to rockets to get themselves up in the air. If you could design a flying machine, what would it be like? What would you use to build it? How would it work?

## Applying the Key Skill
### Plot, Setting, Mood, Narrative Point of View

Use complete sentences to answer the following questions about "The Flight of Icarus."

1. What is the setting?

2. How would you summarize the important events in the plot?

3. What is the mood of the story at the beginning? At the end?

4. From whose point of view is the story told?

# Eagle Flight
### Alonzo Lopez

An eagle wings gracefully
through the sky.
On the earth I stand
and watch.
My heart flies with it.

# PARTS OF A BOOK:
# INDEX, BIBLIOGRAPHY

An **index** is a list of subjects discussed in a book, found at the back of a book. Each subject listed in an index is called a heading or entry. **Main entries** or headings are general subjects. **Subentries** are specific topics related to the main entry.

**ACTIVITY A** Use the sample index below to answer the questions. Write the answers on your paper.

Daedalus
    as engineer, 73
    in Sicily, 76
    legend of Daedalus and
      Icarus, 74—75

Delos, 44
    *See also* Cyclades

Greece, 12—24
    architecture, 27—29
    early history, 25—26
    gods and goddesses
      of, 30—35

Icarian Sea, 42
Icarus
    *See* Daedalus

Lebinthus
    *See* Levinthos

Legends, 60—62
    Egyptian, 63—70
    Greek, 71—82
    *See also* Myths

1. Under what entry should you look to find information about Lebinthus?
2. On what pages should you look to find out about the legend of Daedalus and Icarus?
3. On what pages should you look to find information about the early history of Greece?
4. Under what entry should you look to find more information about legends?

A **bibliography** is a list of books. The list may include sources the author used in writing the book or article. Sometimes a bibliography lists books and articles that the reader may enjoy or use to find out more about a particular subject.

Look at the sample bibliography items below to find out what information they give.

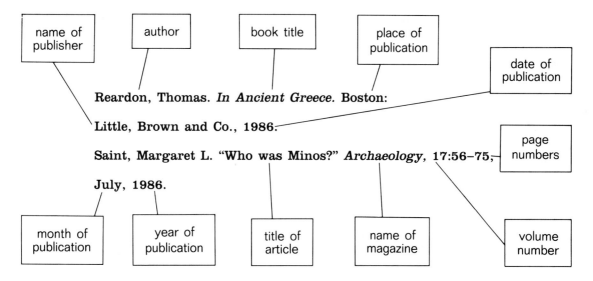

**ACTIVITY B** Use the sample bibliography below to answer the questions. Write the answers on your paper.

Barker, Robin. *The Legends of Crete*. New York: Macmillan, 1984.
Kraft, Catherine. "Where Daedalus Landed," *Smithsonian Magazine*, 17:12–27, April 1986.
Martin, Harold. *Labyrinths*. New York: Dell Publishing Co., Inc., 1981.

1. Who is the author of *Labyrinths*?
2. In what year was *The Legends of Crete* published?
3. In what volume and on what pages of *Smithsonian Magazine* did "Where Daedalus Landed" appear?

# East of the Sun and

# West of the Moon

## RETOLD BY MARGARET H. LIPPERT

**The woodcutter's daughter in this traditional Norwegian folk tale embarked on her first journey riding safely on the back of a great white bear. Her next journey, undertaken alone, will require all of her courage and ingenuity, as well as the assistance of some who she meets along her way, to keep her headed toward her goal.**

There was once a poor woodcutter who had so many children he could hardly provide food and clothing for them all. They were all comely, but the youngest daughter was so beautiful that there was no end to her loveliness.

One Thursday night in the fall of the year they were all gathered round the hearth, busy with one thing and another. The wind whipped through the trees, shaking the walls of their little cottage. Suddenly they were startled to hear three taps on the windowpane. The father went to see who it might be. When he opened the door, he was astonished to see a great White Bear standing before him.

"Good evening to you," said the White Bear.

"And the same to you," answered the woodcutter.

"If your youngest daughter will come and live with me, I will give you everything you need," said the Bear. The woodcutter was delighted to hear that his family might soon be well provided for, and he asked the bear to wait while he spoke with his daughter.

The girl did not want to go with the bear, so the woodcutter asked the bear to come back the next week for an answer. Meanwhile he explained how much better off they would all be if she went, so she decided to go. She packed her few clothes and was ready when the bear returned. Bidding farewell to her family, she took her bundle and climbed onto the back of the bear.

"Are you afraid?" the bear asked.

"No," said she.

"Then," said the bear, "hold tight to my shaggy fur, and you will be safe."

They went into the forest and traveled a long, long way until they came to a steep hill. The bear knocked on the side of the hill, and at once the hill opened. Before them stood a shining castle. They entered, and passed through many rooms where all was of silver and gold. In one room there was a table covered with a beautiful cloth and laid with delectable things to eat. The bear said that he must leave, but that he would see her again in the morning. Then he gave her a silver bell and told her to ring it whenever she wished for anything.

After she had eaten she began to feel sleepy from her long journey. No sooner had she picked up the silver bell to ask for a place to sleep, than she found herself in a lovely bedroom with a bed made with silken sheets and warm comforters. After she lay down and put out the light, she heard someone enter the room next to hers. This was the White Bear, who threw off his bear shape at night. She never knew who it was, though, for he went in each night after dark and before she woke each morning he had left.

All went well for a time, since she had everything she needed, but after a while she grew homesick. The White Bear noticed her sadness, and asked her why she was so unhappy. When he heard how she missed her family he

said, "I will take you to visit them next Sunday. I only ask that you do not tell them about your life here, for if you do you will bring us both misfortune."

On Sunday they set off, and after they had traveled a long way the Bear left her in front of a grand house. Her family ran to greet her. They were eager to see her, and to show her all they had gained because of her. Although they frequently asked her about her life with the White Bear, she remembered his warning, and refused to speak of it. Towards evening they grew more and more curious about how she was living, and begged her to tell them until she could resist no longer.

When her mother heard about the hill, the castle, and the person who slept in the room next to hers, she said, "That might be an ugly troll who lives there. Take this bit of candle and hide it in your dress. Then tonight, go into the room next to yours while he is asleep. Light the candle, so that you might see his face."

The girl took the candle and hid it in her dress. Soon the bear returned to carry her back. On the way he asked if she had told them about her life with him, and she could not say that she had not. "Did your mother suggest that you enter the room next door tonight?" the Bear asked. The girl was silent. "Do not do it," warned the White Bear. "You are happy with me. Trust me, and all will be well."

But that night, her curiosity overwhelmed her. "I can take one look without waking him," she thought.

"The Bear will never know I did not heed his warning." She got up, slipped quietly into the room next to hers, and lighted the candle. Looking down, she was astonished to see on the bed there the handsomest prince anyone had ever laid eyes on. She fell deeply in love with him

at once. She leaned forward to kiss him, but as she did so, three drops of hot tallow fell from the candle onto his shirt. He woke with a start.

"What have you done?" he cried. "Why did you not trust me? I am a prince bewitched by a wicked troll. She made me a White Bear by day. The spell could only be broken if the one I loved trusted me enough to live with me for a year without knowing who I really was. Now I must go back to the troll. She wants me to marry her ugly daughter, a princess who has a nose three yards long."

The girl wept then, and asked to go with him.

"That you cannot do."

"Then may I search for you?" she asked.

"That you may do, but there is no road to get there. I know only that they live in a castle which lies east of the sun and west of the moon."

In the morning, when the girl awoke, both prince and castle were gone. She lay in a green clearing in the midst of the forest, with her bundle of clothes beside her.

She picked herself up and set off, walking for day after weary day, until at last she came to a lofty crag. By it sat an old woman playing with a golden apple. "Can you tell me where is the castle that lies east of the sun and west of the moon?" the girl asked.

"Why, you must be the lass that should have had the prince," said the old woman.

"Yes, I am," replied the girl.

"Then I will try to help you," said the old women. "I don't know where it is myself, but perhaps my neighbor can tell you. You look tired. I will loan you my horse. When you arrive just give it a switch under the left ear and turn it towards home. And take this golden apple," she added, tossing the apple to the girl. "You may find a use for it."

The girl rode on a long, long way until she came to another crag, beside which sat another old woman.

This one was carding with a golden carding-comb. The girl asked the way to the castle that lies east of the sun and west of the moon, but the old women couldn't tell her where it was. "I will loan you my horse," she offered, "for perhaps my neighbor can help you. If you give him a switch under his left ear when you arrive he'll find his way home." Then she gave the girl her golden carding-comb, in case she might find a use for it, and the girl set off.

After a long time the girl came to still another great crag, and another old woman sat under it, spinning with a golden spinning wheel. As before, the girl asked her the way to the castle that lies east of the sun and west of the moon, but like the others, the old woman did not know how to get there. "Perhaps the East Wind can help you," the old woman suggested. "He blows all over the land. Maybe he can blow you there. I will loan you my horse. When you arrive just give him a switch under his left ear and turn him toward home." After the girl had mounted, the old woman handed up her golden spinning wheel. "Take this with you," she said. "Maybe you'll find a use for it."

Then the girl rode for many, many days until she came to the East Wind's house. "You have blown far and wide over the world," she said. "Can you tell me the way to the castle that lies east of the sun and west of the moon?"

The East Wind had often heard of it, but he had never blown that far. "If you would like to climb on my back," he said, "I will take you to my brother, the West Wind. Ask him. He is stronger than I am; he may have blown there."

So the girl climbed onto the back of the East Wind, and soon they were at the house of the West Wind. The

East Wind told his brother that the lass was looking for the castle that lies east of the sun and west of the moon, but the West Wind did not know where to find it. "I can take you to my brother, the South Wind," he said. "Ask him. He is bigger and stronger than I am, and he may have been there."

The West Wind quickly carried the girl to his brother's house, and explained, "This is the girl who loves the prince in the castle that lies east of the sun and west of the moon."

"Often I have heard my older brother talk of that castle," said the South Wind. "Perhaps he has been there. He is the biggest and strongest of us all. Climb on my back, and I will take you there."

The South Wind blew and blew. As they went further and further north, it got colder and colder. At last they heard the North Wind roar: "Who comes there?"

"It is your brother, the South Wind. I have brought a lass who wishes to find the prince in the castle which lies east of the sun and west of the moon. Have you ever been there?"

"Yes, once long ago I blew an aspen leaf thither," answered the North Wind, in icy blasts that chilled the girl to the bone. "If you really wish to go, and if you are not afraid to come along with me, I will take you on my back and see if I can blow you there."

"I wish to go with all my heart," the girl replied. "I am not afraid."

The North Wind rested that night. Very early the next morning they set out, the girl riding on the back of the powerful North Wind. He tore through the sky, causing a fearful storm below. Trees were uprooted, roofs were lifted off houses, crops were ruined. As they passed over the

ocean hundreds of ships foundered. On and on they flew, until by day's end even the ferocious North Wind began to droop. As he dipped lower and lower towards the sea, he asked the girl if she was afraid. "No," she answered.

"We will soon be there," he whispered, and up ahead she could see a dark line of land on the horizon. As they approached he skimmed the tops of the waves, and with his last breath he carried her to the shore. He had used himself up with the effort, and had to rest many days before returning to his home.

The girl looked up, and saw the windows of the castle east of the sun and west of the moon lit by the evening sunset. She began to play with the golden apple, which also shone in the last rays of the sun. A window opened above her, and out stuck the head of the ugliest troll she had ever seen, with a nose three yards long. The girl knew this was the princess that the wicked troll wanted the prince to marry. "I wish to buy that golden apple," screeched the troll.

"It is not for sale for gold nor money," replied the girl, tossing the apple from hand to hand.

"What will you take for it, then?" asked the troll.

"I want to see the prince in the castle."

"Very well, then. Toss it up here." The girl threw the golden apple to the troll, and in return she was soon led into the chamber of the prince. He, however, was sound asleep, and though she shook him, and wept, and called to him, he did not waken. In the morning, the troll princess chased the girl out of the room.

The girl went down to the shore and began to card with her golden carding-comb. Again the window above her was thrown open, and the ugly princess demanded: "Sell me your carding-comb."

"It is not for sale for gold nor money," repeated
the girl.

"What will you exchange for it this time?" questioned
the troll. The girl answered that she wanted only to see
the prince again. The troll agreed, and took the carding-
comb. That night the girl was again led to the room of
the prince, but once again she could not waken him. As
soon as it was light, the troll princess arrived to take the
girl away.

Later that day, the girl began to spin with the golden
spinning wheel under the window of the troll princess.
The window flew open and the princess screamed:
"I must have your spinning wheel. What will you take for
it? I will pay any price you ask."

"It is not for sale for gold nor money," said the girl,
"but I will give it to you if you let me see the prince
again." The princess agreed, and the girl gave her the
spinning wheel.

At the same time, some good folk imprisoned by the
trolls were talking to the prince. They told him that a
maiden had been calling and crying in his room for two
nights. Since he had not wakened, he guessed that the
troll princess had been giving him a sleeping drink each
night. So that evening, when the princess came to give
the prince his dinner, he only pretended to drink.

When the girl came to see the prince that night, she
was overjoyed to find him awake, and told him the
whole story of how she had found him. "You have come
just in time," he told her, "for tomorrow I was to be
married to the ugly troll. You are the only woman in the
world who can set me free. I will complain to the wicked
troll that my wedding shirt has three drops of tallow on it
and propose that I marry whoever can wash them out.

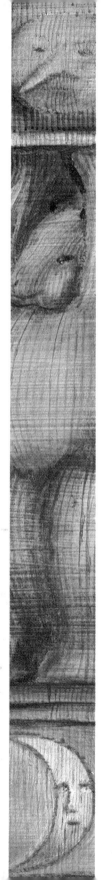

Thinking her daughter can do it, she will agree. But only you can wash them out, for it was you who dripped them there." The night passed quickly, and in the morning the troll princess came for the girl.

Just before the wedding was to take place, the prince announced: "Before I am married, I would like to see what my bride can do."

"Of course," said the wicked troll, looking with pride at her long-nosed daughter.

"My wedding shirt has three drops of tallow on it. I would like to propose that whoever can wash them out will be my wife." The wicked troll agreed, so sure was she that her daughter could do it.

The troll princess began to wash the shirt as hard as she could, but the more she rubbed, the bigger the spots grew. Then the mother tried, but as she scrubbed the spots grew darker than ever. All the other trolls tried, too, but the spots got bigger and blacker until the whole shirt was as black as if it had just been drawn up the chimney.

At last the prince said, "There is a beggar lass outside the gate. Let her in so that she can try."

The moment the girl dipped the shirt in the water, it became as white as snow.

"Why, you are better than all of them!" exclaimed the prince. "Now I have found the true princess. You are the bride for me."

As soon as the wicked troll heard that, she flew into such a rage that she burst on the spot, and the princess with the long nose burst after her. Then all the other trolls burst, too.

As for the prince and the princess, they set free all the good folk who had been imprisoned by the trolls. They took all the gold and silver they could carry, and went as far as they could away from the castle that lay east of the sun and west of the moon.

## Thinking and Writing About the Selection

1. Why did the woodcutter ask his youngest daughter to go with the White Bear?

2. How did the White Bear show that he cared about the woodcutter's daughter?

3. What would have happened if the woodcutter's daughter had trusted the White Bear and followed his instructions?

4. The number three or groups of three are often important in folk tales. How was the number used in "East of the Sun and West of the Moon"?

## Applying the Key Skill
### Sequence of Events

The following incomplete sentences are about events from "East of the Sun and West of the Moon." Complete each sentence and write it on your paper.

1. Before the White Bear took the woodcutter's daughter to visit her family, he asked her _____.

2. As the White Bear was returning with the woodcutter's daughter, he warned her _____.

3. The handsome prince awakened right after _____.

4. The woodcutter's daughter met three women. The first gave her _____, the second gave her _____, and the third gave her _____.

5. The woodcutter's daughter finally reached the troll's castle and talked with the prince on the day just before _____.

# ▪ LANGUAGE ACTIVITY ▪

## WIND WORDS

The woodcutter's daughter met the winds from the North, South, East, and West. These winds were named for the directions from which they came. We also have names for the winds that blow at different speeds. The gentle wind we call a **breeze** may have its origin in the Old Spanish *briza*, meaning "northeast wind." A very strong wind is called a **gale**. **Hurricane** comes from the Carib Indian word for the same kind of storm, *huracan*.

In certain parts of the world there are names for local winds. In our country, a warm, dry wind that descends from the eastern slopes of the Rockies is called a **chinook**. This wind can melt several feet of snow in a few hours. In Europe, the cold, dry, northerly wind that blows down the Rhone Valley is known as the **mistral** (from the Latin words for "master wind").

Parts of southern and eastern Asia are affected by seasonal winds called **monsoons**. During the summer, monsoons blow from the sea toward the land, bringing the rainy season. The winter monsoons bring the dry season by blowing cool, dry air from the land toward the sea. The word *monsoon* comes from the Arabic *mausim*, meaning "season."

From another Arabic word, *sharug* ("east wind"), we have the name **sirocco**. The sirocco begins as a dry, dusty wind in the Sahara, but it becomes moist as it passes over the Mediterranean. It reaches southern Italy and the islands of the Mediterranean as a hot, moist wind from the south.

381

*On top of a high hill, James Henry Trotter lived in an old house with his two aunts, Sponge and Spiker. One summer day, while he was in the garden, James encountered an old man. The man handed James a small paper bag. Inside were sparkling green things that looked like tiny stones. "There's magic in those things," the old man said. "Marvelous things will start happening to you." Then the old man hurried away.*

*James ran through the garden holding the bag, but slipped on the grass under an old peach tree. The paper bag burst open. The bright green things spilled out and sank into the soil. Suddenly something strange and wonderful happened. A peach appeared on the highest branch of the tree. It began to grow before his very eyes. It grew larger and larger until it was the size of a small house. The branch on which it grew bent, until the peach came to rest on the ground.*

*James was drawn to the garden again and again. One night, something magical happened.*

James stood alone out in the open, wondering what to do. The night was all around him now, and high overhead a wild white moon was riding in the sky. There was not a sound, not a movement anywhere.

He could see the giant peach towering over everything else. What a dazzling sight it was! The moonlight was shining and glinting on its great curving sides, turning them to crystal and silver. It looked like a tremendous silver ball lying there in the grass, silent, mysterious, and wonderful.

Then all at once, little shivers of excitement started running over the skin on James's back. *Something else*, he told himself, *something stranger than ever this time, is about to happen to me again soon.* He was sure of it. He could feel it coming.

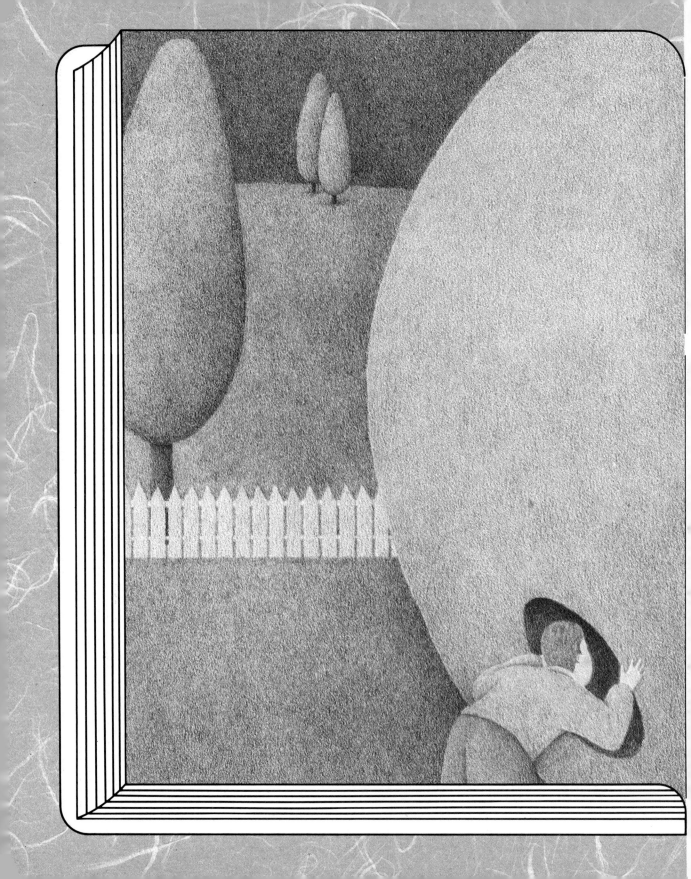

He looked around him, wondering what on earth it was going to be. The garden lay soft and silver in the moonlight. The grass was wet with dew and a million dewdrops were sparkling and twinkling like diamonds around his feet. And now suddenly, the whole place, the whole garden seemed to be *alive* with magic.

Almost without knowing what he was doing, as though drawn by some powerful magnet, James Henry Trotter started walking slowly toward the giant peach. He climbed over the fence that surrounded it, and stood directly beneath it, staring up at its great bulging sides. He put out a hand and touched it gently with the tip of one finger. It felt soft and warm and slightly furry, like the skin of a baby mouse. He moved a step closer and rubbed his cheek lightly against the soft skin. Then suddenly, while he was doing this, he happened to notice that right beside him and below him, close to the ground, there was a hole in the side of the peach.

It was quite a large hole, the sort of thing an animal about the size of a fox might have made.

James knelt down in front of it and poked his head and shoulders inside.

He crawled in.

He kept crawling.

*This isn't just a hole*, he thought excitedly. *It's a tunnel!*

The tunnel was damp and murky, and all around him there was the curious bittersweet smell of fresh peach. The floor was soggy under his knees, the walls were wet and sticky, and peach juice was dripping from the ceiling. James opened his mouth and caught some of it on his tongue. It tasted delicious.

He was crawling uphill now, as though the tunnel were leading straight toward the very center of the gigantic fruit. Every few seconds he paused and took a bite out of the wall. The peach flesh was sweet and juicy, and marvelously refreshing.

He crawled on for several more yards, and then suddenly—*bang*—the top of his head bumped into something extremely hard blocking his way. He glanced up. In front of him there was a solid wall that seemed at first as though it were made of wood. He touched it with his fingers. It certainly felt like wood, except that it was very jagged and full of deep grooves.

"Good heavens!" he said. "I know what this is! I've come to the stone in the middle of the peach!"

Then he noticed that there was a small door cut into the face of the peach stone. He gave a push. It swung open. He crawled through it, and before he had time to glance up and see where he was, he heard a voice saying, "*Look* who's here!" Another one said, "We've been *waiting* for you."

James stopped and stared at the speakers, his face white with horror.

He started to stand up, but his knees were shaking so much he had to sit down again on the floor. He glanced behind him, thinking he could bolt back into the tunnel the way he had come, but the doorway had disappeared. There was now only a solid brown wall behind him.

James's large frightened eyes traveled slowly around the room.

The creatures, some sitting on chairs, others reclining on a sofa, were all watching him intently.

Creatures? Or were they insects?

An insect is usually something rather small, is it not? A grasshopper, for example, is an insect.

So what would you call it if you saw a grasshopper as large as a dog? As large as a *large* dog. You could hardly call *that* an insect, could you?

There was an Old-Green-Grasshopper as large as a large dog sitting on a stool directly across the room from James now.

Next to the Old-Green-Grasshopper, there was an enormous Spider.

Next to the Spider, there was a giant Ladybug with nine black spots on her scarlet shell.

Each of these three was squatting upon a magnificent chair.

On a sofa nearby, reclining comfortably in curled-up positions, there was a Centipede and an Earthworm.

On the floor over in the far corner, there was something thick and white that looked as though it might be a Silkworm. But it was sleeping soundly and nobody was paying any attention to it.

Every one of the "creatures" was at least as big as James himself, and in the strange greenish light that shone down from somewhere in the ceiling, they were absolutely terrifying to behold.

"I'm hungry!" the Spider announced suddenly, staring hard at James.

"*I'm* famished!" the Old-Green-Grasshopper said.

"So am *I*!" the Ladybug cried.

The Centipede sat up a little straighter on the sofa. "*Everyone's* famished!" he said. "We need food!"

Four pairs of round black glassy eyes were all fixed upon James.

The Centipede made a wriggling movement with his body as though he were about to glide off the sofa—but he didn't.

There was a long pause—and a long silence.

The Spider (who happened to be a female spider) opened her mouth and ran a long black tongue delicately over her lips. "Aren't *you* hungry?" she asked suddenly.

387

Poor James was backed up against the far wall, shivering with fright and much too terrified to answer.

"What's the matter with you?" the Old-Green-Grasshopper asked. "You look positively ill!"

"He looks as though he's going to faint any second," the Centipede said.

"Oh, my goodness, the poor thing!" the Ladybug cried. "I do believe he thinks it's *him* that we are wanting to eat!"

There was a roar of laughter from all sides.

"Oh dear, oh dear!" they said. "What an awful thought!"

"You mustn't be frightened," the Ladybug said kindly. "We wouldn't *dream* of hurting you. You are one of *us* now, didn't you know that? You are one of the crew. We're all in the same boat."

"We've been waiting for you all day long," the Old-Green-Grasshopper said. "We thought you were never going to turn up. I'm glad you made it."

"So cheer up, my boy, cheer up!" the Centipede said. "Meanwhile I wish you'd come over here and give me a hand with these boots. It takes me *hours* to get them all off by myself."

James decided that this was most certainly not a time to be disagreeable, so he crossed the room to where the Centipede was sitting and knelt down beside him.

"Thank you so much," the Centipede said. "You are very kind."

"You have a lot of boots," James murmured.

"I have a lot of legs," the Centipede answered proudly. "And a lot of feet. One hundred, to be exact."

"*There* he goes again!" the Earthworm cried, speaking for the first time. "He simply cannot stop telling lies about his legs! He doesn't have anything *like* a hundred of them!

388

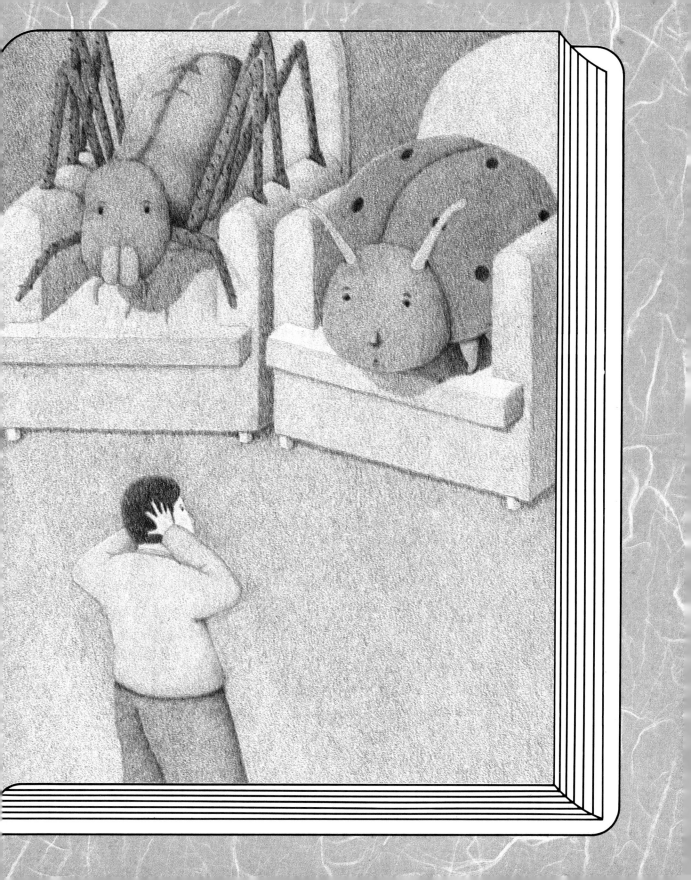

He's only got forty-two! The trouble is that most people don't bother to count them. They just take his word. Anyway, there is nothing *marvelous*, you know, Centipede, about having a lot of legs."

"Poor fellow," the Centipede said, whispering in James's ear. "He's blind. He can't even see how splendid I look."

"In my opinion," the Earthworm said, "the *really* marvelous thing is to have no legs at all and to be able to walk just the same."

"You call that *walking*!" cried the Centipede. "You're a *slitherer*, that's all you are! You just *slither* along!"

"I glide," said the Earthworm primly.

"You are a slimy beast," answered the Centipede.

"I am *not* a slimy beast," the Earthworm said. "I am a useful and much loved creature. Ask any gardener you like. And as for you . . ."

"I am a pest!" the Centipede announced, grinning broadly and looking round the room for approval.

"He is *so* proud of that," the Ladybug said, smiling at James. "Though for the life of me I really cannot understand why."

"I am the only pest in this room!" cried the Centipede, still grinning away. "Unless you count Old-Green-Grasshopper over there. But he is long past it now. He is too old to be a pest anymore."

The Old-Green-Grasshopper turned his huge black eyes upon the Centipede and gave him a withering look. "Young fellow," he said, speaking in a deep, slow, scornful voice, "I have never been a pest in my whole life. I am a musician."

"Hear, hear!" said the Ladybug.

"James," the Centipede said. "Your name *is* James, isn't it?"

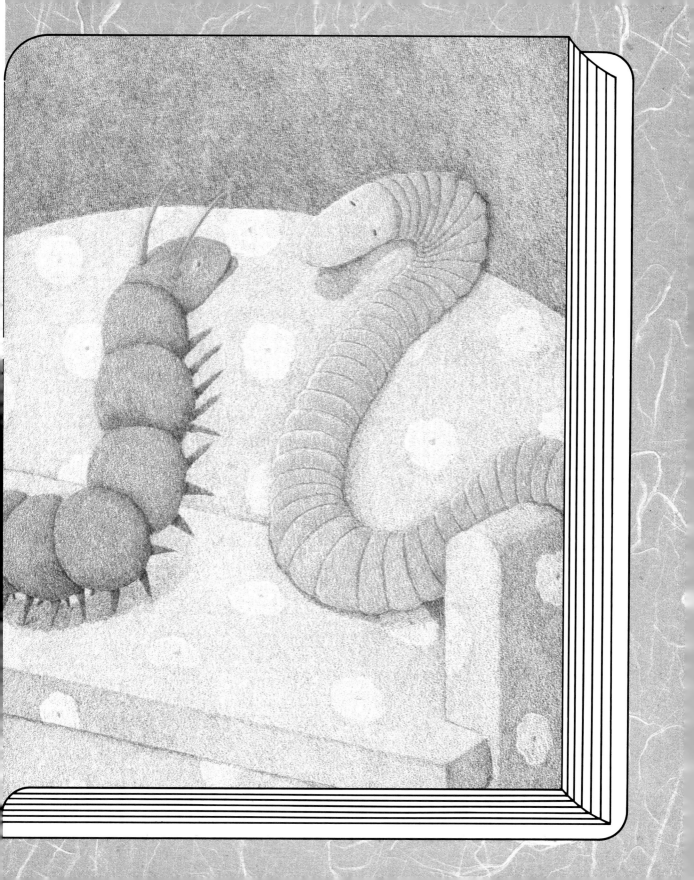

"Yes."

"Well, James, have you ever in your life seen such a marvelous colossal Centipede as me?"

"I certainly haven't," James answered. "How on earth did you get to be like that?"

"*Very* peculiar," the Centipede said. "*Very, very* peculiar indeed. Let me tell you what happened. I was messing about in the garden under the old peach tree and suddenly a funny little green thing came wriggling past my nose. Bright green it was, and extraordinarily beautiful, and it looked like some kind of a tiny stone or crystal . . ."

"Oh, but I know what that was!" cried James.

"It happened to me, too!" said the Ladybug.

"And me!" Miss Spider said. "Suddenly there were little green things everywhere! The soil was full of them!"

"I actually swallowed one!" the Earthworm declared proudly.

"So did I!" the Ladybug said.

"I swallowed three!" the Centipede cried. "But who's telling this story anyway? Don't interrupt!"

"It's too late to tell stories now," the Old-Green-Grasshopper announced. "It's time to go to sleep."

"I refuse to sleep in my boots!" the Centipede cried. "How many more are there to come off, James?"

"I think I've done about twenty so far," James told him.

"Then that leaves eighty to go," the Centipede said.

"*Twenty-two*, not *eighty*!" shrieked the Earthworm. "He's lying again."

The Centipede roared with laughter.

"Stop pulling the Earthworm's leg," the Ladybug said.

This sent the Centipede into hysterics. "Pulling his *leg*!" he cried, wriggling with glee and pointing at the Earthworm. "Which leg am I pulling? You tell me that?"

"We really *must* get some sleep," the Old-Green-Grasshopper said. "We've got a tough day ahead of us tomorrow. So would you be kind enough, Miss Spider, to make the beds?"

Then *click*—and out went the light.

James Henry Trotter lay there in the darkness with his eyes wide open, listening to the strange sleeping noises that the "creatures" were making all around him, and wondering what on earth was going to happen to him in the morning. Already, he was beginning to like his new friends very much. They were not nearly as terrible as they looked. In fact, they weren't really terrible at all. They seemed extremely kind and helpful in spite of all the shouting and arguing that went on between them.

"Good night, Old-Green-Grasshopper," he whispered. "Good night, Ladybug—Good night, Miss Spider—" But before he could go through them all, he had fallen fast asleep.

\*     \*     \*

"We're off!" someone was shouting. "We're off at last!"

James woke up with a jump and looked about him. The creatures were all out of their hammocks and moving excitedly around the room. Suddenly, the floor gave a great heave, as though an earthquake were taking place.

"Here we go!" shouted the Old-Green-Grasshopper, hopping up and down with excitement. "Hold on tight!"

"What's happening?" cried James, leaping out of his hammock. "What's going on?"

"At this moment," said the Ladybug, "our Centipede, who has a pair of jaws as sharp as razors, is up there on top of the peach nibbling away at that stem. In fact, he must be nearly through it, as you can tell from the way

393

we're lurching about. Would you like me to take you under my wing so that you won't fall over when we start rolling?"

"That's very kind of you," said James, "but I think I'll be all right."

Just then, the Centipede stuck his grinning face through a hole in the ceiling and shouted, "I've done it! We're off!"

"The journey begins!" shouted the Centipede.

"Who knows where it will end," muttered the Earthworm, "if *you* have anything to do with it. It can only mean trouble."

"Nonsense," said the Ladybug. "We are now about to visit the most marvelous places and see the most wonderful things! Isn't that so, Centipede?"

"There is no knowing what we shall see!" cried the Centipede.

One second later . . . slowly, oh most gently, the great peach started to lean forward and steal into motion. The whole room began to tilt over and all the furniture went sliding across the floor, and crashed against the far wall. So did James and the Ladybug and the Old-Green-Grasshopper and Miss Spider and the Earthworm, also the Centipede, who had just come slithering quickly down the wall.

Now the peach had broken out of the garden and was over the edge of the hill, rolling and bouncing down the steep slope at a terrific pace. Faster and faster and faster it went, and the crowds of people who were climbing up the hill suddenly caught sight of this terrible monster plunging down upon them and they screamed and scattered to right and left as it went hurtling by.

At the bottom of the hill it charged across the road, knocking over a telegraph pole and flattening two parked automobiles as it went by.

Then it rushed madly across about twenty fields, breaking down all the fences and hedges in its path. It went right through the middle of a herd of fine Jersey cows, and then through a flock of sheep, and then through a paddock full of horses, and then through a yard full of pigs. Soon the whole countryside was a seething mass of panic-stricken animals stampeding in all directions.

The peach was still going at a tremendous speed with no sign of slowing down, and about a mile farther on it came to a village.

Down the main street of the village it rolled, with people leaping frantically out of its path right and left, and at the end of the street it went crashing right through the wall of an enormous building and out the other side, leaving two gaping round holes in the brickwork.

This building happened to be a famous factory where they made chocolate, and almost at once a great river of warm melted chocolate came pouring out of the holes in the factory wall. A minute later, this brown sticky mess was flowing through every street in the village, oozing under the doors of houses and into shops and gardens.

But the peach rushed on across the countryside—on and on and on, leaving a trail of destruction in its wake. Cowsheds, stables, pigsties, barns, bungalows, hayricks, anything that got in its way went toppling over like a nine-pin. A man sitting quietly beside a stream had his fishing rod whisked out of his hands as it went dashing by, and a woman called Daisy Entwistle was standing so close to it as it passed that she almost had the skin taken off the tip of her long nose.

Would it ever stop?

Why should it? A round object will always keep on rolling as long as it is on a downhill slope, and in this case the land sloped downhill all the way until it reached the

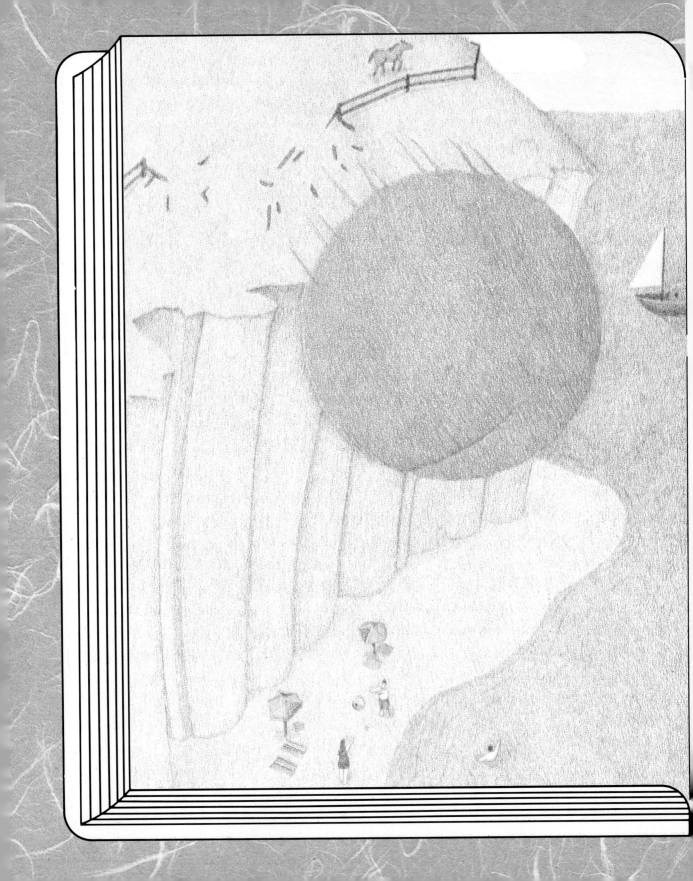

ocean—the same ocean that James had begged his aunts to be allowed to visit the day before.

Well, perhaps he was going to visit it now. The peach was rushing closer and closer to it every second, and closer also to the towering white cliffs that came first.

These cliffs are the most famous in the whole of England, and they are hundreds of feet high. Below them, the sea is deep and cold and hungry. Many ships have been swallowed up and lost forever on this part of the coast, and all the men who were in them as well. The peach was now only a hundred yards away from the cliff—now fifty—now twenty—now ten—now five—and when it reached the edge of the cliff it seemed to leap up into the sky and hang there suspended for a few seconds, still turning over and over in the air . . .

Then it began to fall . . .

Down . . .

Down . . .

Down . . .

Down . . .

Down . . .

*SMACK!* It hit the water with a colossal splash and sank like a stone.

But a few seconds later, up it came again, and this time, up it stayed, floating serenely upon the surface of the water.

*As the Ladybug said, James and his new friends are "now about to visit the most marvelous places and see the most wonderful things!" You can find out about their adventures if you read the rest of* **James and the Giant Peach.**

## *Encounters*

An encounter is a meeting, often an unexpected one. Encounters may lead to a discovery or a new understanding. In *Encounters*, you read about people who discovered something new or unexpected about themselves or about people they thought they knew and understood. You also read about people who were changed as a result of their encounters. Perhaps you have discovered that reading can lead you to memorable encounters with characters, authors, and stories you will not soon forget.

## Thinking and Writing About *Encounters*

1. The Leonids appear every thirty-three years. If you don't see them at a certain time, you may have a chance to try again. Many events happen only once. Imagine that you could travel back in time to meet a person or witness an event. Whom or what would you choose? Why?
2. Thomas in "The House of Dies Drear" and Kate in "A Game of Catch" both had unusual encounters. Do you think they could explain what had happened to them in such a way that others would believe them? What difficulties might they have?
3. Sometimes feelings can be powerful forces. How was this true for Peter Grayson in "Canyon Winter"?
4. Rodney said he was proud of Clutz even though they had lost the moonball game. Have you ever been proud of yourself, a friend, or a team after encountering defeat? Describe your experience.
5. Daedalus gave a warning to his son in "The Flight of Icarus." The White Bear gave a warning to the woodcutter's daughter in "East of the Sun and West of the Moon." How did each character respond to the warning? How were the consequences for both characters similar? How were they different?
 6. Write about an encounter that you have had. Describe what you learned about yourself or another person.

## Introducing Level 11

# FORCES

The forces of nature are constantly at work upon the earth, building it up and wearing it away. The stories in this unit are about the forces of wind, water, volcanoes, and earthquakes, and the changes they cause. You will read about slow changes like the carving of a valley, and sudden changes like the destruction of a mountaintop. How do these powerful forces affect our lives?

*Nature is often hidden; sometimes overcome; seldom extinguished.*

**Francis Bacon**

# FLOAT DOWN THE TAMARACK

### DAVID BUDBILL

Daniel and Seth grew up in the wilderness. As young boys, they had been taught to survive outdoors: how to live off the land, paddle a canoe, fish, and identify animals.

When Daniel and Seth were twelve, they set off on a long-awaited adventure—a trip by canoe down Tamarack Brook into the wild and lonely heart of Bear Swamp. They knew it would be rough going. But the promise of catching the trout that lived there would, they hoped, make the trip worthwhile.

The idea for the trip had come one cold and snowy night last winter when Seth, his parents, and Mr. Bateau (bä tō') were visiting at Daniel's house. That night Mr. Bateau got to telling stories about the old days when he was logging the edges of Bear Swamp. He told a story about finding a huge beaver pond in the middle of the swamp. "That was the biggest beaver dam I ever saw. I fished there once too, and I caught a speckled trout. Big as my arm!"

Mr. Bateau was a great storyteller. Everyone loved to listen to him talk, but no one really believed his stories, especially one about an eighteen-inch trout—no one except Seth and Daniel.

"Big fish in there. But fishermen say it's too hard to get to. The alders too thick; the grass too high and that muddy muck, it's terrible. The only way you get there is in spring when the water is high. You take a canoe down the brook, right through the alders. You have to be rugged to get there!"

That winter evening the boys decided. They could do it and they would, come spring.

As they pushed off from the gravel bar, the boys realized Mr. Bateau hadn't been kidding. They could see the brook weave its narrow, twisted way through the knotted tangle of alders and marsh grass. It was impossible to paddle the canoe. The brush was too thick, the stream too crooked and, in spots, too shallow. They had to use their paddles as poles to push the canoe along.

Soon the alders were so thick and low across the stream that they had to lie down in the canoe and pull themselves along by grabbing low-hanging branches. They had dreamed of paddling quietly along the stream, but this was work. The branches slapped them across the face and caught in their clothes. The canoe began to fill with broken twigs, dead grass, and leaves.

Slowly the alders began to thin out. Then there weren't any branches anywhere. The marsh grass came right down to the brook. The brook flowed broad and quiet. The boys sat up for the first time and actually paddled the canoe.

A little farther downstream, where the banks were high, there was a smooth, wet groove in the clay bank. It was an otter slide, a place where the big minklike animals came to play, to slide down the slippery clay and into the brook over and over again, just for the joy of it.

"Boy! I'd like to see an otter," Seth said. "I've never seen one. Have you?"

"Nope. I would, too."

As the boys made their way easily downstream, Daniel exclaimed, "Now this is more like it!"

"Well, don't get your hopes up," Seth said. "Look ahead." About a hundred yards downstream the open place ended abruptly in another incredible tangle of alders.

If their first stretch of rough going had been a bad dream, this was a nightmare. Not only were the alders thicker, but there were old beaver dams every few feet. The boys were out of the canoe more than in it.

For some stretches they had to walk through the stream pulling the canoe behind them, dragging it over the stumps and through the branches.

The alders began thinning out again. Then it happened. All of a sudden the alders were gone, and as far as they could see ahead of them, the brook wound broad and quiet through a flat plain of old stumps and marsh grass. Far at the other end, almost half a mile ahead, was a huge beaver pond, its smooth surface glittering in the sun, and at the far end of the pond the boys could see the dam, that half-moon miracle of woven birch and alder branches.

The boys sat in the canoe and glided along the broad stream. It was as if they had come through a terrible storm and this was the eye, the still center. As they moved along, the only sound they heard was the quiet dip of their paddles.

Now for the first time the boys didn't have to struggle against the swamp. They could look around, and what they saw amazed them. Both boys lived in the wild country, but this place made their farms, their fields, seem tame by comparison. Here there was no sign of humanity—no tin cans, no power lines, nothing. It was as if human beings had never been here before, as if they were the first ones ever to see this place.

As the boys floated noiselessly, they felt out of place. They were aware, somewhere inside, that they were strangers here. This was a world of wild creatures, of water, grass, and trees, a world that neither knew nor cared for people. It was an exciting place to be, and also a little frightening.

Alongside the canoe a big beaver swam easily upstream. He was so close, the boys could have reached out and touched him. They could see his dark eyes blinking in the canoe's wake, his thick, almost black, soaking fur, and his huge orange teeth. Wherever he was going, he was in no hurry. He seemed totally unconcerned with the boys' presence. Then he ducked quietly under the water's skin, his big, hairless tail rising in a quick swish, and was gone.

At that moment Daniel accidentally bumped the side of the canoe with his paddle, and the noise echoed across the swamp. Suddenly there was a great crack and then a number of splashes. Another beaver had seen the boys; he had slapped a warning with his flat tail across the water, and all of the other beavers in the pond immediately headed for the safety of their underwater homes. It was the last the boys would see of any beaver that day.

The boys had almost forgotten they had come to fish. But now the broad, deep water made them think of trout, big trout. They paddled quickly across the pond, beached the canoe at the beaver dam, and got out. Their legs were stiff. They brushed off the sandy swamp muck, got their fishing tackle ready, and climbed back into the canoe.

The beaver house stood about a hundred feet out in the pond from the dam. The boys knew the water would be deepest between the house and the dam. Quietly now they positioned the canoe over the deep water, baited their hooks, and cast them across the water. Daniel's worm hadn't sunk six inches when he had a strike! Then Seth did too. All the trouble, all the struggle had been worth it for this moment! The pond was alive with trout, or so they thought. As Daniel lifted his fish into the canoe he cried, "Oh! No! Dace." Seth had the same disappointing fish on his line.

Black-nosed dace are large members of the minnow family, a food fish for trout, but the dace always get to the bait first.

The boys were disgusted. All this way, all that trouble, and for what? A bunch of dace, something they could catch any-where. They tried again, and again they caught dace. Something had to be done; some way had to be found to get around the dace and down to the trout. That was it! Down. Maybe the trout were under the dace, in the deeper water. The boys added weights to their lines.

The worms sank rapidly now, all the way to the bottom, through almost six feet of water. In that much water there could be big trout. Nothing. The boys sat waiting, floating on the quiet skin of water. Waiting. Waiting. Then slowly, very slowly, Daniel's line began to move away from the canoe, then back, then away again. Something was down there, down in that dark water, something was on! Daniel set the hook. It was a small fish, but Daniel didn't care; he wanted to know what kind. Slowly, carefully he brought it to the top, pulling gently against the fish's desperate struggle to get free. Trout!

Again and again their baits sank to the bottom and hooked

trout. There wasn't much size to the fish, all of them between six and eight inches, but that was the best size for eating. They would be perfect for lunch.

Lunch. In the excitement the boys had almost forgotten how hungry they were, but now their stomachs demanded attention.

"Let's bring in our lines and go cook lunch," Daniel said. "We've got eight. That's plenty."

"Good idea. I'm starved!"

Daniel stowed his rod in the canoe and got ready to paddle towards the dam. "What's the matter, Seth?" Seth was yanking on the line.

"I'm hung up, I guess. Must have hooked a stump or something. Only it moves a little when I pull hard on it."

"Probably you're caught on a limb and it gives a little."

Daniel maneuvered the canoe around to the other side of the snag so Seth could get a better angle to free himself. Seth pulled. Again the snag moved slightly.

"It's no use," Seth said. "I'll have to break my line."

Then the snag moved again and Seth was free, or so he thought. When he had his bait almost to the surface, his reel began to spin, and the line raced away from the canoe! In the next instant a huge trout broke the water, leaped into the air, turned a somersault, and disappeared again into the pond.

"Yeow!" Seth shouted. "That's no snag!"

The battle was on. The big trout raced from the one side of the pond to the other. He leaped into the air. He dove down to the bottom. He raced toward the canoe, then away, then back again.

"We're in trouble!" Daniel shouted. "We didn't bring a net! We'll never get him over the edge of the canoe without one! He'll break your line!"

"What'll we do?" Seth was almost in tears. This was the one they had been waiting for. He had to have him.

"I'll try to get us to the dam. It's our only chance. You stay with him."

Their only hope of landing a fish this big without a net was to play him until he was exhausted, then drag him ashore onto the beaver dam. Daniel slowly, carefully, moved the canoe toward the shore. When they reached the dam, both boys got out, and Seth continued struggling with his fish.

After almost half an hour, the big trout flopped helplessly as Seth reached down through the shallow water and grabbed twenty inches of beautiful, speckled muscle and fight.

"Big as my arm!" Seth shouted.

"Bigger," Daniel said. "Let's have lunch."

"Are you kidding? Let's go find another one of these!"

"Come on. I'm starved." Daniel was a little jealous. He wished he'd been the one to catch the big trout.

410

As they got their cooking gear together, all Seth could say was, "What a battle! What a fish! Did you see the way he jumped? Did you see it?"

And all Daniel could say was, "I saw it."

A small brook entered the beaver pond near the dam. The boys could see where it wound its way down through the big spruce and fir trees and into the swamp. The water in the pond was brown from silt and pollen. The boys worked their way up the brook, out of the swamp, and into the cool shade of the evergreen trees. They found a place where there was a broad, clean gravel bar, the perfect spot for a safe fire. Here the brook bubbled quiet and clear over clean stones.

As Daniel arranged stones for a fireplace, Seth went in search of dead, dry wood. He was still talking to himself about his big trout. When the fire was going, he gutted the eight small trout, rinsed them in the brook, and laid them aside on a smooth flat stone. Seth took the frying pan from the backpack and began frying bacon. The bacon would be good between bread and butter, and a little of the left-over grease was just what was needed for frying trout. When the bacon was cooked, Daniel covered each trout with corn-meal. The meal would make a crisp, delicious crust on the fried fish.

Now the boys sat back, re-laxed, and ate. This was a still, peaceful place. The only sounds were the gentle gurgle of the brook, the wind moving easily through the tops of the big trees, and an occa-sional chickadee who sang to interrupt the noontime quiet. And such smells: the sweet, deli-cate summertime odor of spruce and fir, the smell of wood smoke, the smell of bacon and trout frying. There couldn't be a better way to have lunch.

"You know what?" Seth said. "We ought to build a camp right here, like the one on Otter Creek. We could hike down here from the upper crossroads, stay a day or two, fish the pond, then move on down to the river camp."

"That'd be good," Daniel replied lazily. "We could be gone three or four days. It would be a real test of how good we were in the woods."

The boys dreamed on. They made plans. Dreaming about things was as much fun as doing them—in fact, often it was more fun. In dreams there never seemed to be bugs or mud. There were never any mishaps or mistakes, everything went just right. The boys were silent for a long time.

"Hey!" Seth shouted. "We could sit here all day. But if we want another monster, we'd better get going."

They poured water on the fire, then held the ashes in their hands to make sure they were cold. They washed the pots in the stream, packed the backpack, and headed toward the canoe.

Seth and Daniel fished hard that afternoon, and each boy caught his legal limit of twelve trout. But they never again had the thrill of another monster. The sun began to sink. It was time to go, but Seth kept saying, "One more try! One more try!"

Finally the threat of darkness and the thought of the long struggle back drove the boys to put away their gear and head upstream. The trip out of the swamp was worse than the trip in, but the boys didn't mind. They had what they had come for, a story and a memory.

## Thinking and Writing About the Selection

1. Mr. Bateau said that the trip to Bear Swamp would be rugged. Was he right? Explain your answer.
2. Why did Seth and Daniel add weights to their lines?
3. Why do you think there are legal limits for the number of trout that can be caught?
4. What do you think the author meant when he said that the boys "had what they had come for, a story and a memory"?

## Applying the Key Skill
### Sequence of Events

The sentences below tell about events in "Float Down the Tamarack." Write the sentences in the correct sequence.

Seth and Daniel decided to take a canoe trip to Bear Swamp.

The boys came to a section of the brook where the alders were thick and there were old beaver dams every few feet.

Daniel caught a dace.

Seth played the trout until it was exhausted.

The boys had to pull the canoe through the brook by grabbing branches.

The boys saw a huge beaver pond.

Mr. Bateau caught a big speckled trout in Bear Swamp.

The alders disappeared, and the brook became broader and deeper.

Seth thought he might have hooked a tree stump.

The boys dreamed about building a camp near the beaver pond.

# THE CHANGING RIVER

### Laurence Pringle

*Water is a powerful natural force. Rushing water can pound boulders into pebbles and cut into the sides of mountains. Even gently flowing water can carry tons of soil for many miles. In this article, you will discover how the water in rivers changes the land, wearing it away and building it up.*

If you hiked the entire length of a river, you would see many changes along the way. Many rivers begin in mountains or in hilly country. Flowing rapidly downhill, the river's water has great force. It cuts a V-shaped valley in the land. The river flows at the bottom of the V, swirling around boulders and plunging over waterfalls.

If you visit such a river in the spring, you may hear it at work. There are grinding sounds, booms, and thuds. This is flood time, and the river runs with great power. The force of the water tears boulders loose and tumbles them along. Some are split in half. Rough edges are knocked off. Slowly but surely, the river wears boulders down to stones, stones down to pebbles, and pebbles down to sand grains. The lighter materials

415

are carried along by the current. The river also carries soil that washes in from the surrounding land. All of these sediments scrape along the river's channel.

In this way, the river wears away the bottom and sides of its channel. Gradually the river valley gets deeper and wider. Of course, the river doesn't make an entire valley by itself. The Grand Canyon, for example, wasn't carved by the Colorado River alone. As the Colorado cut its channel in the land, it exposed slopes of soil and rock on both sides. Small streams, rain, and wind began slowly wearing away the slopes. All of these forces working together have carved the Grand Canyon.

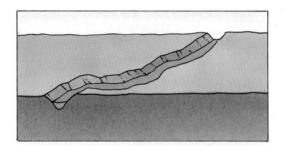

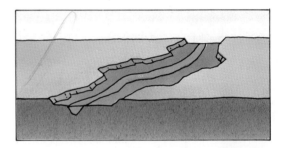

A young, fast-flowing river (left) cuts a V-shaped valley in the land. As time passes, a river flows more slowly and begins to cut sideways, forming a U-shaped valley.

As time passes, a river cuts deep enough so that it doesn't dash downhill as quickly as before. The water moves with less energy. It doesn't cut much deeper into the valley bottom. Instead, it starts to cut sideways. The valley becomes U-shaped rather than V-shaped.

Eventually the river's current is not strong enough to carry all of its load of gravel, sand, mud, and other sediments. The material settles to the bottom, especially in areas where the current is slowest. You may see signs of this, such as sand bars, along the shore.

The river may change course, flowing first on one side of its valley, then on the other. These changes take place over long periods of time. But there is evidence

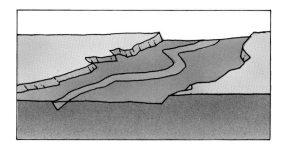
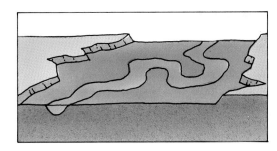

**As a river accumulates gravel and other sediments, it slows down. Sandbars are formed as sediment is deposited. A river may change its course several times over the years.**

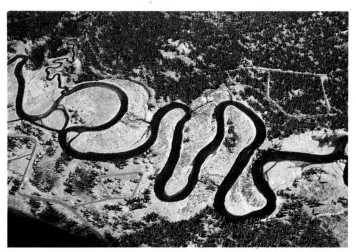

that they do happen. Photographs taken from airplanes and satellites show that rivers have changed their courses over thousands of years. You can also see these changes by comparing new and old maps. In the early days of this country, both the Mississippi and Missouri rivers were used as boundaries between states. If you compare modern maps with old ones, you will find that these rivers have moved miles from where they used to be. In the same way, a river you explore may be changing its course.

In times of flood, a river may spread over the entire floor of its valley. The area covered by water is called the *flood plain*. Then the water recedes, leaving the sediments on the land. Flood plains are especially good farmland, since the soil is rich in minerals brought from farther up the river valley. The flood plain may be as

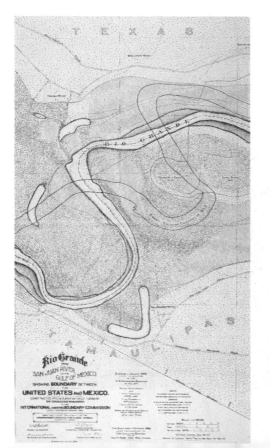

Left: The map shows how the Rio Grande, which forms part of the border between Mexico and the United States, has changed course. Below: The Missouri River spreads out over its flood plain after the spring rains.

much as 60 miles (96 km) wide along a big river like the Mississippi. A flood plain is really part of a river, even though it is covered with water only in time of flood.

When a river plunges down from mountainous country, it often follows a straight path. A slow-moving river on nearly flat land follows a different pattern. It may meander all over. From the air, a meandering river looks something like a snake wiggling along the ground. As the river meanders, it forms big loops. In time of flood, the river may take a "short cut" across the land, cutting off the loop. The river runs straight, leaving the loop off to one side. Often these loops continue to hold water. They are called *oxbow lakes*.

Perhaps you live near a river's mouth, where the river ends. Some rivers end where they join another river. Many rivers end when they flow into the sea. Some rivers carry big loads of sediments to the sea. Most of this material is dropped in a wide triangular area called a *delta*. The Mississippi flows into the Gulf of Mexico with more than 700 million tons (630 million

**Left: A slow-moving river often forms oxbow lakes.
Below: A view of the Mississippi River Delta.**

metric tons) of sediments each year. Each year the Mississippi Delta grows another 300 feet (90 m) out into the Gulf. The river has been doing this for millions of years.

A river is much more than a steady flow of water to the sea. It is a powerful force that helps change the shape of the land.

Rivers have been at work a long time, changing the land through which they flow. The changes take many years, so we often aren't aware of them. But once you know something about the ways of a river, you may see signs of running water at work almost anywhere. A small stream acts much like a big river. You may find one that has formed a meandering pattern in a meadow. In the spring, the meadow may be the stream's flood plain.

You may see other, smaller "rivers" at work in a schoolyard, field, or other place where rainwater flows over bare soil. Watch the patterns of running water during or just after a heavy rain. Perhaps you can find a place where a delta is forming. Whatever you see, you can be sure you will observe how running water changed the soil.

## Thinking and Writing About the Selection

1. A river runs with great power during flood time. What effect does the force of the water have on rocks?

2. What are sediments? Give some examples.

3. What do you think will happen to the southern boundary of Mississippi as the Mississippi Delta gets bigger?

 4. Find a place in your neighborhood where rainwater has flowed over bare soil. Write a description of how the water has changed the land.

## Applying the Key Skill
### Main Idea

Find the paragraphs listed below in "The Changing River." Then write the statement that best expresses the main idea of the paragraph.

1. the second paragraph, which begins: "If you visit such a river in the spring . . ."

   a. In the spring, some rivers are powerful enough to split boulders.

   b. During flood time, the force of the river wears down boulders and stones.

   c. As time passes, boulders become stones, stones become pebbles, and pebbles become grains of sand.

2. the seventh paragraph, which begins: "In times of flood, a river may spread . . ."

   a. A flood plain is rich in minerals and makes good farmland.

   b. When a river spreads over the entire floor of its valley, it forms a flood plain.

   c. A flood plain is part of the river that forms it.

# The River

There was a river that rose
   in the cool of the morn,
It leaped down the side of the mountain,
   and ran through the meadows and corn:
But it came at the last to a cave
   by the edge of the sea,
And it fell through the darkness, and vanished
   Forever from me.

I am sad for the river that fell
   through the darkness away;
From the fields full of corn, from the sun,
   from the light of the day.
I could weep for the river that danced
   in the light of the day,
And sunk through the darkness, and vanished
   Forever away.

James Stephens

# Lakes, Levees, and Levers

In the last selection, you found out that a river is always changing. Let's take a closer look at some of the words that describe rivers and the features they help create.

A **tributary** is a stream or river flowing into a larger river. Tributaries add their water to that of the larger river as they flow into it. A **distributary** is a branch of a river that flows away from the main stream and does not return to it.

A **meander** is a twist or turn in a river's course. It gets its name from the river Meander in Turkey, which twists and turns before entering the Aegean Sea. Often a meander is "cut off," and an **oxbow lake** is formed. The name comes from the lake's similarity in shape to an oxbow, a U-shaped piece of wood that fits under and around the head of an ox and attaches to the yoke.

During flood time, water spills over a river bank and deposits sediments. Often a great deal of the sediments are deposited close to the river, forming natural **levees**. *Levee*, meaning "ridge or raised area," comes from the French word *lever*, "to raise." Natural levees help confine a river within its channel during floods.

Rivers carrying large loads of sediments may drop this material when they flow into a lake or sea at their mouth. Often a great triangular plain is formed. Such a plain came to be called a **delta** because of the similarity of its shape to the Greek letter Δ, or delta.

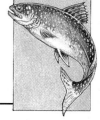

423

# MAIN IDEA

You have learned that the most important idea of a paragraph is called the **main idea**. Sometimes a writer states the main idea in a single sentence. At other times, the most important information in a paragraph is given in two sentences. You must combine the information from both sentences to state the main idea.

Read the following paragraph from "Float Down the Tamarack."

> Mr. Bateau was a great storyteller. Everyone loved to listen to him talk, but no one really believed his stories, especially one about an eighteen-inch trout—no one, that is, except Seth and Daniel.

Part of the main idea is found in the first sentence, and part is found in the second sentence. Information from both sentences can be combined to state the main idea: Mr. Bateau was a great storyteller, but no one except Seth and Daniel really believed his stories.

**ACTIVITY A** Read the paragraphs below. Then write the sentence that best states the main idea of each.

1.  Many fast-flowing rivers have their sources in the Rocky Mountains. These rivers are dammed to provide water for irrigation and to generate electricity. Hoover Dam, on the Colorado River between Nevada and Arizona, is one of the largest dams. Another is Hungry Horse Dam on the Flathead River in Montana.

a. Two of the largest dams in the Rocky Mountains are Hoover Dam and Hungry Horse Dam.
b. Many fast-flowing rivers in the Rocky Mountains are dammed to irrigate land and to generate electricity.
c. The sources of many rivers, including the Colorado and the Flathead, are in the Rocky Mountains.

2. The Nile is the longest river in the world. It flows north through the eastern part of the Sahara to empty into the Mediterranean Sea. The Aswan High Dam was built on the Nile. An artificial lake called Lake Nasser was created behind the dam. It is the largest artificial lake in the world. The dam controls the floodwaters of the Nile. The silt that used to be deposited in the fields now stays in Lake Nasser. Without the silt to enrich the soil, farmers must now buy expensive fertilizers for their fields.

a. The Aswan High Dam controls the flooding of the Nile but also prevents its silt from enriching farm land.
b. The Nile is the longest river in the world and Lake Nasser is the largest artificial lake in the world.
c. Before the Aswan High Dam was built, farmers along the Nile did not have to buy fertilizers.

**ACTIVITY B** Read the paragraph below. Then use your own words to state the main idea.

Deep valleys and canyons are carved by running water. The Grand Canyon in Arizona is an example. It was formed by the Colorado River. Layers of brilliantly colored rocks can be seen in the canyon walls. The Grand Canyon is 18 miles (29 km) wide and one mile (1.6 km) deep.

# THE *Big Wave*

## PEARL S. BUCK

*Pearl Buck wrote this introduction to her book*
*The Big Wave.*

In Japan one summer's day, I saw the tidal
wave come sweeping in from the sea. I saw an
ancient village swept away and only an empty
beach remain. The village should never have
been built there in the first place. Two hundred
years ago, the records tell me, the village was
swept away and again and again it has happened. Yet every time, those who survive the
big wave come back to build once more the
little village lying low between two mountains
and surrounded on two sides by the sea.

Today the head of the village, an aging
man, thinks I wrote The Big Wave about him.
All his family was swept away when he was a
boy, and only he is left. Well, I did not really
write my story about him but about someone
like him, a boy named Jiya (jē′yä), and his
friend, the farmer's son, Kino (kē′nō). Kino lived
on a farm, high on the terraced hill above the
village. Jiya, a fisherman's son, lived on the
edge of the sea. Both boys must learn to live
with danger, for Kino's father would sometimes
say, "On any day the ocean may rise into storm
and the volcano burst into flame."

On days when the sky was bright and the winds mild, the ocean lay so calm and blue that it was hard to believe that it could be cruel and angry. Yet even Kino never quite forgot that under the warm blue surface the water was cold and green. When the sun shone, the deep water was still. But when the deep water moved and heaved and stirred, ah, then Kino was glad that his father was a farmer and not a fisherman.

And yet, one day, it was the earth that brought the big wave. Deep under the deepest part of the ocean, miles under the still green waters, fires raged in the heart of the earth. The icy cold of the water could not chill those fires. Rocks were melted and boiled under the crust of the ocean's bed, under the weight of the water, but they could not break through. At last the steam grew so strong that it forced its way through to the mouth of the volcano. That day, as he helped his father plant turnips, Kino saw the sky overcast halfway to the zenith.

"Look Father!" he cried. "The volcano is burning again!"

His father stopped and gazed anxiously at the sky. "It looks very angry," he said. "I shall not sleep tonight."

All night while the others slept, Kino's father kept watch. When it was dark, the sky was lit with red and the earth trembled under the farmhouses. Down at the fishing village, lights in the little houses showed that other fathers watched too. For generations fathers had watched earth and sea.

Morning came, a strange fiery dawn. The sky was red and gray, and even here upon the farms cinders and ash fell from the volcano. Kino had a strange feeling, when he stepped barefoot upon the earth, that it was hot under his feet. In the house the mother had taken down everything from the walls that could fall or be broken, and her few good dishes she had packed into straw in a basket and set outside.

"Shall we have an earthquake, Father?" Kino asked as they ate breakfast.

"I cannot tell, my son," his father replied. "Earth and sea are struggling together against the fires inside the earth."

No fishing boats set sail that hot summer morning. There was no wind. The sea lay dead and calm, as though oil had been poured upon the waters. It was a purple gray, and beautiful, but when Kino looked at it he felt afraid.

"Why is the sea such a color?" he asked.

"Sea mirrors sky," his father replied. "Sea and earth and sky—if they work together against us, it will be dangerous indeed."

"Where are the gods at such a time?" Kino asked. "Will they not be mindful of us?"

"There are times when the gods leave us to take care of ourselves," his father replied. "They test us, to see how able we are to save ourselves."

"And if we are not able?" Kino asked.

"We must be able," his father replied. "Fear alone makes us weak. If you are afraid, your hands tremble, your feet falter, and your brain cannot tell hands and feet what to do."

No one stirred from home that day. Kino's father sat at the door, watching the sky and the oily sea, and Kino stayed near him. He did not know what Jiya was doing, but he imagined that Jiya, too, stayed by his father. So the hours passed until noon.

At noon his father pointed down the mountainside. "Look at Old Gentleman's castle," he said.

Halfway down the mountainside on the knoll where the castle stood, Kino now saw a red flag rise slowly to the top of a tall pole and hang limp against the gray sky.

"Old Gentleman is telling everyone to be ready," Kino's father went on. "Twice have I seen that flag go up, both times before you were born."

"Be ready for what?" Kino asked in a frightened voice.

"For whatever happens," Kino's father replied.

At two o'clock the sky began to grow black. The air was as hot as though a forest fire were burning, but there was no sign of such a fire. The glow of the volcano glared over the mountaintop, blood-red against the black. A deep-toned bell tolled over the hills.

"What is that bell?" Kino asked his father, "I never heard it before."

"It rang twice before you were born," his father replied. "It is the bell in the temple inside the walls of Old Gentleman's castle. He is calling the people to come up out of the village and shelter within his walls."

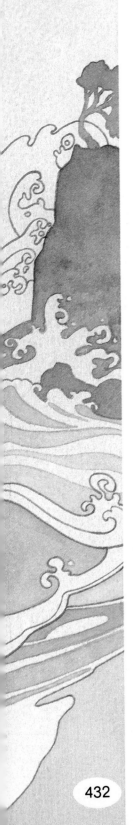

"Will they come?" Kino asked.

"Not all of them," his father replied. "Parents will try to make their children go, but the children will not want to leave their parents. Mothers will not want to leave fathers, and fathers will stay by their boats. But some will want to be sure of life."

The bell kept on ringing urgently, and soon out of the village a trickling stream of people nearly all of them children, began to climb toward the knoll.

"I wish that Jiya would come," Kino said. "Do you think he will see me if I stand on the edge of the terrace and wave my white girdle cloth?"

"Try it," his father said.

"Come with me," Kino begged.

So Kino and his father stood on the edge of the terrace and waved. Kino took off the strip of white cloth from about his waist that he wore instead of a belt, and he waved it, holding it in both hands, high above his head.

Far down the hill Jiya saw the two figures and the waving strip of white against the dark sky. He was crying as he climbed, and trying not to cry. He had not wanted to leave his father, but because he was the youngest one, his older brother and his father and his mother had all told him that he must go up the mountain. "We must divide ourselves," Jiya's father said. "If the ocean yields to the fires you must live after us."

"I don't want to live alone," Jiya said.

"It is your duty to obey me, as a good Japanese son," his father told him.

Jiya had run out of the house, crying. Now when he saw Kino, he decided that he would go there instead of to the castle, and he began to hurry up the hill to the farm. Next to his own family he loved Kino's strong father and kind mother. He had no sister of his own and he thought Setsu was the prettiest girl he had ever seen.

Kino's father put out his hand to help Jiya up the stone wall and Kino was just about to shout

out his welcome when suddenly a hurricane wind broke out of the ocean. Kino and Jiya clung together and wrapped their arms about the father's waist.

The purple rim of the ocean seemed to lift and rise against the clouds. A silver-green band of bright sky appeared like a low dawn above the sea.

"May the gods save us," Kino heard his father mutter. The castle bell began to toll again, deep and pleading. Ah, but would the people hear it in the roaring wind? Their houses had no windows toward the sea. Did they know what was about to happen?

Under the deep waters of the ocean, miles down under the cold, the earth had yielded at last to the fire. It groaned and split open and the cold water fell into the middle of the boiling rocks. Steam burst out and lifted the ocean high into the sky in a big wave. It rushed toward the shore, green and solid, frothing into white at its edges. It rose, higher and higher, lifting up hands and claws.

"I must tell my father!" Jiya screamed.

But Kino's father held him fast with both arms. "It is too late," he said sternly.

And he would not let Jiya go.

In a few seconds, before their eyes the wave had grown and come nearer and nearer, higher and higher. The air was filled with its roar and shout. It rushed over the flat still waters of the ocean and before Jiya could scream again it reached the village and covered it fathoms deep

in swirling wild water, green laced with fierce white foam. The wave ran up the mountainside, until the knoll where the castle stood was an island. All who were still climbing the path were swept away—black, tossing scraps in the wicked waters. The wave ran up the mountain until Kino and Jiya saw the wavelets curl at the terrace walls upon which they stood. Then with a great sucking sigh, the wave swept back again, ebbing into the ocean, dragging everything with it, trees and stones and houses. They stood, the man and the two boys, utterly silent, clinging together, facing the wave as it went away. It swept back over the village and returned slowly to the ocean, sinking into a great stillness.

Upon the beach where the village stood not a house remained, no wreckage of wood or fallen stone wall, no little street of shops, no docks, not a single boat. The beach was as clean of houses as if no human beings had ever lived there. All that had been was now no more.

Jiya gave a wild cry and Kino felt him slip to the ground. He was unconscious. What he had seen was too much for him. What he knew, he could not bear. His family and his home were gone.

Kino began to cry and Kino's father did not stop him. He stooped and gathered Jiya into his arms and carried him into the house, and Kino's mother ran out of the kitchen and put down a mattress and Kino's father laid Jiya upon it.

"It is better that he is unconscious," he said gently. "Let him remain so until his own will wakes him. I will sit by him."

"I will rub his hands and feet," Kino's mother said sadly.

Kino could say nothing. He was still crying and his father let him cry for a while. Then he said to his wife:

"Heat a little rice soup for Kino and put some ginger in it. He feels cold."

Now Kino did not know until his father spoke that he did feel cold. He was shivering and he could not stop crying. Setsu came in. She had not seen the big wave, for her mother had closed the windows and drawn the curtains against the sea. But now she saw Jiya lying white-pale and still.

"Is Jiya dead?" she asked.

"No, Jiya is living," her father replied.

"Why doesn't he open his eyes?" she asked.

"Soon he will open his eyes," the father replied.

The mother came in with hot rice soup and Kino drank it. He felt warm now and he could stop crying. But he was frightened and sad.

"What will we say to Jiya when he wakes?" he asked his father.

"We will not talk," his father replied. "We will give him warm food and let him rest. We will help him to feel he still has a home."

"Here?" Kino asked.

"Yes," his father replied. "I have always wanted another son, and Jiya will be that son. As soon as he knows that this is his home, then we must help him to understand what has happened."

## Thinking and Writing About the Selection

1. Why did Jiya's father tell him to leave the village and go up the mountain?
2. What were the warning signs that the big wave would come?
3. What did Kino's father mean when he said that Jiya should not be disturbed "until his own will wakes him"?
4. How do you think Kino will try to help Jiya understand that he has a new home?

## Applying the Key Skill
### Sequence of Events

The following incomplete sentences are about events in "The Big Wave." Complete each sentence with the words *before*, *after*, or *as*. Write the complete sentences.

1. Kino noticed the overcast sky ___ he and his father were planting turnips.
2. Old Gentleman rang the bell ___ he raised the red flag.
3. Jiya saw Kino and Kino's father ___ he started walking up the hill.
4. ___the earth split open, cold water poured over the boiling rocks.
5. ___the water hit the hot rocks, it turned to steam.
6. The big wave swept over the village ___ it ran up the mountainside.

# HAIKU

FOUR POEMS

The waves are so cold
a rocking gull can scarcely
fold itself to sleep.

BASHO

Tides of a spring sea,
tide after indolent tide,
drifting on and on . . .

BUSON

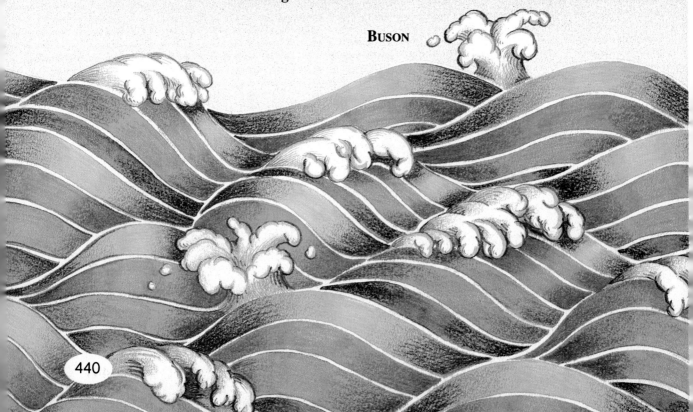

Would my house were on the cliff
Of Suminoye!
I should be happy always watching
The white waves drawing near
To the shore of the open sea.

ANONYMOUS


Each time a wave breaks,
    The raven
        Gives a little jump.

NISSHA

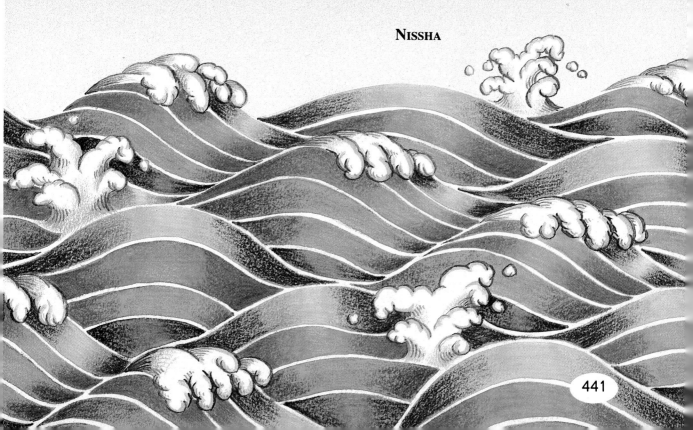

# GRAPHS

A **graph** is a way of presenting information that can help you to make comparisons easily. One kind of graph is a bar graph. A **bar graph** uses bars to give information. You can compare information by comparing the length of the bars.

**ACTIVITY A**  Use the bar graph below to answer the questions. Number your paper from 1 to 4. Write the answers on your paper.

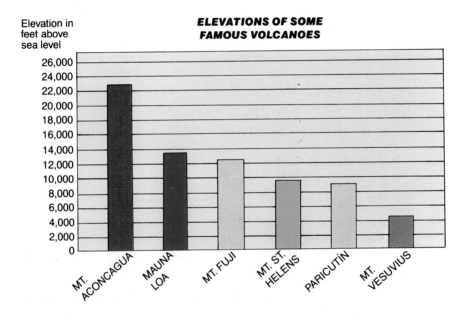

1. What is the highest volcano shown on the graph? About how high is it?
2. Which volcano shown on the graph has about the same elevation as Mount St. Helens?
3. How many volcanoes shown on the graph are higher than Mount St. Helens? How many are lower?
4. About how many feet higher than Mount St. Helens is Mount Aconcagua?

442

Another kind of graph is a line graph. A **line graph** uses lines to connect points on the graph. Line graphs are useful for showing information about something over a period of time.

**ACTIVITY B** Use the line graph below to answer the questions. Number your paper from 1 to 4. Write the answers on your paper.

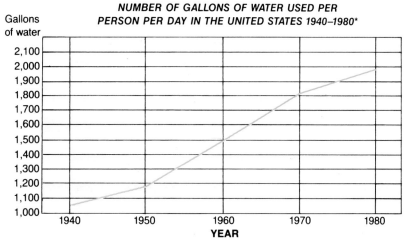

Gallons of water

**NUMBER OF GALLONS OF WATER USED PER PERSON PER DAY IN THE UNITED STATES 1940–1980***

YEAR

*Figure represents total number of gallons used in the country—including industry and agriculture—divided by total population.

1. In what year was the number of gallons of water used per person per day the highest? The lowest?
2. About how many gallons of water per person per day were used in 1950?
3. About how many more gallons of water per person per day were used in 1960 than in 1940?
4. Choose the phrase that best completes this statement: The number of gallons of water used per person per day ____.

   a. nearly doubled between 1940 and 1980
   b. was about one third as much in 1940 as it was in 1970
   c. increased by about 300 gallons between 1940 and 1950

# WHY MOUNT ST. HELENS

Like the nearby peaks of Mount Rainier, Mount Hood, and Mount Baker, Mount St. Helens is part of the scenic Cascade Mountains. As long as anyone could remember, Mount St. Helens looked like a picture postcard, as peaceful and as permanent as a mountain could be. But strong forces were at work under the surface.

Below: Snow-covered Mount St. Helens before the eruption.
Right: Clouds of ash and steam pour from the cone.

444

# BLEW ITS TOP  JAN RASMUSSEN

For many people living in Washington State, in nearby Oregon, or even as far away as Idaho, the date May 18, 1980, is one they will never forget. On this date, 9,677-foot (2,903-m) Mount St. Helens in Washington State shook with the force of two earthquakes and spit out a deadly blast of hot gas, steam, and particles from its top northern slope.

For eleven and a half hours the mountain threw out all the gases and ash that had been building up inside. The force was equal to that of ten million tons of TNT. When it was over and the smoke and ash had settled,

the majestic mountain had lost 1,277 feet (389.23 m) from its top.

To most Americans the eruption was a surprise. To geologists who knew the crater and its history, the thunderous explosion was no surprise.

Why did Mount St. Helens erupt? Why weren't geologists surprised? Was it the first time? Will it erupt again? To answer these questions we must understand the makeup of the earth's surface.

## BENEATH THE SURFACE

Imagine a pond in the winter covered with a layer of ice. When spring arrives, the water

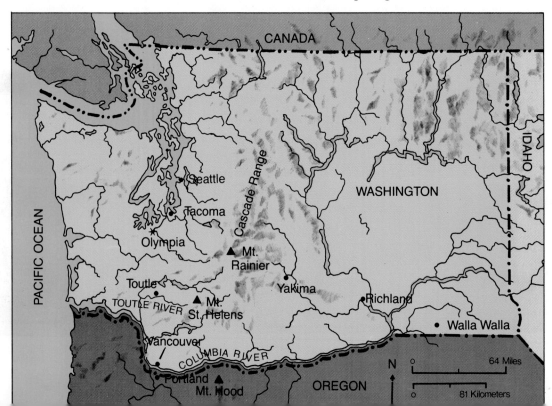

Above: The eruption begins with a landslide.
Below: Ten seconds later the north side of the mountain is blown away.

beneath the ice warms and begins to flow more easily. The sheet of ice thins and cracks into pieces of ice that float on the water's surface.

The earth's crust, or outer layer, looks similar to the cracked ice on the ponds. But instead of cracked ice, the earth's crust is made of large slabs of rock, called *tectonic plates*.

Like the water beneath the ice on the pond, the area of the earth beneath the crust, called the *mantle*, is never still. And because the mantle is never still, the plates that cover the mantle are constantly moving, slipping and sliding over and under each other.

Sometimes one plate will overlap another, pushing the bottom plate deeper into the earth's mantle. This lower plate is heated and melts into liquid rock and gases. This mixture of melted rock and gases is called *magma*. Magma forces its way to the earth's surface when it is pushed by pressures in the mantle and crust.

Have you ever shaken a soda bottle with your thumb over the top? When this is done, gas inside the bottle expands and needs to escape. This is what

Clouds of ash hide the north side of the mountain. The explosion left a crater 1.2 miles (1.9 km) wide and 2.4 miles (3.8 km) long.

happens inside the earth. Great pressures form. The magma and gas work their way up through cracks and openings in the plates toward the earth's surface. Finally, they push through a weak spot, releasing the pressure like the soda that gushes out when you remove your thumb from the bottle.

In the case of Mount St. Helens, the tectonic plate in the Pacific Ocean, called the Juan de Fuca (hwän dā fü' kä) plate, pushed under the North American plate. This movement pushed the North American plate

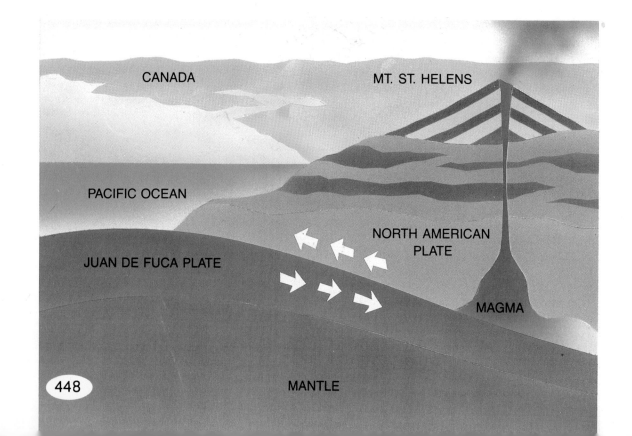

CANADA

MT. ST. HELENS

PACIFIC OCEAN

JUAN DE FUCA PLATE

NORTH AMERICAN PLATE

MAGMA

MANTLE

Scientists set up seismographs to record and monitor changes in the volcano. Information from the monitors is relayed to the University of Washington and then to the Vancouver Forest Service Volcano Information Center.

upward, helping to create the Cascade Mountain range in Washington State. Mount St. Helens is only one of twenty volcanoes in the Cascade Mountains. It happens to be in a place where large pressures build up and rise to the earth's surface. The eruptions of 1980 were not the first for Mount St. Helens. The last eruption was 123 years before, in 1857.

Sensitive equipment allows geologists to learn what is happening inside a volcano. Though they cannot tell to the day when an eruption will occur, they can

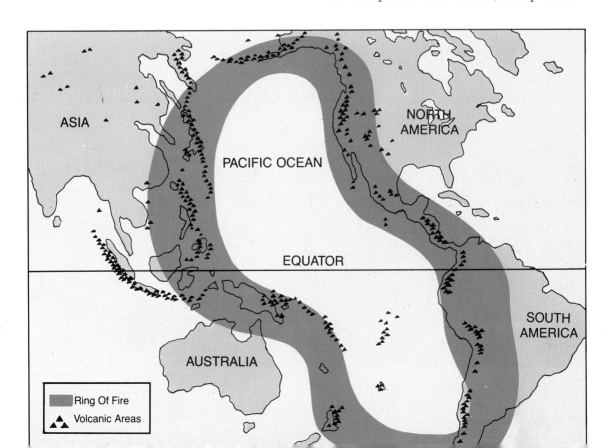

ASIA

NORTH AMERICA

PACIFIC OCEAN

EQUATOR

SOUTH AMERICA

AUSTRALIA

Ring Of Fire
▲▲ Volcanic Areas

make a prediction based on studied information. For example, in 1979 geologists had warned that Mount St. Helens would probably erupt before the end of this century. Prior to the giant explosion on May 18, the volcano had shook and spit in preparation for two months. Using very strong binoculars, geologists observed glowing red spots in the crater. These were signs of a lava dome just under the surface. (Magma that reaches the surface is called *lava*.) Geologists also measured the growth of a bulge on the north side of Mount St. Helens.

They didn't know exactly when or how strong it would be, but they knew an eruption was coming. However, no one was sure what sort of eruption it would be.

## What It Was Like

The magazine COBBLESTONE asked its readers who lived near Mount St. Helens to tell what the eruption was like. They gave these eyewitness accounts.

"We live about 90 miles (144.8 km) from Mount St. Helens," wrote Wendy Jackson of Yakima, Washington. "I got to see the eruption of May 18th. The day

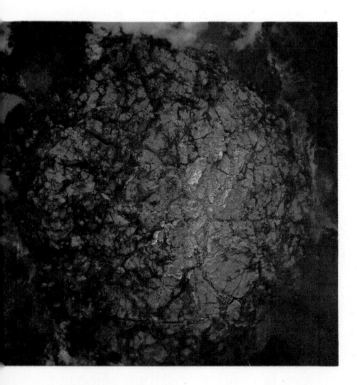

Magma is created in a zone within the upper mantle of the earth where temperatures are more than 2,000° F. (1,093° C). In this photo, the molten rock shows through cracks inside the crater of the volcano.

started with blue sky and sunshine. I was outside that morning. I heard a loud BOOM! I didn't think much of it as I live by an airport and hear jets breaking the sound barrier quite often. Before long I saw a big black cloud coming toward Yakima. I heard thunder and saw lightning. I thought a storm was coming. I went into the house. Mommy turned on the radio. We heard Mount St. Helens had blown. I got my dad and brother out of bed. We all ran outside to see the cloud. We were out for about two minutes when ash started to fall; it

burned my head because of the ash being in my hair, so we went in and washed up, and washed the ash out of my hair. It was a while before we could go back outside to play and start school again.

"After the ash started falling there was a strong smell of sulfur. It was really awful. A few days later my mom and dad went out to clean up the ash. It was really heavy—a three-pound coffee can full of ash weighed seven pounds."

Scott Qualley, also of Yakima, wrote: "As we were driving to church that Sunday morning, it looked like a storm was moving in. During church we were all told to go home because the

After the explosion came the enormous job of cleaning up. Crews in Yakima, Washington, removed 600,000 tons of ash.

DON'T BE FOOLED BY SUBSTITUTES

ST. HELENS DUST 50¢ GAL

FACE MASKS

mountain had erupted and ash was predicted to fall. On the way home we noticed that gray spots began to appear on the window, and before we knew it the sky turned pitch black and ash was pouring like rain. The volcano-like storm lasted all day.

"The next morning everything was covered with about one inch of ash. There was no school that whole week because of the ash. We had to shovel the ash like snow to get it off our lawn, roof, steps, roads, parking lots, and sidewalks. Even today, almost a year later, you can still see piles of ash along the roads.

"P.S. I saved 32 jars of ash."

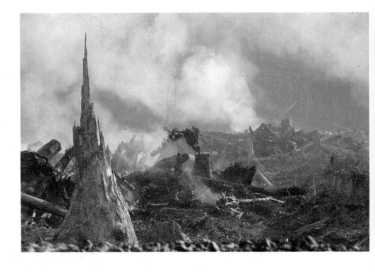

After the eruption the area was a smoking ruin. But only four months later, hardy fireweed had begun the mountain's renewal.

## WILL IT HAPPEN AGAIN?

After all the pressure has been released, the lava that is at the opening of the volcano cools. As it cools, the lava hardens and forms a plug, again blocking pressure. As long as there is movement inside the earth between the Juan de Fuca plate and the North American plate, it is very probable that the entire process will repeat itself sometime in the future. There is no sure evidence that enough pressure has been released to quiet the volcano. In the meantime, scientists continue to keep watch on the mountain and learn as much as they can from what may be, for them, a once-in-a-lifetime experience.

## Thinking and Writing About the Selection

1. What are tectonic plates?
2. Why do tectonic plates move?
3. What is the difference between magma and lava?
4. If you could talk to geologists who are observing Mount St. Helens, what questions would you ask them?

## Applying the Key Skill
### Judgments

Answer the following questions, using information from "Why Mount St. Helens Blew Its Top." Write your answers in complete sentences.

1. What information allowed geologists to know that Mount St. Helens was going to erupt?
2. Why are eyewitness accounts important sources of information about an event?
3. What information supports the following judgment?

   It is important for scientists to continue watching Mount St. Helens.
4. What information does not support the following judgment?

   Mount St. Helens will probably never erupt again.

# REPORT

### Prewrite

Mount St. Helens is only one of many active volcanoes in the world. You are going to write a report about volcanoes. The topic of volcanoes is much too large for one report, so you will write about one part of the subject. The subject of your report will be: Eruptions of Major Volcanoes.

Look at the chart below: There are four categories of information for six major volcanoes. Some categories have been completed. You must find the information to complete the others.

## ERUPTIONS OF MAJOR VOLCANOES

| Volcano | Location | Last Eruption | Earlier Eruptions | Other Information |
|---|---|---|---|---|
| Mount St. Helens | Washington, USA | 1984 | 1857, 1980 | |
| Nevado de Ruiz | Colombia, SA | November, 1985 | | |
| Kilauea | | | | |
| Paricutín | | | | |
| Mount Etna | | | | |
| Mount Fuji | | | | |

You may replace any volcano on the list, but your report should include information on at least six major volcanoes.

**Write**

1. Reread the information on your chart.
2. The first paragraph of your report should introduce your topic. Tell about the volcanoes and their locations in the world.
3. The second paragraph should present information about the last eruption and about earlier eruptions. Make comparisons in your report. For example, you might compare the number of years between eruptions for one volcano.
4. The third paragraph should present the information from the other category that you added to the chart.
5. Try to use Vocabulary Treasures in your report.
6. Now write the first draft of your report.

> ### VOCABULARY TREASURES
>
> | | |
> |---|---|
> | comparison | crater |
> | evidence | spectacular |
> | erupt | |

**Revise**

Read your report. Have a friend read it, too. Think about this checklist as you revise.

1. Did your first paragraph clearly state the topic of your report?
2. Did you check the information in the report to be sure it was correct? If not, do so now, especially the dates you use and the figures in your comparisons.
3. Does each paragraph have a main idea sentence with details that help explain that main idea?
4. Check your spelling and capitalization of names and places.
5. Now rewrite your report to share.

# PREFIXES

**Prefixes** are word parts that are added to the beginning of base words. A new word is made when a prefix is added to a base word. A special group of prefixes have numerical meanings. Some of these numerical prefixes are based on multiples of ten. Because they are often used with the basic units of measurement in the metric system, we call them metric prefixes.

| metric prefix | meaning | numeral |
|---|---|---|
| **centi-** | hundred; one-hundredth of | 100; 1/100 |
| **deca-, deka-** | ten | 10 |
| **deci-** | one-tenth of | 1/10 |
| **kilo-** | one thousand | 1,000 |
| **milli-** | one-thousandth of | 1/1,000 |

The basic units of measurement in the metric system are the gram (for weight), the liter (for volume), and the meter (for length or distance). Below are some examples of how metric prefixes are used with these base words.

A centigram equals one-hundredth of a gram.
A decaliter equals ten liters.
A decimeter equals one-tenth of a meter.
A kilogram equals one thousand grams.
A millimeter equals one-thousandth of a meter.

**ACTIVITY A** Number your paper from 1 to 5. Write the word or words that correctly complete each sentence.

1. A centimeter equals _____ meter(s).
2. A milligram equals _____ gram(s).
3. A deciliter equals _____ liter(s).
4. A kilometer equals _____ meter(s).
5. A milliliter equals _____ liter(s).

**ACTIVITY B** Use the metric table to answer these questions. Number your paper from 1 to 5. Write the answers on your paper.

1. How many grams equal one kilogram?
2. How many centimeters equal one meter?
3. How many milliliters equal one liter?
4. How many decimeters equal one meter?
5. How many centigrams equal one gram?

Metric prefixes are used not only with the basic units of measurement in the metric system, but with other root words and word parts as well.

**ACTIVITY C** Number your paper from 1 to 5. Write the answers on your paper.

1. If *gon* means "side," how many sides does a dekagon have?
2. A *watt* is a unit of electrical power. How many watts are in a kilowatt?
3. If *pede* means "foot," what does the word *millipede* mean?
4. What is another name for the coin we call a penny that is worth one-hundredth of a dollar?
5. How many years are there in a decade?

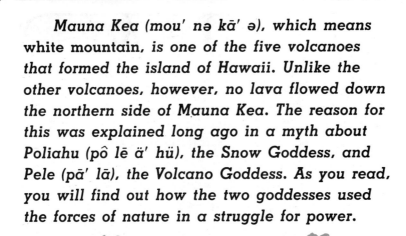

*Mauna Kea (mou' nə kā' ə), which means white mountain, is one of the five volcanoes that formed the island of Hawaii. Unlike the other volcanoes, however, no lava flowed down the northern side of Mauna Kea. The reason for this was explained long ago in a myth about Poliahu (pô lē ä' hü), the Snow Goddess, and Pele (pā' lā), the Volcano Goddess. As you read, you will find out how the two goddesses used the forces of nature in a struggle for power.*

# A STRANGE SLED RACE

## A HAWAIIAN MYTH RETOLD BY
## VIVIAN L. THOMPSON

Poliahu and her snow maidens one day covered their dazzling snow mantles with mantles of golden sunshine. They took their long, slender sleds to the race course below the snowfields. There a narrow, grassy track had been laid, dropping swiftly toward the sea.

High, tinkling laughter filled the air as the maidens urged the goddess to race. Poliahu was

very willing. She made a running start, threw herself upon her sled, and plunged down. Far below she came to a stop, marked the spot, and lifted her sled aside.

One after another the snow maidens followed, but none reached the goddess's mark. As they gathered below they discovered a stranger in their midst, a handsome woman dressed in black mantle and robe.

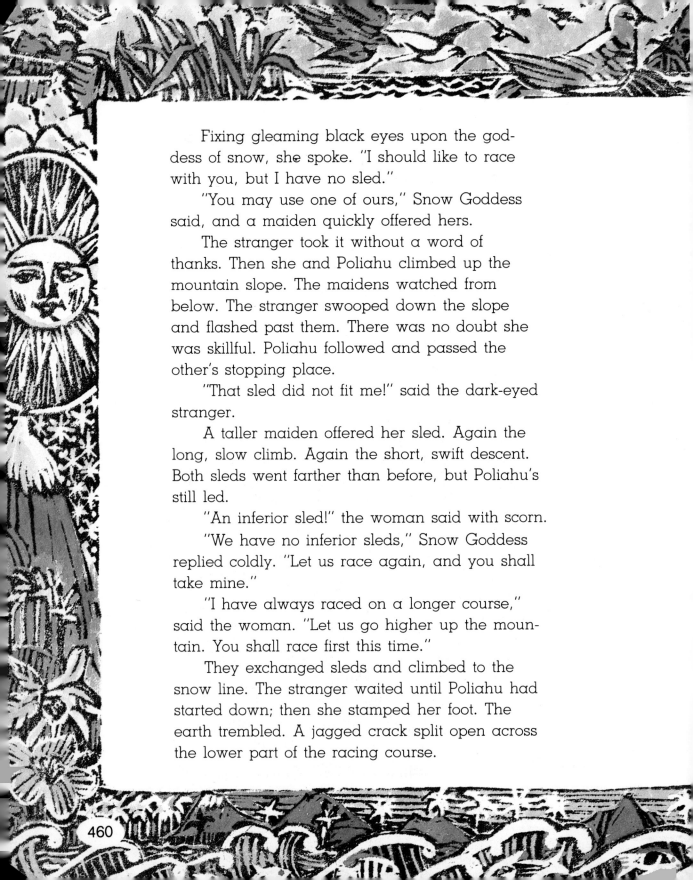

Fixing gleaming black eyes upon the goddess of snow, she spoke. "I should like to race with you, but I have no sled."

"You may use one of ours," Snow Goddess said, and a maiden quickly offered hers.

The stranger took it without a word of thanks. Then she and Poliahu climbed up the mountain slope. The maidens watched from below. The stranger swooped down the slope and flashed past them. There was no doubt she was skillful. Poliahu followed and passed the other's stopping place.

"That sled did not fit me!" said the dark-eyed stranger.

A taller maiden offered her sled. Again the long, slow climb. Again the short, swift descent. Both sleds went farther than before, but Poliahu's still led.

"An inferior sled!" the woman said with scorn.

"We have no inferior sleds," Snow Goddess replied coldly. "Let us race again, and you shall take mine."

"I have always raced on a longer course," said the woman. "Let us go higher up the mountain. You shall race first this time."

They exchanged sleds and climbed to the snow line. The stranger waited until Poliahu had started down; then she stamped her foot. The earth trembled. A jagged crack split open across the lower part of the racing course.

The snow maidens, watching below, lost sight of their goddess as steam rose from the crack and formed a curtain. They ran up the slope.

For a moment, the steam cleared. They caught a glimpse of Poliahu racing toward the widening crack. The woman in black was close behind her, standing upright on her speeding sled. In horror they saw her black robe turn red and her eyes glow like burning coals. They knew now! She was Pele—Volcano Goddess!

She stamped again. They felt the molten lava come rumbling through underground

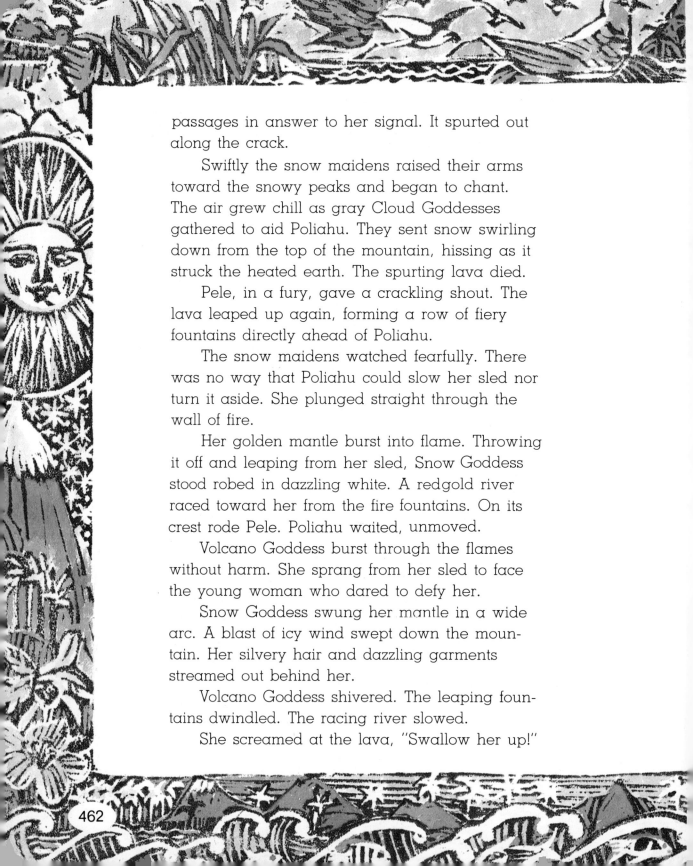

passages in answer to her signal. It spurted out along the crack.

Swiftly the snow maidens raised their arms toward the snowy peaks and began to chant. The air grew chill as gray Cloud Goddesses gathered to aid Poliahu. They sent snow swirling down from the top of the mountain, hissing as it struck the heated earth. The spurting lava died.

Pele, in a fury, gave a crackling shout. The lava leaped up again, forming a row of fiery fountains directly ahead of Poliahu.

The snow maidens watched fearfully. There was no way that Poliahu could slow her sled nor turn it aside. She plunged straight through the wall of fire.

Her golden mantle burst into flame. Throwing it off and leaping from her sled, Snow Goddess stood robed in dazzling white. A redgold river raced toward her from the fire fountains. On its crest rode Pele. Poliahu waited, unmoved.

Volcano Goddess burst through the flames without harm. She sprang from her sled to face the young woman who dared to defy her.

Snow Goddess swung her mantle in a wide arc. A blast of icy wind swept down the mountain. Her silvery hair and dazzling garments streamed out behind her.

Volcano Goddess shivered. The leaping fountains dwindled. The racing river slowed.

She screamed at the lava, "Swallow her up!"

But the lava fountains died. The lava river grew sluggish. Still deadly, it flowed to the very feet of Snow Goddess. She flung her arms wide. The river split in two, leaving her unharmed in the center. It made its way beyond her, moving slowly down to the sea. There it formed a long, flat point of land, known to this day as Leaf-of-Smooth-Lava.

Volcano Goddess stared, unable to believe what she saw. Her red mantle turned black again. Her glowing eyes dulled. Shivering with cold, she disappeared as mysteriously as she had come.

High, tinkling laughter filled the air once more as the Snow Goddess and her maidens picked up their sleds and returned to their snowy home.

Pele never again crossed over Mauna Kea to Poliahu's side of the island, although she still sent lava pouring down the southern side.

## Thinking and Writing About the Selection

1. Who was the stranger who challenged Poliahu to a sled race?

2. When Pele caused the earth to tremble and crack, what natural event occurred?

3. Why do you think Pele never returned to Poliahu's side of Mauna Kea?

 4. The Cloud Goddesses helped Poliahu to defeat Pele. If Pele had received help, perhaps she would have overtaken the Snow Goddess. Imagine that goddesses did come to the aid of Pele. Describe them and their powers. Write a new ending for the myth.

## Applying the Key Skill
### Context Clues

Find the words listed below in "A Strange Sled Race." Based on context clues, define each word in a sentence. Then check your definitions in a dictionary.

1. dazzling     2. swiftly
3. mantle       4. chant
5. crest        6. sluggish
7. urged        8. scorn
9. peaks        10. slope

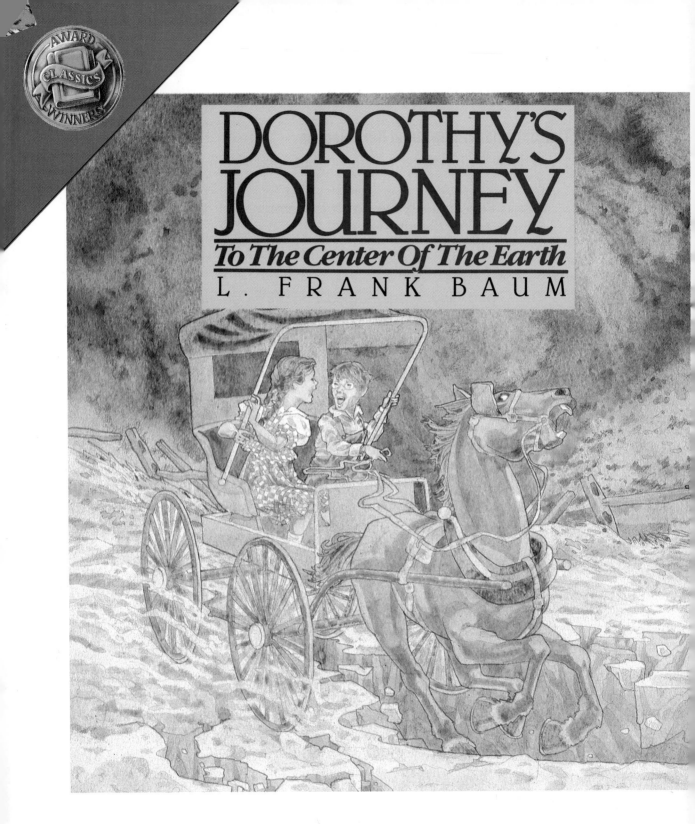

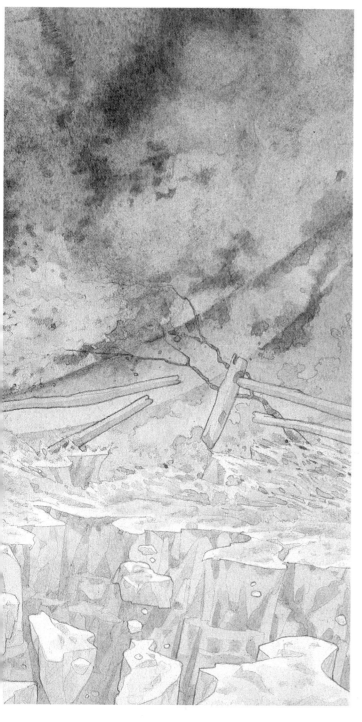

 *L. Frank Baum's The Wizard of Oz has fascinated readers of all ages since it was first published in 1900.* Over the years, readers have written to the author pleading for more Oz books. The Wizard of Oz thus became the first in a series of fourteen books.

In the fourth book of the series, *Dorothy and the Wizard in Oz,* Dorothy and her cousin Zeb were riding in a horse-drawn buggy when suddenly an earthquake struck. The ground beneath them split wide open. Dorothy, Zeb, and the buggy tumbled down through space until they reached the middle of the earth. To their amazement, they discovered a city of glass, the home of the Mangaboos. From the beginning, Dorothy and Zeb thought the Mangaboos were unusual. They looked very much like people, but were they? The story you are about to read begins just after the earthquake. The adventure is about to start.

When Dorothy recovered her senses they were still falling, but not so fast. The top of the buggy caught the air like a parachute or an umbrella filled with wind, and held them back so that they floated downward with a gentle motion.

Dorothy sighed and started to breathe easier. She began to realize that she had merely started upon another adventure. With this thought in mind, Dorothy took heart and leaned her head over the side of the buggy to see where the strange 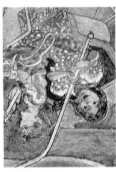 light was coming from. Far below her she found six great glowing balls suspended in the air. The central and largest one was white, and reminded her of the sun. Around it were arranged, like the five points of a star, the other five brilliant balls; one being rose colored, one violet, one yellow, one blue, and one orange.

Just then the buggy tipped slowly over upon its side, the body of the horse tipping also.

But they continued to fall, all together, and Zeb and Dorothy had no difficulty in remaining upon the seat, just as they were before. Then they turned bottom side up, and continued to roll slowly over until they were right side up again. During this time the horse Jim struggled frantically, all his legs kicking the air.

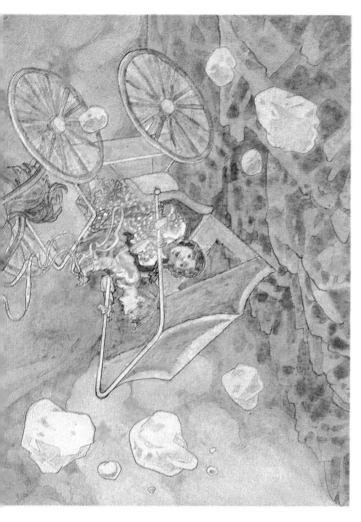

But on finding himself in his former position the horse said, in a relieved tone of voice, "Well, that's better!"

Dorothy and Zeb looked at one another in wonder.

"Can your horse talk?" she asked.

"Never knew him to, before," replied Zeb.

"Those were the first words I ever said," called out the horse, who had overheard them. "I can't explain why I happened to speak then."

Swiftly they drew near to the flaming colored suns, and passed close beside them. The light was then so bright that it dazzled their eyes. They covered their faces with their hands.

"We've got to come to the bottom some time," remarked Zeb, with a deep sigh. "We can't keep falling forever."

"Of course not," said Dorothy. "We are somewhere in the middle of the earth, and the chances are we'll reach the other side of it before long. But it's a big hollow, isn't it?"

"Awful big!" answered Zeb.

"We're coming to something now," announced the horse.

At this they both put heads over the side of the buggy and looked down. Yes, there was land below them; and not so very far away, either. But they were floating very, very slowly— so slowly that it could no longer be called a fall.

They saw a landscape with mountains and plains, lakes and

rivers, very like those upon the earth's surface. But the scene was splendidly colored by the lights from the six suns. Here and there were groups of houses that seemed made of clear glass because they sparkled so brightly.

"I'm sure we are in no danger," said Dorothy.

"We'll never get home again, though!" declared Zeb, with a groan.

"Oh, I'm not so sure of that," replied Dorothy. "But don't let us worry over such things."

The boy became silent, and soon both were fully occupied in staring at the strange scenes below them. They seemed to be falling right into the middle of a big city which had many tall buildings with glass domes and sharp-pointed spires. They floated gently down upon a broad, flat roof, and came to a stop at last.

When Jim felt something firm under his feet, the poor beast's legs trembled so much that he could hardly stand. But Zeb at once leaped out of the buggy onto the roof. He was so awkward and hasty that he kicked over Dorothy's birdcage, which

rolled out upon the roof so that the bottom came off. At once a kitten crept out of the upset cage, sat down upon the glass roof, and yawned and blinked its round eyes.

"Where's my milk?" asked the kitten, looking up into Dorothy's face.

"Oh, Eureka! Can you talk?"

"Talk! Am I talking? Good gracious, I believe I am. Isn't it funny?" asked the kitten.

"It's all wrong," said Zeb, gravely. "Animals ought not to talk."

"I can't see that it's wrong," remarked Jim. "At least, it isn't

as wrong as some things. What's going to become of us now?"

"I don't know," answered Zeb, looking around him curiously.

The roof beside them had a great hole smashed through it. A nearby steeple had been broken off short, and the fragments lay heaped beside it. Other buildings were cracked in places or had corners chipped off from them. But not a sound had broken the stillness since the strangers had arrived, except that of their own voices.

Suddenly a man appeared through a hole in the roof next to the one they were on. The man had taken a step or two across the glass roof before he noticed the presence of the strangers; but then he stopped abruptly. There was no expression of either fear or surprise upon his face, yet he must have been both astonished and afraid. After his eyes had rested upon the horse for a moment, he walked rapidly to the furthest edge of the roof, and walked into space as calmly as if he were on firm ground.

Dorothy watched the man walking rapidly through the air

toward the ground. Soon he reached the street and disappeared through a glass doorway into one of the glass buildings.

"How strange!" she exclaimed.

"Yes; but it's a lot of fun, even if it *is* strange," remarked the kitten. Dorothy turned to find her pet walking in the air a foot or so away from the edge of the roof.

"Come back, Eureka!" she called, in distress, "You'll certainly be killed."

"I have nine lives," said the kitten, purring softly as it walked around in a circle and then came back to the roof.

"Does the air bear up your weight?"

"Of course, can't you see?" Again the kitten wandered into the air and back to the edge of the roof.

"It's wonderful!" said Dorothy. "Perhaps we can walk on the air ourselves."

"Why don't you walk down?" asked Eureka.

"Will you try it, Zeb?" asked Dorothy.

Dorothy stretched out a hand to him and Zeb put one foot out and let it rest in the air a little over the edge of the roof. It seemed firm enough to walk upon, so he took courage and put out the other foot. Dorothy followed him, and soon they were both walking through the air, with the kitten frisking beside them.

"Come on, Jim!" called Zeb. "It's all right."

Jim had crept to the edge of the roof to look over, and being a sensible horse and quite experienced, he made up his mind that he could go where the others did. So, he trotted off the roof into the air. His great weight made him fall faster than the children walked, and he passed them on the way down. But when he came to the glass pavement, he alighted so softly that he was not even jarred.

"Well, well!" said Dorothy, drawing a long breath. "What a strange country this is."

People began to come out of the glass doors to look at the new arrivals. There were men and women, but no children at all. They did not smile nor did they frown, or show either fear or surprise or curiosity or friendliness. They simply stared at the

472

strangers, paying most attention to Jim and Eureka, for they had never before seen either a horse or a cat.

Pretty soon a man joined the group who wore a glistening star in the dark hair just over his forehead. He seemed to be a person of authority, for the others pressed back to give him room. After turning his eyes first upon the animals and then upon

the children, he said to Zeb: "Tell me, intruder, was it you who caused the Rain of Stones?"

"No, sir; we didn't cause anything. It was the earthquake."

"What is an earthquake?"

"I don't know," said Zeb, who was still confused. But Dorothy, seeing his perplexity, answered:

"It's a shaking of the earth. In this quake a big crack opened and we fell through—horse and buggy, and all—and the stones shook loose and came down with us."

"The Rain of Stones has done much damage to our city," the

473

Prince said, "and we shall hold you responsible for it. Now you must follow me."

He turned and walked down the street, and after a moment's hesitation Dorothy caught Eureka in her arms and climbed into the buggy. Zeb took his seat beside her, took the reins, and said: "Gid-dap, Jim."

The glass city had several fine streets, for a good many people lived there. But when they had passed through these, they came upon a broad plain covered with gardens and watered by many brooks. There were paths through these gardens, and over some of the brooks were glass bridges.

Dorothy and Zeb now got out of the buggy and walked beside the Prince, so that they might see and examine the flowers and plants better.

"Who built these lovely bridges?" asked Dorothy.

"No one built them," answered the man with the star. "They grow."

"Did the glass houses in your city grow, too?"

"Of course," he replied. "But it took many years for them to grow as large and fine as they

are now. That is why we are so angry when a Rain of Stones comes to break our towers and crack our roofs."

"Can't you mend them?" she asked.

"No; but they will grow together again, in time, and we must wait until they do."

"If you will come with me to one of our folk gardens, I will

ground. In the center of each plant grew a daintily dressed Mangaboo, for the clothing of all these creatures grew upon them and was attached to their bodies.

The growing Mangaboos were of all sizes. On some of the bushes might be seen a bud, a blossom, a baby, a half-grown person, and a ripe one. This sight explained to Dorothy why she had seen no children among the Mangaboos.

"Where did you grow?" asked Dorothy.

"I will show you," said the Prince. "Step this way, please."

He led them within another circle of hedge, where grew one large and beautiful bush.

"This," said he, "is the Royal Bush of the Mangaboos. All of our Princes and Princesses have grown upon this one bush from time immemorial."

They stood before it in silent admiration. On the central stalk stood poised the figure of a girl.

"Who is this?" asked Dorothy.

The Prince had been staring hard at the girl on the bush. Now he answered, with a touch of uneasiness in his cold tones:

"She is a Royal Princess.

show you the way *we* grow in the Land of the Mangaboos."

The little party of strangers followed the Prince across a few of the glass bridges and along several paths until they came to a garden enclosed by a high hedge.

Inside the hedge they came upon row after row of large and handsome plants with broad leaves that curved nearly to the

When she becomes fully ripe I must turn over my rule of the Mangaboos to her."

"Isn't she ripe now?" asked Dorothy.

He hesitated.

"Not quite," said he, finally. "It will be several days before she needs to be picked, or at least that is my judgment. I am in no hurry to resign my office, you may be sure."

"I'm sure the Princess is ready to be picked," asserted Dorothy, gazing hard at the beautiful girl on the bush. "She's as perfect as she can be."

"Never mind," answered the Prince, hastily, "she will be all right for a few days longer. It is best for me to rule until I can dispose of you strangers, who have come to our land uninvited."

"What are you going to do with us?" asked Zeb.

"That is a matter I have not quite decided upon" was the reply.

The words of the Prince were not very comforting, and as he spoke them he turned away and left the garden. The children were about to follow him when

Dorothy whispered, "Suppose we pick the Royal Princess. I'm quite sure she's ripe, and as soon as she comes to life she will be the Ruler, and may treat

"Pull!" cried Dorothy, and as they did so the royal lady leaned toward them, and the stems snapped and separated from her feet.

The beautiful creature passed her hands over her eyes an instant and after a look around the garden made those present a gracious bow and said, "I thank you very much."

"We salute your Royal Highness!" cried Dorothy and Zeb.

Just then the voice of the Prince was heard calling upon them to hasten. A moment later he returned to the garden, followed by a number of his people.

Instantly the Princess turned and faced him. When he saw that she was picked, the Prince stood still and began to tremble.

"Sir," said the Royal Lady, with much dignity, "You have wronged me greatly, and would have wronged me still more had not these strangers come to my rescue. I have been ready for picking all the past week, but because you were selfish and desired to continue your unlawful rule, you left me to stand silent upon my bush."

us better than that heartless Prince intends to."

So together they leaned over the bush, and each of them seized one hand of the lovely Princess.

"I did not know that you were ripe," answered the Prince, in a low voice.

"Give me the Star of Royalty!" she commanded.

Slowly he took the shining star from his own brow and placed it upon that of the Princess. Then all the people bowed low to her, and the Prince turned and walked away alone. What became of him our friends never knew.

The people of Mangaboo now formed themselves into a procession and marched toward the glass city to escort their new ruler to her palace and to perform those ceremonies proper to the occasion. But while the people in the procession walked upon the ground, the Princess walked in the air just above their heads to show that she was a superior being and more exalted than her subjects.

Meanwhile Dorothy and Zeb rode to the great square in their buggy. They soon came to the large door of a domed hall.

"It doesn't look very homelike," said Dorothy, gazing around at

the bare room. "But it's a place to stay, anyhow."

"What are those holes up there?" asked Zeb, pointing to some openings that appeared near the top of the dome.

"They look like doorways,"
said Dorothy.

With this she began walking
in the air toward the high openings, and Zeb followed. They
were nearly out of breath when
they came to the doorways leading into halls in the upper part
of the house. Following these
halls they discovered many
small rooms opening from them.
Some were furnished with glass
benches, tables, and chairs. But
there were no beds at all.

"I wonder if these people ever
sleep," said Dorothy.

"Why, there seems to be no
night at all in this country," Zeb
replied. "Those colored suns are
exactly in the same place they
were when we came, and if
there is no sunset there can be
no night."

"Very true," agreed Dorothy.
"But it is a long time since I
have had any sleep, and I'm
tired. So I think I shall lie down
upon one of these hard glass
benches and take a nap."

Zeb walked down again to
unharness Jim, who, when he
found himself free, rolled over a
few times and then settled down
to sleep, with Eureka nestling
comfortably beside his big, bony
body. Then the boy returned to
one of the upper rooms, and in
spite of the hardness of the glass
bench he was soon deep in
slumberland.

## Thinking and Writing About the Selection

1. What was the "Rain of Stones"?
2. In what ways were the Mangaboos different from Dorothy and Zeb?
3. Do you think the Princess will treat Dorothy and Zeb more kindly than the Prince had? Give reasons to support your answer.

 4. L. Frank Baum created the Land of the Mangaboos by imagining a place that he had never seen. Think about the details he used to make the place seem real. Then imagine a magical world of your own. Write a description of it and include the details that will let others "see" it.

## Applying the Key Skill
### Sequence of Events

The following incomplete sentences are about events in "Dorothy's Journey to the Center of the Earth." Complete each sentence with the words *before*, *after*, or *as*. Write the complete sentences.

1. Jim began to talk ___ the buggy passed close to the six great glowing balls of light.
2. The Prince told Dorothy and Zeb to follow him ___ Dorothy explained how they had come to the land of the Mangaboos.
3. The Prince would have to resign his office ___ the Princess was picked.
4. ___ the Prince placed the Star of Royalty on the brow of the Princess, all the people bowed low.
5. ___the people marched toward the glass city, the Princess walked in the air just above their heads.

# L. FRANK BAUM

"The imaginative child will become the imaginative man or woman most apt to create, to invent, and therefore to foster civilization."

L. Frank Baum had already written, edited, and published both an amateur newspaper and a literary magazine by the time he was eighteen. In his twenties he also dabbled in acting, raising chickens, and newspaper reporting. Then he became manager of a chain of theaters, and wrote several plays. Later, he operated a variety store, published a magazine, and even sold axle grease! Years later, Baum (the youngest of seven children) gave credit to his sister Harriet for encouraging him to write.

Baum's first Oz book, *The Wizard of Oz*, grew out of his experience of telling stories to his own children. Inventing characters came easily to him, but, he said, "the plot and plan of adventures take considerable time to develop. When I get at a thing of that sort I live with it day by day, jotting down on odd slips of paper the various ideas that occur . . . . (Then) I must rewrite it, stringing the incidents into consecutive order . . . ."

Baum spent 17 years writing the Oz books. At one point he quit, only to be called back by demanding readers. He died shortly after finishing his last Oz book, *Glinda of Oz*, in 1919. His last words were "Now I can cross the Shifting Sands," a reference to the desert outside the land of Oz.

**More to Read** *The Wizard of Oz, The Road to Oz, Glinda of Oz*

# DANGERS UNDERGROUND

## MARY ZETTELMIER

*A cave can be a fascinating place to explore, but it can also be a confusing maze of passageways. Experienced cavers know that there are wonders and dangers under the ground.*

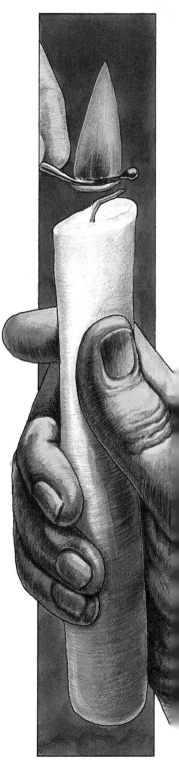

It was still early in the morning when the lanky sixteen-year-old adjusted the burlap bag on his shoulder, glanced quickly around the Virginia countryside, and dropped into the hole at his feet that was almost concealed by a mass of low bushes. He and his brother had found the hole the day before, and he knew it opened into a large passageway that looked as if it wound its way for miles underground.

He had wanted to explore the cave yesterday, but they hadn't had the right equipment with them for spelunking. Now he had returned alone with the things he needed to really see what was in the dark confines of the cave: two large candles and plenty of matches, several of the blueberry muffins his mother had made for breakfast, some beef jerky to chew on if he should stay longer than planned, and a piece of charcoal. His wool jacket and thick boots would keep him warm and dry underground. He felt ready for adventure.

The only thing he hadn't done, in fact, was tell anyone where he was headed. His brother had said they would explore the cave together sometime next week, but the boy couldn't see waiting that long. He knew he was breaking the most important rules for spelunkers—first, never go underground alone, and second, let someone on the surface know of your plans for entering a cave—but it was too nice a day to worry, and he'd be back before anyone missed him.

He lit the first candle and started groping his way down the narrow path. Away from the daylight at the entrance, the cave was pitch black. He could see no farther than the flicker his candle threw out, and more than once he hit his head sharply on rock ledges hanging out over the path.

"Whoo . . . whoo . . . whoo," he called softly. The cave echoed back at him, "whoo . . . who," and from a distant hall came an even fainter "whoooo . . . ."

When the path turned, he marked a large X on the gray-white cave wall with his charcoal. That was the method he had chosen to find his way out when he was ready to go home. As he slowly moved forward, he thought about what his brother had told him, "Caves are living things, always changing and growing. Dripping water makes beautiful rock formations, and sometimes rivers or streams rush through the underground rooms. Wind blows in through the entrance hole or any other surface openings, and together the wind and the water change the cave throughout the years. Many creatures live in caves. Watch for them."

Crouching under an overhanging ledge, the boy heard a noise in the still, lonesome blackness. It was a sound he knew; the trickle of water. He rounded the next turn of the hallway and lowered his candle to see a small stream winding its way through that passage and into the next. He made another X at the turning and then, very carefully, wedged his candle between a rock and the wall. He slid his hand along the slippery wall and into the stream. The water felt only a little cooler than the air, and he remembered that caves, protected as they are by thick layers of earth and rock, stay about the same temperature all year round.

He let his fingers dangle in the cool water and was suddenly surprised to feel something alive moving around in his hand, something that felt like little minnows. He had never seen any of the cave creatures his brother had told him about, and he decided to try to catch some of them. It was a struggle, but he finally managed to scoop up a handful and, keeping them in his cupped hands, held them up to the candle. They wriggled and squirmed so that it was hard to study them, but he could see that they were white and had no eyes. Otherwise they looked like ordinary small fish. He thought for a minute. Of course, what would they need eyes for? They never went out in the sunshine, and there certainly wasn't any light for them to see by here, in the black confines of the inner earth.

Placing the fish back in the water, he picked up his candle and began to make his way along the edge of the stream. Sometimes the trail narrowed so that he had to step into the stream, getting his boots wet. And no matter how carefully he felt for ledges jutting out over the path, he occasionally found one with his head instead of his hand. But never mind—he was learning, and that was the important thing.

Finally, when he had almost decided to turn back, the hallway opened into a huge room. By moving his candle around, he saw an enormously high ceiling. Slowly he circled around the edge of the room, marveling at the beauty of the grotto. Limestone

formations seemed to flow like rippling waterfalls down the cavern walls and others hung, ropelike, from the ceiling. Best of all, there was a huge stalagmite growing up from the floor in the very center of the room, formed long ago by water seeping through the ceiling. The water, containing carbonic acids absorbed from plant roots and soil above the cave, had dripped onto the floor and evaporated, leaving tiny crystals that had gradually built up to form this giant. His brother had told him all about it, and even as he watched, one drop of water dripped onto the stalagmite. He wondered how long it would be before another drop joined the first. Ten minutes? Ten hours? His brother said stalagmites only grew about an inch every hundred years, and he decided not to wait around for any more droplets.

As he started to move on, something slithered across his feet, startling him. At the same moment, his candle stub gave a last flicker and burned out completely, and he was left in total darkness. He let out a small gasp. Its echo bounced eerily back to him from across the room, and he shuddered as he felt the cold blackness all around him.

"Hold on there. Don't get scared," he muttered to himself, groping in his bag for his second and last candle and a match to light it with. When the light once more flickered in the room, he leaned against the wall, suddenly tired and hungry. Inside the cave he had lost all track of time. It was another world altogether from that above ground.

He chewed on a little beef jerky and ate a muffin while he rested. He knew he must start back soon. If one candle had brought him to this strangely beautiful room it would certainly take one more to return him to the entrance. He swallowed the last of his muffin, and,

taking another long look around, he turned and started back the way he had come.

It was easy enough to find the hallway through which he had entered the grotto, but when he came to an intersection where two paths met, he became confused. There was no charcoal X on the wall. Apparently he had not noticed the second path before. He decided to try the right-hand way and see what happened. Now it occurred to him that he had not seen any of his charcoal markings on the walls for a long time. Why hadn't he been more careful about placing them regularly? And, more important, why hadn't he told his brother or a friend that he was exploring the cave? He wondered what time it was.

He knew the dangers of spelunking: poisonous gases, sudden flooding from storms on the surface, diseases carried by bats and other cave animals, and, worst of all, the danger of losing your way. And now he had let himself get lost!

This could not be the right passage, he was sure of that. Where were the large outcroppings of rock that he had so often bumped his head on when he was coming in? This hall was clear of overhanging ledges. He must backtrack and try the other way.

This candle was burning down more quickly, it seemed, than the first one. He reached the intersection where he had taken the wrong turn and hurried up the left-hand path, casting his light about for any signs of his X markings. Nothing.

A few steps more and something ran across his boot. He started, and then saw a large lizard scrambling up the wall. He wondered briefly if that creature, too, had no eyes, but he was too concerned with finding his way out to examine it.

Suddenly, he thought he saw something familiar on the wall far ahead. His candle didn't shine brightly enough to be sure, but it looked like one of his big charcoal Xs. With a sigh of relief, he hurried along even faster, not daring to think what he would do if his candle burned out.

He hadn't gone far when all of a sudden he heard a deafening noise. His heart pounding, he pressed against the wall as thousands of large bats filled the passageway. The candle flickered, then went out in the draft created by their wings. He could feel the bats swarming around him and over him as they passed through the hall. It must be sunset time, he realized suddenly. His brother had told him that early every evening the bats swarmed out of their caves to find food.

Then he had another, happier thought. If the bats were on their way out, then he must be headed in the right direction, too! Encouraged, he reached in his knapsack for a match and relit his candle. The bats had all flown past him by now, and he pressed forward quickly, following them along the quiet passageway. A large X stood out on the wall ahead, and when the passage turned to the right, he could see a speck of daylight far in the distance. He was approaching the twilight area, that space just inside the opening of a cave where daylight can still be seen. He breathed a sigh of relief. He wasn't lost after all—but he had come uncomfortably close to it. Next time, he would tell his brother where he was going, or, better yet, bring him along. Now he wanted to leave as quickly as possible, but there was one last thing he had to do. Taking his knife from his pocket, he carved his name and the date of his exploration on the wall just inside the cave entrance: *G. Washington—1748.*

## Thinking and Writing About the Selection

1. What natural forces change caves?
2. Why did George Washington mark X's on the walls of the cave?
3. Why was Washington encouraged when he saw the bats?
4. If you were getting ready to explore a cave, what precautions would you take? What preparations would you make?

## Applying the Key Skill
### Judgments

Use complete sentences to answer the following questions about "Dangers Underground."

1. Washington broke two of the most important rules for spelunkers. What are the rules, and why are they important?
2. What information helped Washington to judge when it was time for him to leave the grotto?
3. What possible dangers do spelunkers face when they explore caves? Which do you think is the worst? Why?
4. What information in the story might have helped you to figure out that the spelunker was George Washington?
5. What might you do to find out if this story is based on a true incident from George Washington's life? Where might you look?

# A Bat is Born

A bat is born
Naked and blind and pale.
His mother makes a pocket of her tail
And catches him. He clings to her long fur
By his thumbs and toes and teeth.
And then the mother dances through the night
Doubling and looping, soaring, somersaulting—
Her baby hangs on underneath.
All night, in happiness, she hunts and flies.
Her high sharp cries
Like shining needlepoints of sound
Go out into the night and, echoing back,
Tell her what they have touched.
She hears how far it is, how big it is,
Which way it's going:
She lives by hearing.
The mother eats the moths and gnats she catches
In full flight; in full flight

The mother drinks the water of the pond
She skims across. Her baby hangs on tight.
Her baby drinks the milk she makes him
In moonlight or starlight, in mid-air.
Their single shadow, printed on the moon
Or fluttering across the stars,
Whirls on all night; at daybreak
The tired mother flaps home to her rafter.
The others all are there.
They hang themselves up by their toes,
They wrap themselves in their brown wings.
Bunched upside down, they sleep in air.
Their sharp ears, their sharp teeth, their
        quick sharp faces
Are dull and slow and mild.
All the bright day, as the mother sleeps,
She folds her wings about her sleeping child.

                              Randall Jarrell

## DIRECTIONS

George Washington encountered danger underground partly because he did not follow his brother's directions. How might his experience have been different if he had followed directions?

All of us follow directions at one time or another if we want the things we make or do to turn out successfully. **Directions** are a set of instructions about how to proceed or how to act in order to reach a particular goal or achieve a certain result. You may have followed directions when making a kite, putting together a bicycle, or baking a cake.

You know that sometimes directions are made up of several steps, or actions. When you are following directions, it is important to remember these two things:

1. Do each step given in the directions.
2. Do the steps in the order in which they are given.

If you leave out a step or do the steps in the wrong order, you probably won't be successful in what you are trying to do or make.

In "Dangers Underground," you read that the crystals that form stalagmites build up a layer of about one inch every hundred years. That's a long time to wait! You can "grow" your own crystals in a much shorter time. Just follow the directions on the next page.

ACTIVITY A   Read the directions below. Then use complete sentences to answer the questions that follow.

## Making Crystals

### Materials Needed

salt, string, saucer, spoon, water, pot, hot plate, measuring cup, pot holder, magnifying glass

1. Heat a half-cup of water until it is very hot, but not boiling.
2. Add a small amount of salt to the hot water and stir.
3. Keep adding salt in small amounts until no more salt will dissolve.
4. Pour the saltwater into the saucer.
5. Place the string in the saltwater. Let some of the string hang over the sides of the saucer.
6. Put the saucer in a dry place where the temperature stays about the same throughout the day.
7. In three days, pour off the liquid in the saucer. Pick up the string. It should have crystals attached to it. Examine the crystals with a magnifying glass.

---

1. Why was a pot holder included in the list of materials needed?
2. How much water should you use? How much salt?
3. Should you put the string in the saucer before or after you pour in the saltwater?
4. Would a windowsill be a good place to put the saucer? Why or why not?

When directions are numbered, it is easy to keep track of the order, or sequence. Sometimes directions appear in a paragraph. Writers may use signal words such as *first, next,* and *then* to help readers figure out the correct order. Illustrations can also help make directions easier to follow.

**ACTIVITY B** Read the directions below. Then use complete sentences to answer the questions that follow.

## A Garden of Crystals

You can grow a garden of crystals in your own home. All you need are: 6 tablespoons of water, 1 tablespoon of ammonia, 6 tablespoons of laundry bluing, 6 tablespoons of salt, and 6 pieces of charcoal (the kind used in barbecue grills).

First, mix the water, ammonia, bluing, and salt together in a bowl. Be careful with the ammonia. It has a strong smell that can make your eyes water. Pour the liquids carefully so they do not splash out of the bowl.

Next, put the charcoal in a pie pan. Then, pour the liquid over the charcoal. Put the pie pan in a warm place where the water will evaporate quickly. When the water has evaporated, you will see a garden of crystals!

1. What materials are needed in addition to those mentioned in the first paragraph?

2. Why do you think the writer included the information about the smell of ammonia?

3. Do you think it would make a difference if you mixed the bluing into the water before you mixed the ammonia? Why or why not?

4. Why should the pie pan be put in a warm place?

**ACTIVITY C** Write a set of directions for one of the following. You may want to number each step in the directions. Illustrations could help your reader, too.

1. Booting up a computer

2. Making a paper airplane

3. Getting from your school to the local library

4. Making applesauce

5. Making a clay bowl

6. Getting from your home to school

7. Creating an origami flower or bird

8. Making popcorn

# THE ENDLESS CAVE

Marilyn Z. Wilkes

Illinois

Indiana

Ohio

Louisville

Lexington

W. Va.

Frankfort

Kentucky River

Licking River

Owensboro

Kentucky

Lincoln's Birthplace

Va.

Mammoth Cave National Park

Lake Cumberland

Bowling Green

Tennessee

Long ago, the sea covered the land in Kentucky. Plants and animals lived in and around the water. When they died, the sea slowly filled with their bodies, layer upon layer. Years passed, and the layers turned into limestone and other rocks.

In time, the land rose and the sea retreated. Then water in streams and rivers seeped through the ground and nibbled at the soft rock, gently, endlessly. It carved a secret wonderland of caves with strange formations and winding passages. Part of this hidden world has been discovered and mapped by the cavers who explored Mammoth Cave. As you read this selection, think about the natural forces that formed the underground wonders in Mammoth Cave.

### Early History of Mammoth Cave

About 4,000 years ago, when only Indians lived in Kentucky, Mammoth Cave was much the same as it is today. Early people often used caves as shelters from the weather and as hiding places from wild animals. But these Indians also explored. We know that from the black smoke left on the stones by their torches, from the objects they left behind, from the prints of their feet in the hardened mud, and from the remains of people like "Lost John".

"Lost John" was an Indian miner who came to Mammoth Cave for gypsum (jip' sǝm), a white, chalk-like mineral. Gypsum can be mixed with water and then heated to make a white paint. Early Indians used this paint on their bodies during religious ceremonies. "Lost John" entered the cave wearing sandals and carrying a lighted bundle of cane. He stuck his torch into the dirt and began scraping the sparkling gypsum from

499

a giant rock with a stone tool. But under that rock, a pebble that had held it in place for countless ages now moved. The boulder fell onto "Lost John," crushing him.

"Lost John" was found by two Mammoth guides in 1935 while they were building trails. Because of the dry, cool air, his body had become a mummy. By counting the rings in one of his teeth, it was shown that "Lost John" was about 45 years old when he died. He had been dead almost 2,300 years!

Kentucky remained an unsettled place until the late 1700s. At that time, hunters and farmers began to trickle in. One of the first to discover Mammoth Cave, they say, was a hunter named Houchins. One day in 1799, Houchins was chasing a bear. The bear ran into a hole in a hillside; it was the entrance to Mammoth Cave.

Others probably knew of the cave before that, and many heard about it a short time later. That was when calcium nitrate (kal' sē əm nī' trāt), or saltpeter, was discovered in its dirt floor.

The saltpeter came from the droppings of millions of bats that had lived in Mammoth Cave through the ages. Why was it important? To make gunpowder.

The new United States of America was again at war with England, the War of 1812. The English had blocked all ships entering American ports, including ships carrying saltpeter. Seeing a chance to get rich, Hyman Gratz and Charles Wilkins, who had purchased Mammoth Cave in 1812, brought slaves to mine the dirt. The nitrate was boiled out of the dirt and sent up-river to Philadelphia gunpowder factories. It was backbreaking work. But without the saltpeter from Mammoth Cave, we might sing "God Save the Queen" before ball games instead of "The Star-Spangled Banner"!

# The First Great Caver

Black slaves were important in the history of Mammoth Cave, and none was more important than 16-year-old Stephen Bishop. He was brought to Mammoth Cave in 1838 by his owner, Franklin Gorin. Gorin had just bought the cave and a nearby hotel for $5,000. He planned to make the property a tourist attraction. He wanted Bishop to become a guide.

Stephen Bishop was a handsome young man of great intelligence and curiosity. He was lean, athletic, and not very tall—useful qualities in a caver. He quickly learned the ins and outs of cave guiding and began taking visitors through the miles of passages. Wearing a brown hat, striped pants, and a jacket, Bishop carried an oil lantern in one hand, a basket of food in the other, and a can of lamp oil on a strap over his shoulder. It sounds difficult, but he enjoyed his work and grew interested in what lay beyond the paths he now knew so

Stephen Bishop

Early exploring parties in Mammoth Cave

well. He began to explore on his own, finding cane torches and even the bones of ancient explorers. Then, in the summer of 1838, Stephen Bishop squeezed past a huge rock called Giant's Coffin and discovered a small room. A happy Franklin Gorin named it Gorin's Dome.

The event brought many would-be explorers to Mammoth Cave. Bishop took one of them, H. C. Stevenson, on a trip to Bottomless Pit. No one had ever gone past it because of the 6-foot (1.8 m) leap to the other side. But Bishop laid two wooden ladders across it. Then he sat down on one and inched his way across. Stevenson followed on the other, and the two set off along a dry stream bed. The tunnel grew smaller, forcing them to stoop. Smoke from the oil lamps burned their lungs, and the light was dim. It was muddy, and they could smell and hear water near by. They came to a valley and saw a dark river below. They named it the River Styx (stiks) after the river that ran through the Underground in Greek and Roman mythology.

After that, Stephen Bishop became famous as the first great caver in America. He seemed willing to risk any danger and push through any opening to make a new discovery.

In less than a year, Bishop's explorations doubled the known length of Mammoth Cave. Newspapers were full of stories about him, and tourists were arriving by the wagon load. Then Dr. John Croghan of Louisville made Gorin an offer. He would buy Mammoth Cave for $10,000. Gorin agreed.

Croghan enlarged the hotel and even got the state to build roads right to its door. By 1840, Mammoth Cave was the biggest attraction in Kentucky, and Stephen Bishop was its star. He spent more and more time ex-

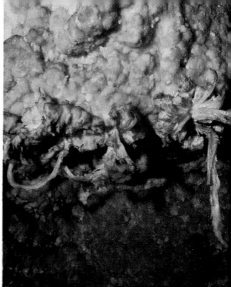

ploring, finding Mammoth Dome, Lake Lethe (lē' thē), and Echo River.

In July, 1841, Bishop took two men on a trip across Echo River. About 2 miles (3.2 km) past the far shore, they came to a passage 6 feet (1.8 m) high and 60 feet (18 m) wide. The ceiling was crusted with shiny white gypsum "flowers" and snowball-like lumps. They called it the Snowball Room.

Croghan was thrilled. He asked Bishop to draw a map of everything he had found. The map was so good that copies were made for use at Mammoth Cave. Three years later it was published, and Bishop became even more famous.

Dr. Croghan now decided to turn part of Mammoth Cave into a hospital for those who had tuberculosis. This was a lung disease for which no cure was known. Croghan thought the cool saltpeter air might help, since some saltpe-

ter miners lived very long lives. Inside the cave, he had stone huts built for the sick. But within a year, several patients had died, and the rest were not getting better. Nothing could have been worse for them than the damp, cold, dark of the cave. The hospital was closed.

In 1849, Dr. Croghan died of tuberculosis himself, and Mammoth Cave passed to his family. In his will, he gave Stephen Bishop freedom in seven years. Bishop stayed at Mammoth Cave, married, and had a son. But he didn't want to wait seven years to be free. He began saving to buy his freedom. He wished to take his family to Liberia, a new black nation on the coast of Africa, and become a lawyer.

Stephen Bishop was freed in 1856, but he never went to Liberia. He grew ill and died in July, 1857, and was buried near his beloved cave.

## Kentucky Cave Wars

Mammoth Cave now went through a quiet time. There were many tourists, but few explorers. Attention turned to neighboring Flint Ridge, where in 1895 Lute Lee and Henry Lee discovered Colossal Cave. Its entrance was about a mile and a half (2.4 km) from Mammoth. People began to wonder if Colossal Cave and Mammoth were somehow connected. It was a question that would not be answered for nearly 80 years.

Meanwhile, in 1921, a clever engineer named George Morrison decided that Mammoth Cave must extend beyond the area owned by the Croghan family. He bought land down the road, blasted a new entrance into the cave, and went into the tourist business himself. This touched off what was known as the Kentucky Cave Wars. Every farmer who owned a cave now saw a

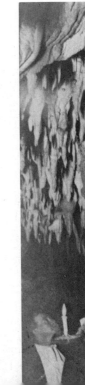

chance to cash in. They put up billboards and ticket stands along the highway and chased visitors' cars. They stole each other's signs and fought over customers.

One young farmer named Floyd Collins found the beautiful Crystal Cave on his father's property. But the cave was too far up the road to draw tourists, so he decided to follow George Morrison's example. He made a deal with three farmers south of Morrison's place. If Floyd could develop a cave on their land, he would get half the profits.

He set to work in January, 1925, moving rocks and digging in Sand Cave. Then, at the bottom of a tight passage, he kicked a large rock. It fell on his ankle and held him fast. By the next day it was known that he was trapped, and efforts were begun to free him. But day after day passed without success. Fifteen days later, a shaft was finally dug, but it was too late. Floyd Collins was dead, a victim of the Cave Wars.

**Exploring the River Styx**

**A group of tourists viewing the cave by candlelight a century ago**

## A National Park

It was clear that the Mammoth and Flint Ridge caves needed more protection than they were getting from cave owners interested only in profits. Like most of nature, a cave is a delicate thing. Stalactites and stalagmites that took thousands of years to form could be broken off in one thoughtless moment, and often were. The answer was a national park, but it would not be easy to get the land. Then, in 1926, the last of the Croghan family died, and the Mammoth Cave National Park Association was formed. The needed laws were passed by the 1930s, and about 45,000 acres (18,000 hectares) were finally put together.

It was the time of the Great Depression, however, and few tourists were coming to Mammoth Cave. To stir up interest, new explorations were begun. Following a likely lead past Echo River, through miles of difficult passages, four cave guides hit the jackpot. Carl and Pete Hanson and Leo and Claude Hunt crawled out of a tunnel and dropped into "another world." White gypsum crystals covered the ceiling, walls, and floor for hundreds of feet. There were sparkling "flowers," from tiny blossoms to long "lilies," and clouds of what looked like cotton candy. There were curling crystal ribbons hanging from the walls and clusters of tiny needles. "This is Paradise," said one of the men, and so it was named. In New Discovery, as the whole area was called, they also found beautiful dripstone and flowstone, rock that looks like curtains and waterfalls. It was a wonderful addition to Mammoth Cave, and the publicity helped the park association's efforts. Finally, on July 1, 1941, Mammoth Cave became a national park.

## The Longest Cave

Interest in caving was high around the world, and a contest heated up between the Mammoth and Flint Ridge systems and the Holloch Cave of Switzerland. Which would prove to be the longest? The key was to find a connection between the caves of Flint Ridge—Salts, Crystal, Unknown, and Colossal—and the huge Mammoth group.

Never mind that exploring national park land was not permitted. A secret expedition was begun, and several connections were made. By 1955, Flint Ridge was known to be the longest system in the world, but there was surely more to find. The Cave Research Foundation was set up to give the cavers scientific backing. In 1959, the government finally agreed to let them explore.

By 1964, cavers in Flint Ridge had come to within 800 feet (240 m) of Mammoth valley before being stopped by fallen rock. They were determined to break through.

In this time-lapse photo, a flare lights a room in the cave.

**Pat Crowther**

A group led by John Wilcox tried in May, 1972, without success. In July, a scientist named Pat Crowther squeezed through a narrow crawlway called the Tight Spot. She came out above a waterfall flowing toward Mammoth Cave. A tunnel led that way. A month later, Pat and her team returned. After twelve hours, they found an arrow carved in a mudbank and the name "Pete H." It was the spot where Pete Hanson and Leo Hunt had ended a trip from Mammoth Cave! This was it! They hurried on through waist-deep water but had to turn back after several more hours.

On September 9, 1972, the Wilcox team, including Pat Crowther, tried again. Water in the passage was less than a foot from the ceiling. Wilcox held his breath and ducked through, followed by the others. They were in a big black chamber. "I see a tourist trail!" shouted Wilcox. There was also a metal handrail.

They had done it! They were in Mammoth Cave, in Cascade Hall, once open to the public but now closed. It was 7.2 miles (11.5 km) from where they had begun, but one of the group, Cleve Pinnix, had a surprise. As a Mammoth park ranger, he carried several keys. He pulled one out and turned on a nearby elevator. And that's how the first group ever to enter Mammoth Cave from Flint Ridge made its exit—straight up!

The Mammoth-Flint Ridge cave system is now known the world over as number one, with more than 295 miles (472 km) of passages mapped thus far. But is the search at an end? How many secrets still lie waiting for determined cavers? The possibilities are endless.

## Thinking and Writing About the Selection

1. Why was Stephen Bishop called the first great caver in America?

2. Why did some people want Mammoth Cave to become a national park?

3. What might cavers discover in the Mammoth-Flint Ridge system in years to come?

4. Suppose you are a cave scientist who is putting together a team to explore a cave. You decide to place an ad in a magazine for interested and qualified cavers. Write the ad, describing the kind of person you would want for your team.

## Applying the Key Skill
### Context Clues

Read the sentences below. Use context clues to figure out the meaning of each underlined word. Write each word and its meaning. Then check your definitions in a dictionary.

1. During the War of 1812, English ships blockaded American ports. Ships carrying valuable supplies such as saltpeter were turned back.

2. The saltpeter needed to make gunpowder was found in abundant supply in Mammoth Cave. The saltpeter came from the droppings of millions of bats over a period of thousands of years.

3. Dr. Croghan tried to turn Mammoth Cave into a tuberculosis sanitorium. However, the conditions in the cave made the patients become worse, and several died.

4. The walls of the cave scintillated as the lights shone on the crystals and smooth stones.

# MNEMONIC FOR SPELUNKING

### Eve Merriam

From the cavern of my mind
Here's a remembrance clue
That was passed along to me
Now I pass it on to you:

Stalactites from the ceiling show;
Stalagmites from the *ground up grow*

# SPELUNKERS AND SPELEOLOGISTS

The Greeks had a word for *cave*, just as they had a word for most things. Their word was *spelaion*. From the Greek root we have several modern words related to caves.

**speleology**—the scientific study of caves
**speleologist**—a scientist who studies caves
**spelunking**—the activity or hobby of exploring caves
**spelunker**—one who explores caves for a hobby

The words *stalactite* and *stalagmite* can also be traced back to a single Greek word. Each developed from a slightly different form of the word, as is explained in the brackets following the definitions below.

**stalactite**—a formation resembling an icicle, hanging down from the ceiling of a cave, usually made up of calcium carbonate deposited by water seeping through the rock above. [Latin *stalactites*, from Greek *stalaktos*, ''oozing out in drops,'' from *stalassein*, ''to drip.'']

**stalagmite**—a formation resembling a cone, built up on the floor of a cave by calcium carbonate dripping from the ceiling. [Latin *stalagmites*, from Greek *stalagma*, ''a drop,'' from *stalagmos*, ''dropping or dripping,'' from *stalassein*, ''to drip.'']

The formation of stalactites and stalagmites is really part of the same process. Some of the water oozing from the ceiling of a cave deposits calcium carbonate there to form stalactites. But some of the water drops or drips to the floor below. The calcium carbonate deposited there builds up to form stalagmites.

511

## DIAGRAMS

A **diagram** is a special kind of illustration. It can show the different parts of something, show how something is put together, or show how something works. Diagrams often accompany articles to help you better understand what the author is talking about. The diagram below, for example, may give you a clearer idea of some of the things you read about in "The Endless Cave."

Most diagrams have a title that tells what the diagram shows. The names of the different parts of the diagram are indicated by labels.

There are several different kinds of diagrams. The one below is a sectional diagram. It gives a view of a cave such as Mammoth Cave as it would appear if a cut were made through the earth.

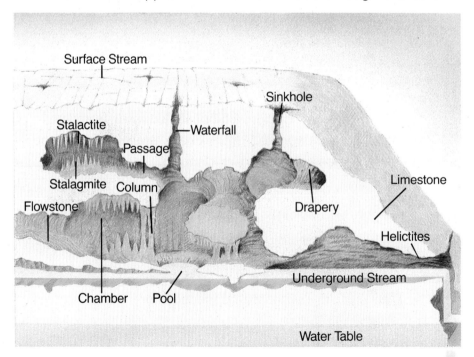

**ACTIVITY** Number your paper from 1 to 8. Refer to the diagram to complete each sentence below. Write the word or words that correctly complete each sentence on your paper.

1.  The cave shown in the diagram has been formed in a kind of rock called _____.

    a.  flowstone          b.  limestone          c.  chamber

2.  The water of the surface stream enters the cave as a _____.

    a.  pool               b.  passage            c.  waterfall

3.  The pointed formations that extend down from the ceiling of the cave are called _____.

    a.  stalactites        b.  stalagmites        c.  columns

4.  The large underground rooms in a cave are called _____.

    a.  passages           b.  sinkholes          c.  chambers

5.  The underground stream in the diagram flows to the surface at the _____.

    a.  water table        b.  pool               c.  sinkhole

6.  The water table is found _____ the underground stream.

    a.  above              b.  at the same        c.  below
                               level as

7.  A _____ may join to form a column.

    a.  passage and a chamber          b.  stalactite and
    c.  helictite and a stalagmite         a stalagmite

# Cave Of The Ancestors

Jean Craighead George

*The Florida Everglades is one of the largest swamp areas on the earth. It is a world of snakes, alligators, turtles, and birds. Huge cypress trees tower above a jungle of reeds and other plants. The Seminole Indians call this place the pa-hay-okee (pä hā ō' kē). They have lived in and around the Everglades since the 1830s.*

*In this story, a young Seminole woman named Billie Wind sets out to explore the pa-hay-okee. As the story begins, she is floating in a dugout canoe, looking for a place to spend the night. There is something in the air, however. The animals seem to sense it, too, and even the sounds in the swamp seem different. What is nature trying to tell her?*

The snakes liked the hot temperature. They slithered through the water, hunting delicacies. They moved swiftly, one after another, on both sides of the boat, their pointed heads above water, making ripples.

"There are an awful lot of snakes out here," Billie Wind finally said to herself. "And they all seem to be moving west to east across Lost Dog Slough. And that's strange."

And the alligators were restless. On other trips down the slough, she had seen them hang quietly at the surface, eyes jutting above the water, watching and waiting for food. Today they were zigzagging beneath the surface of the water. She did not know why. Probably because it was hot, so hot in fact that she finally pulled her black hair over her face to make shade and stopped exerting herself. She lay back in the dugout and let the current carry her.

She drifted only a few feet a minute, for the water of the Everglades creeps. It is a slow river. Once, it seeped out of Lake Okeechobee, before canals were dug to drain the land south of the lake for farming. Now the river comes from rainfall only. It is one hundred miles long and seventy-five miles wide and ends in Florida Bay.

The sounds of the glades were strange this day. Squawks, screams, croaks, and pipings floated across the humid air. As she listened and dozed, her mind wandered back to the Space Center, where she and her brother had spent two winters with their father, Iron Wind. Iron Wind worked on the launcher for the Voyager spaceships that explored the planets.

When Iron Wind worked at night Billie would wait for him outside the Space Life lab. She would stare up at the stars and wonder which one had a sapphire-blue planet with an Everglades and a girl like herself looking out toward her.

The dugout bumped into a clump of alligator flags, tall plants with single leaves growing like flags atop the bare stems. The plants got their name from these leaves and the fact that they usually surrounded alligator pools. Taking heed of this, she paddled around the plants into a clump of willows, drifted past the willows and came upon an alligator trail she had never seen before. She stood up to better see where it led. The

trail wound for miles across the glittery pa-hay-okee to a green island.

"That's where I will spend the night," she said.

Billie Wind poled along the alligator trail. It wound and twisted through the reeds, crossed sloughs, then beelined through the saw grass for many miles.

The white clouds became purple thunderheads. They roiled and flashed lightning. For the first time in almost two years she hoped they would not pour down rain although the glades needed it.

"Are you going to rain?" she asked the clouds by way of testing the voice of the thunderbird god. "Answer me!" A clap of thunder banged overhead with such force that she jumped. "I'm sorry. I'm sorry," she called. "I believe you are there. I believe you are there." Then she grinned.

About a hundred yards from the island she stopped. The wind changed; a cooler breeze nudged her face. She headed for a small beach under a cabbage palm.

Out of the water rose a tail so large it could have belonged to a whale. It was sheathed in heavy armor and spiked with sharp ridges. The monstrous tail came straight toward her. She dropped to the bottom of the dugout as a mammoth alligator struck the stern of the boat. It rocked, tipped, but not quite over, then hit the beach with a crack. Billie Wind jumped ashore as a fifteen-foot alligator slammed his jaws closed on the rear of the boat. The wood splintered.

"You! You!" She jabbed her pole at the monster. He grunted, spat out the wood and sank beneath the surface of the water.

Shaking from the scare, she pulled the dugout up on the shore, saw that the damage was slight and tied it to the cabbage palm. She threw her deerskin pouch over her shoulder, pushed back the limbs of a shrub and stepped into a hauntingly beautiful forest.

A few feet into the forest she came upon a cocoplum bush laden with plumlike fruits. She paused and popped the tart fruits into her mouth. Then she wended her way through a valley of ten-foot-high conte ferns and found herself in a mossy glade. Its odor was fresh with the smell of growing things. Nearby an enormous strangler fig dropped cascades of roots from its limbs, forming corridors and caverns.

She crossed the glade to a cluster of strap ferns with their long thin leaves. She pushed past them and came upon a circle of soft lichens and moss. She swung her pouch to the ground.

"This is my magic spot. I will sleep here and listen to the animals talk."

She selected two trees about six feet apart, from which she would sling her hammock. She was pulling it from her pack when she heard a strange wind.

She stood up. It whined like something alive.

"But it isn't a bird or a beast." Curious, she wended her way among vines and figs, across the island toward the sound. Pushing back the shoreline bushes, she looked out on the endless expanse of saw grass. There was no water gleaming. The blades were brown and dead. Gray clouds rolled and billowed.

"Rain," she cheered. "It really *is* going to rain. These clouds are not teasing." As she ran back to gather up her possessions she kept an eye out for a shelter. A deep sinkhole that looked like an open well caught her attention. It was almost fifteen feet deep and wide "and probably has caves in it, as most sink-holes do," she said as she let herself down a few feet to a ledge in the pit.

Below she saw her reflection in a pool.

"Water. That's good. Water erodes caves." Another ledge lay below the first and she dropped to that. From there it was an easy scramble to the bottom of the pit, where a huge log lay half submerged in the pool. She stepped on it, bent down and peered into a cave.

She leaped from the log into a cave. The sandy floor was pocked with the inverted funnels of ant lions. The little insects sit at the bottom of these funnels that are really traps, waiting for traveling ants to slip and slide down. The pits are pitched at such a steep angle the ants cannot climb out. They fall prey to the little killers.

"The ant lions tell me something," she said. "They build pits only in dry places; so this cave is dry. Good."

She returned to her possessions and, slinging the pouch over her shoulder, hurried toward the pit. A deer, ears back, eyes wide with fright, bolted across the mound. It ran full speed for the far side of the is-land where her dugout was beached.

"What's the matter with you?" she called to the deer. "Is the storm that bad?" The deer was silent.

A marsh rabbit bounded over the ferns, running full out for the far side of the island. He zigged and zagged as rabbits do to confuse an enemy.

An owl took off toward the east. Overhead, a flock of wood storks frantically winged in the same direction. They squawked as they kept in touch with each other.

"What's going on?" she called to them.

Hardly had she spoken than she was struck by a blast of hot air, more searing than the one she had felt in the boat. It smelled of burning grass. And then she knew. She knew why the animals ran and why the island seemed to rise.

"Fire," she gasped. "This is no thunderstorm. The prairie is burning."

Now she could see flames through the trees. Running to the shore, she pushed back the limbs and looked out. Orange blazes licked the sky like serpents' tongues. They shot downward and devoured the grass.

"The boat!" She turned and ran. Near the pit she thought better of escaping in the dugout. "I can't paddle hard enough. The fire is coming too fast."

The cave was her only hope. Letting herself over the edge of the sinkhole, she clambered down to the log. She jumped into the water to wet herself down so she would not burn, and ran into the cave. Creeping deep into the cave, she hugged her calves and dropped her head onto her knees.

After a long while she looked up. The island was a fire box. Green limbs came to a boil and exploded like bullets. Flames ran up and around the trees like slithering serpents: millions and millions of them. A burning limb fell into the pit, struck the water, hissed like a snake and went out.

A deer screamed.

Fires in the Everglades are necessary. Billie Wind knew this. They burned seedling trees out of the pa-hay-okee so that only grass would grow. They thinned out the underbrush on the islands, and because the fires were frequent, they never became hot enough to burn the island trees. Hardwood hammocks like the one Billie Wind was on were protected by moisture from the plants, and they rarely if ever burned. The fires were simply not hot enough to penetrate them. And this had gone on for twenty thousand years. Then practical people fought and put out the Everglades fires. The underbrush grew dense and thick. Now, when fires start in the glades they burn hot, and they sweep through the islands, killing the trees and burning down into the rich humus.

The fire that roared above Billie Wind glowed like a blast furnace. It created rising winds that carried sticks and limbs high into the sky.

Inside the cave Billie Wind watched uneasily as flaming limbs dropped from the smoke clouds into the pit. A turtle plunged off the rim and splashed into the water. Lizards dropped like rain from the hot trees, and an armadillo crept to a ledge. His armoured back was singed and sooty. He lifted his head, slipped and fell ten feet into the water. He did not come up.

Snakes slithered down the wall of the pit. Billie Wind counted more than a dozen before she lowered her eyes and curled up in a ball to sleep. She could not.

She wondered if her tribe could see the fire, and if so, would they try to rescue her?

"They won't," she remembered sadly. "I was curious once too often. Mary will tell them I went south down Lost Dog Slough instead of west. They will not look for me. They will think I am safe. Fires burn as the wind blows. This wind is from west to east."

She lay very still watching the reflected flames dance in the water and listening to the crackle and roar of the fire.

An hour before dawn, Billie Wind, who had not slept all night, lifted her head and looked up at the fire. It still raged. She pushed farther back in the cave. As she moved, her hand struck something hard and round. She brought it close to her face for inspection. It was a clay bowl.

"Burial ground," she said. "This is a burial ground of the Seminoles. I should not be here." Nervously she went to the entrance and held the bowl in the light of the fire shining down from above. Around its rim were feathery drawings. Her fingers ran lightly over the coils of clay that formed the dark bowl. It was gritty to her touch. The grittiness was typical of bowls fired in sand by the ancient Indians.

"Calusa," she said. "This is a Calusa pot." She glanced around the cave. "This place is very old; very, very old. The Calusas were killed off four hundred years ago.

"And it is not a burial ground. Burial pots are broken to let the spirits out.

"Someone lived here. Some ancient ancestor lived in this cave." The light flared up and she crawled

around the room on hands and knees curious to see and learn. Near the far wall she found a conch shell. A hole had been drilled through it, and the tough, thick lip had been ground to a sharp edge.

"A pick," she said. "Hey, ancestor, you had a pick. Who were you and why were you down here in this cave?" She rocked back on her heels and saw that there was a long niche chipped into the wall.

"A bed." She climbed into it, stretched out and discovered that her head and feet touched the walls. "The ancestor was not much taller than I," she observed. Then a thought occurred to her. She felt for human bones. To her relief she found none. "You did not die here," she said aloud. "You lived, and so will I."

As the sun came up the mood of the fire changed. The crackle and roar became a soft hum. The mist of morning was drifting across the island and seeping down into the pit. The air smelled of smoke and tree resin. Billie Wind coughed, took off her scarf and dipped it in the water. She held it over her nose and mouth to filter out the smoke. Lying on her belly, facedown, she breathed the heavy, cold air that still lay along the floor of the cave.

As the morning waned, the smoky mist vanished, leaving the air almost fresh. Billie Wind removed her filter, sat up and breathed deeply. A new sound was on the wind. It was a hiss, and behind the hiss a splat.

"Rain!" she cried. "I hear rain. I'm all right. I'm all right."

Taking off her sneakers, clutching the bowl to her chest, she climbed into the bed of the ancient person. She closed her eyes and this time she did sleep.

## *Forces*

The earth is constantly changing. Some forces act upon the earth in violent ways, changing the surface quickly and dramatically. Other forces work slowly to create gradual changes. In *Forces*, you read about the changes caused by wind and water, volcanoes and earthquakes. You found out how scientists observe, measure, and record these changes. You also read about how natural forces affect people and their way of life. Perhaps you now think about our planet in a different way. You understand the powerful forces that are at work transforming it every day.

## Thinking and Writing About *Forces*

1. In what ways is water both a destructive and a constructive force? How does water wear away the land? How does it build up the land?

2. What forces created the tidal wave described in "The Big Wave"?

3. How did the eruption of Mount St. Helens change the landscape? How did it affect those who lived nearby?

4. L. Frank Baum imagined a city of glass and six suns below the earth's surface. What do you think it is like far beneath the earth? What do scientists think?

5. If you could accompany a group of spelunkers and speleologists as they explore a cave, would you go? Why or why not?

 6. "A Strange Sled Race" is a myth that offers an explanation for the origin of volcanoes. Write a myth to explain how one of these natural occurrences came to be: a hail storm, a hurricane, an avalanche, a flood.

This glossary can help you to pronounce and find out the meanings of words in this book that you may not know.

The words are listed in alphabetical order. Guide words at the top of each page tell you the first and last words on the page.

Each word is divided into syllables. The way to pronounce each word is given next. You can understand the pronunciation respelling by using the key. A shorter key appears at the bottom of every other page.

When a word has more than one syllable, a dark accent mark (′) shows which syllable is stressed. In some words, a light accent mark (′) shows which syllable has a less heavy stress.

The following abbreviations are used in this glossary:

*n.* noun      *v.* verb      *adj.* adjective      *adv.* adverb      *pl.* plural

The glossary entries are adapted from the Macmillan *School Dictionary* and the Macmillan *Dictionary*.

# PRONUNCIATION KEY

## Vowel Sounds

/a/ bat
/ā/ cake, rain, day
/ä/ father
/är/ car
/ãr/ dare, hair
/e/ hen, bread
/ē/ me, meat, baby, believe
/èr/ term, first, worm, turn
/i/ bib
/ī/ kite, fly, pie, light
/ir/ clear, cheer, here
/o/ top, watch

/ō/ rope, soap, so, snow
/ô/ saw, song, auto
/oi/ coin, boy
/ôr/ fork, ore, oar
/ou/ out, cow
/u/ sun, son, touch
/ù/ book, pull, could
/ü/ moon
/ū/ cute, few, music
/ə/ about, taken, pencil, apron, helpful
/ər/ letter, dollar, doctor

## Consonant Sounds

/b/ bear
/d/ dog
/f/ fish, phone
/g/ goat
/h/ house, who
/j/ jar, gem, fudge
/k/ car, key
/l/ lamb
/m/ map
/n/ nest, know
/p/ pig
/r/ rug, wrong

/s/ city, seal
/t/ tiger
/v/ van
/w/ wagon
/y/ yo-yo
/z/ zoo, eggs
/ch/ chain, match
/sh/ show
/th/ thin
/th/ those
/hw/ where
/ng/ song

# A

**a·ban·doned** (ə ban′ dənd) *adj.* left behind or alone; deserted.

**a·broad** (ə brôd′) *adv.* out of one's country; in a foreign land.

**a·brupt·ly** (ə brupt′ lē) *adv.* suddenly; unexpectedly.

**ab·sorbed** (ab sôrbed′, ab zôrbd′) *adj.* very interested.

**ad·e·quate·ly** (ad′ ə kwət lē) *adv.* sufficiently; satisfactorily.

**ad·ren·a·line** (ə dren′ əl in) *n.* a hormone in the body that makes the heart beat faster and quickens the rate of breathing when a person is experiencing stress or danger, helping him to deal more effectively with an emergency.

**ad·ver·tise** (ad′ vər tīz′) *v.* **ad·ver·tised, ad·ver·tis·ing.** to make a public announcement describing the good qualities of a product, service, idea, or the like, in such a way as to make people want to buy it or support it.

**a·gent** (ā′ jənt) *n.* a person having power to do business for others.

**air** (ār) *v.* to tell or to the public.

**al·der** (ôl′ dər) *n.* a tree or shrub that grows in cool, moist regions of the Northern Hemisphere. Most alders have scaly bark and oval leaves.

**am·ble** (am′ bəl) *v.* **am·bled, am·bling.** to walk at a relaxed, easy pace.

**a·mi·no ac·id** (ə mē′ nō as′ id) *n.* any of a group of organic acids composed of carbon, hydrogen, oxygen, and nitrogen. Amino acids are needed by organisms to make protein.

**am·mo·nia** (ə mōn′ yə) *n.* a colorless compound of nitrogen and hydrogen having a strong odor. A solution of ammonia in water is used as a household cleaner.

**an·cient** (ān′ shənt) *adj.* very old.

**an·gle** (ang′ gəl) *n.* the space between two lines or surfaces that meet; amount or degree of slope.

**a·non·y·mous** (ə non′ ə məs) *adj.* of unknown authorship or origin; without any name given.

**A·pol·lo** (ə pol′ ō) *n. Greek Mythology.* god of manly beauty, poetry, music, prophecy, and healing; also considered god of the sun and, as such, was god of light.

Apollo

---

a bat, ā cake, ä father, är car, ār dare; e hen, ē me, ėr term; i bib, ī kite, ir clear; o top, ō rope, ô saw, oi coin, ôr fork, ou out; u sun, u̇ book, ü moon, ū cute; ə about, taken

**ap·par·ent·ly** (ə pār′ ənt lē) *adv.* obviously; seemingly.

**ap·pa·ri·tion** (ap′ ə rish′ ən) *n.* **1.** something strange, startling, or unexpected that comes suddenly into view. **2.** a ghost; phantom.

**ap·point·ment** (ə point′ mənt) *n.* **1.** an arrangement to meet or see someone at a certain time or place. **2.** the act of naming or selecting someone for an office or position.

**ap·prox·i·mate·ly** (ə prok′ sə mit lē) *adv.* nearly; about.

**arc** (ärk) *n.* a curved line.

**ar·chi·tect** (är′ kə tekt′) *n.* a person whose profession is to design and supervise the construction of buildings or other structures.

**architect**

**ar·roy·o** (ə roi′ ō) *n.* a dry bed of a stream; gully.

**ar·ti·fi·cial** (är′ tə fish′ əl) *adj.* not natural; made by humans.

**as·pir·ing** (əs pī′ ring) *adj.* seeking ambitiously to attain something; ambitious.

**as·say** (ə sā′) *v.* to test (an ore, mineral, or the like) by chemical means to determine the nature or quality of its ingredients.

**as·sert** (ə sėrt) *v.* to state firmly and clearly; affirm.

**as·sure** (ə shùr′) *v.* **as·sured, as·sur·ing.** to make certain; convince.

**at·mos·phere** (at′ məs fir′) *n.* the mass of gases surrounding the earth or any other planet.

**at·ti·tude** (at′ ə tüd) *n.* a manner of thinking, acting, or feeling.

**auc·tion** (ôk′ shən) *n.* a public sale at which things are sold to the highest bidder.

**au·thor·i·ty** (ə thôr′ ə tē) *n., pl.* **au·thor·i·ties.** the power or right to act, command, or make decisions.

**au·to·mat·ic** (ô′ tə mat′ ik) *adj.* operating by itself.

# B

**bat·ten** (bat′ ən) *v.* to prepare or strengthen something.

**bee·line** (bē′ līn′) *v.* **bee·lined, bee·lin·ing.** to go directly to; make a beeline for.

**blind·er** (blīn′ dər) *n.* either of a pair of flaps attached to a horse's bridle to prevent it from seeing sideways.

**blinder**

**board·er** (bôr′ dər) *n.* a person who gets meals, or meals and lodging, for pay.

**bot·a·nist** (bot′ ə nist) *n.* an expert in botany, the science or study of plants.

**bound·less** (bound′ lis) *adj.* having no limits; vast.

**bow** (bou) *n.* the front end of a boat, ship, or aircraft.

**box can·yon** (boks′ kan′ yən) *n.* a canyon with steep walls that is usually closed upstream with a similar wall.

**box canyon**

**brack·ish** (brak′ ish) *adj.* somewhat salty; briny.

**buck·skin** (buk′ skin′) *n.* a strong, soft, yellowish-tan leather, made from the skins of deer or sheep.

**bu·reau** (būr′ ō) *n.* **1.** an office or agency. **2.** a chest of drawers, especially for clothes.

**bur·lap** (bėr′ lap) *n.* a coarse fabric often used to make sacks.

**but·ler** (but′ lər) *n.* a male servant, usually the head servant in a household.

**by·line** (bī′ līn′) *n.* a line at the beginning of an article in a newspaper or magazine with the writer's name.

# C

**ca·lam·i·ty** (kə lam′ ə tē) *n., pl.* **ca·lam·i·ties.** an event that causes great misfortune; disaster.

**cal·ci·um car·bo·nate** (kal′ sē əm kär′ bə nāt) a natural compound made of calcium, carbon, and oxygen and found in plant ashes, bones, and shells.

**cal·ci·um ni·trate** (kal′ sē əm nī′ trāt) a chemical compound made up of calcium, nitrogen, and oxygen, also referred to as **saltpeter, lime saltpeter,** or **Norwegian Saltpeter.**

**cal·cu·late** (kal′ kyə lāt′) *v.* **cal·cu·lat·ed, cal·cu·lat·ing. 1.** to figure out beforehand by reasoning; estimate. **2.** to determine by using mathematics; compute.

**cal·lig·ra·phy** (kə lig′ rə fē) *n.* beautiful or elegant handwriting.

**calligraphy**

**can·vas** (kan′ vəs) *n., pl.* **can·vas·es. 1.** a piece of canvas on which a painting, especially an oil painting, is done. **2.** a heavy cloth made of cotton, flax, or hemp.

**can·yon** (kan′ yən) *n.* a deep valley with steep sides, usually with a stream running through it.

**car·bon·ic ac·id** (kär bon′ ik as′ id) *n.* a weak acid formed when carbon dioxide dissolves in water.

**card** (kärd) *v.* to comb or brush wool in preparation for spinning.

**car·go** (kär′ gō) *n., pl.* **car·goes, car·gos.** the goods or merchandise carried by a ship, plane, or vehicle.

**ca·si·no** (kə sē′ nō) *n.* a card game.

**cau·tion** (kô′ shən) *n.* care with regard to danger or risk.

---

a **bat**, ā **cake**, ä **father**, är **car**, âr **dare**; e **hen**, ē **me**, ėr **term**; i **bib**, ī **kite**, ir **clear**; o **top**, ō **rope**, ô **saw**, oi **coin**, ôr **fork**, ou **out**; u **sun**, ù **book**, ü **moon**, ū **cute**; ə **about, taken**

**ce·leb·ri·ty** (sə leb′ rə tē) *n., pl.* **ce·leb·ri·ties.** a person who is well known or much publicized.

**cen·ti·pede** (sen′ tə pēd′) *n.* a small animal that resembles a worm, having a flattened, long body made up of many segments, each bearing a pair of legs.

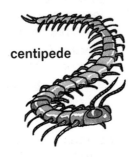
centipede

**cen·tu·ry** (sen′ chər ē) *n., pl.* **cen·tu·ries.** a period of one hundred years.

**cer·e·mo·ni·al** (sãr′ ə mō′ nē əl) *adj.* **1.** used in connection with a ceremony, a formal act or acts done on a special occasion. **2.** relating to ceremony; formal.

**cham·ber** (chām′ bər) *n.* an enclosed space.

**chan·nel** (chan′ əl) *n.* the deepest part of a stream, river, or other waterway.

**chant** (chant) *v.* to sing or shout over and over, usually with a strong rhythm.

**chauf·feur** (shō′ fər, shō fėr′) *n.* a person whose work is driving an automobile, especially a limousine.

**chore** (chôr) *n.* a small or minor job.

**ci·ca·da** (si kā′ də) *n., pl.* **ci·ca·das, ci·ca·dae** (si kā′ dē). a large insect with two pairs of transparent wings. The male makes a loud, shrill sound by means of two vibrating plates on its abdomen.

**cinch** (sinch) *v.* to fasten firmly.

**ci·pher·ing** (sī′ fər ing) *adj.* doing or having to do with arithmetic.

**cir·cuit** (sėr′ kit) *n.* **1.** a system or part of a system of electronic parts through which an electric current flows. **2.** the act of going around; revolution.

**cir·cum·fer·ence** (sėr kum′ fər əns) *n.* the outer boundary of something.

**Civ·il War** (siv′ əl wôr′) *n.* in the United States, the war between the North and the South from 1861 to 1865.

**clan** (klan) *n.* a group of families in a community who claim to be descended from the same ancestor.

**class·ic** (klas′ ik) *n.* a work of art or literature considered to be of such high quality or excellence that it serves as a standard or model.

**clas·si·fied ad** (klas′ ə fīd′ ad′) *n.* a small advertisement, usually one arranged in a special section of a newspaper or magazine.

**classified ad**

**cleft** (kleft) *n.* a space or opening made by splitting; crack.

**clip·per ship** (klip′ ər ship′) *n.* a fast-sailing cargo ship developed in the United States in the nineteenth century, having a narrow beam and, usually, three square-rigged masts.

**clove** (klōv) *n.* the dried, unopened flower bud of a tropical evergreen tree, used as a spice.

**cog·wheel** (kog′ hwēl′) *n.* a wheel with a row of teeth on it; gear.

**co·in·ci·dence** (kō in′ si dəns) *n.* a remarkable occurrence of events at the same time and apparently by mere chance.

**Col·i·se·um** (kol′ ə sē′ əm) *n.* an ancient outdoor circular theater in Rome, Italy. Also Colosseum.

**Coliseum**

**co·los·sal** (kə los′ əl) *adj.* extremely large; gigantic; immense.

**col·umn** (kol′ əm) *n.* feature article that appears regularly in a newspaper or magazine.

**Co·man·che** (kə man′ chē) *n.* a member of a tribe of North American Indians formerly living in the southern part of the Great Plains, now living in Oklahoma.

**come·ly** (kum′ lē) *adj.* pleasing in appearance; good looking.

**com·et** (kom′ it) *n.* a heavenly body that circles the sun and often has a visible tail of gases.

**com·mer·cial** (kə mèr′ shəl) *n.* advertising message on radio or television.

**com·par·i·son** (kəm pār′ ə sən) *n.* the act of comparing or studying in order to find likenesses or differences.

**com·plex** (kom′ pleks) *n.* a group of houses or apartment buildings identified together.

**com·pli·ment** (kom′ plə mənt) *n.* an expression of admiration or praise; flattering comment.

**con·ceal** (kən sēl′) *v.* to put or keep out of sight; hide.

**con·cen·trate** (kon′ sən trāt′) *v.* **con·cen·trat·ed, con·cen·trat·ing.** to direct all of one's efforts or attention.

**con·cen·tra·tion** (kon′ sən trā′ shən) *n.* close attention.

**conch** (kongk, konch) *n., pl.* **conchs** (kongks) or **conch·es** (kon′ chiz). the large spiral shell of a saltwater animal.

**conch**

**con·fi·dence** (kon′ fə dəns) *n.* **1.** faith in oneself; self-assurance. **2.** firm trust or faith; reliance.

**con·fines** (kon′ fīnz) *n., pl.* boundaries; borders; limits.

**con·spire** (kən spīr′) *v.* **con·spired, con·spir·ing.** to work or act together to get something done.

**con·sult·ant** (kən sul′ tənt) *n.* a person who gives professional advice.

---

a b**a**t, ā c**a**ke, ä f**a**ther, är c**a**r, år d**a**re; e h**e**n, ē m**e**, ér t**e**rm; i b**i**b, ī k**i**te, ir cl**e**ar; o t**o**p, ō r**o**pe, ô s**a**w, oi c**o**in, ôr f**o**rk, ou **ou**t; u s**u**n, u̇ b**oo**k, ü m**oo**n, ū c**u**te; ə **a**bout, tak**e**n

**con·sum·er** (kən süm′ ər) *n.* someone who buys and uses up things for sale.

**con·tent·ed·ly** (kən ten′ tid lē) *adv.* in a contented or satisfied way.

**con·ti·nen·tal di·vide** (kon′ tə nent′ əl di vīd′) *n.* an elevation in western North America formed by the various peaks of the Rocky Mountains, separating rivers flowing eastward from those flowing westward.

**con·ven·tion** (kən ven′ shən) *n.* a formal meeting for a particular purpose.

**con·vince** (kən vins′) *v.* **con·vinced, con·vinc·ing.** to cause someone to believe or feel certain; persuade.

**course** (kôrs) *n.* **1.** a line, route, or path in which something moves. **2.** progress.

**cour·te·ous** (kėr′ tē əs) *adj.* polite; showing good manners.

**crag** (krag) *n.* steep, jagged, or projecting rock or cliff.

crag

**cra·ter** (krā′ tər) *n.* a bowl-shaped hollow or hole at the mouth of a volcano.

**Crete** (krēt) *n.* a Greek island in the eastern Mediterranean Sea, southeast of Greece.

**crev·ice** (krev′ is) *n.* a narrow crack in something.

**crock·er·y** (krok′ ər ē) *n.* clay cookware.

**cul·tur·al** (kul′ chər əl) *adj.* of or relating to the culture, or way of life, of a particular people.

**cu·ri·o** (kūr′ ē ō′) *n.* an object valued because it is strange, rare, or unusual.

**cur·rent** (kėr′ ənt) *n.* a portion of a body of water or air flowing in the same path.

**cy·press** (sī′ prəs) *n.* a cone-bearing tree found especially in swampy lands in the southern United States.

**cypress**

# D

**dace** (dās) *n.* a minnow commonly found in small streams of North America and Europe.

**Da·ko·ta Ter·ri·to·ry** (də kō′ tə tär′ ə tôr′ ē) a former territory of the United States, made up of what is now North Dakota and South Dakota.

**day care** (dā′ kār′) *n.* a type of child care in which a child or children are taken care of, usually by trained adults during the temporary absence of a parent or parents.

**dead end** (ded′ end′) *n.* a street, alley, or passage closed at one end.

**de·flect** (di flekt′) *v.* to cause to turn aside or change direction; bend from a straight course.

**de·fy** (di fī′) *v.* **de·fied, de·fy·ing.** to resist boldly and openly.

**de·lec·ta·ble** (di lek′ tə bəl) *adj.* pleasing or delightful to eat; delicious.

**del·i·ca·cy** (del′ ə kə sē) *n., pl.* **del·i·ca·cies. 1.** a rare or choice food. **2.** fineness of structure, quality, texture, or form; daintiness.

**del·i·cate·ly** (del′ ə kit lē) *adv.* in a fine or dainty manner; lightly.

**De·los** (dē′ lös) *n.* a Greek island in the Aegean Sea. Delos is the smallest of a group of Greek islands called the Cyclades (si′ klə dēz).

**del·ta** (del′ tə) *n.* **1.** an area of land formed by a river depositing silt, sand, and pebbles at its mouth. A delta is usually triangular in shape. **2.** the fourth letter of the Greek alphabet, corresponding to English D, d.

**del·ver** (delv′ ər) *n.* a person who makes a careful investigation or searches for information.

**de·mand** (di mand′) *n.* **1.** the desire for a product together with the ability to buy it. **2.** the act of demanding.

**dem·on·strate** (dem′ ən strāt′) *v.* **dem·on·strat·ed, dem·on·strat·ing.** to show by example.

**de·pot** (dē′ pō) *n.* a railroad station.

**de·scend** (di send′) *v.* to move from a higher place to a lower one.

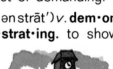

**depot**

**de·sert** (di zėrt′) *v.* to leave, abandon.

**de·spair** (di spār′) *n.* a complete loss of hope.

**des·per·ate** (des′ pər it, des′ prit) *adj.* ready or willing to take any risk.

**des·per·ate·ly** (des′ pər it lē) *adv.* **1.** deeply; extremely. **2.** in a reckless or hopeless way; rashly.

**de·tect** (di tekt′) *v.* to discover.

**de·ter·mined** (di tėr′ mind) *adj.* having a fixed purpose; resolved.

**de·vice** (di vīs′) *n.* something made or invented for a particular purpose.

**de·vour** (di vour′) *v.* **1.** to waste or destroy. **2.** to eat up with great greed or vigor.

**dig·ni·ty** (dig′ nə tē) *n., pl.* **dig·ni·ties.** nobility of character; stateliness.

**di·lem·ma** (di lem′ ə) *n.* a situation that requires a choice between two or more things that are equally unsatisfactory; difficult choice.

**di·men·sion** (di men′ shən) *n.* a type or kind of experience.

**dis·as·trous** (di zas′ trəs) *adj.* causing much suffering, distress, or loss.

**dis·pose** (dis pōz′) *v.* **dis·posed, dis·pos·ing.** to make inclined or willing. **to dispose of.** to get rid of; throw away.

**dog·eared** (dôg′ ird) *adj.* having pages with corners turned down.

---

a **bat,** ā **cake,** ä **father,** är **car,** ãr **dare;** e **hen,** ē **me,** ėr **term;** i **bib,** ī **kite,** ir **clear;** o **top,** ō **rope,** ô **saw,** oi **coin,** ôr **fork,** ou **out;** u **sun,** u̇ **book,** ü **moon,** ū **cute;** ə **about, taken**

**dome** (dōm) *n.* a round roof resembling a hemisphere, built on a circular or many-sided base.

dome

**dor·mer** (dôr' mər) *n.* a window that projects from a sloping roof.

**douse** (dous) *v.* **doused, dous·ing. 1.** *Informal.* to put out; extinguish. **2.** to plunge into water or other liquid.

**down·stage** (down' stāj') *adv.* toward the footlights; in or to the front of the stage.

**downstage**

**drip·stone** (drip' stōn') *n.* calcium carbonate in the form of stalactites and stalagmites.

**drought** (drout) *n.* a long period of dry weather; prolonged lack of rainfall.

**dunk** (dungk) *v.* to dip (something to eat) into a liquid.

**dwin·dle** (dwin' dəl) *v.* **dwin·dled, dwin·dling.** to become gradually smaller or less.

# E

**earth·quake** (ėrth' kwāk') *n.* a movement of the ground, caused by the sudden shifting of rock along a fault or crack in the earth's surface, or by volcanic disturbances.

**Ech·o** (ek' ō) *n. Greek Mythology.* a mountain nymph who was deprived by the goddess Hera of her power of speech, except to repeat the final words of others.

**ed·it** (ed' it) *v.* to make (written material) ready for publication by correcting or revising.

**ed·i·tor** (ed' ə tər) *n.* a person who edits, or prepares written material for publication.

**ee·ri·ly** (ir' i lē) *adv.* weirdly; strangely.

**Eif·fel** (ī' fəl) *n.* the name of a famous metal tower in Paris, France. **The Eiffel Tower.**

**Eiffel Tower**

**e·lu·sive** (i lü' siv) *adj.* difficult to catch or grasp.

**e·merge** (i mėrg') *v.* **e·merged, e·merg·ing.** to come into view.

**em·i·grant** (em' ə grant) *n.* a person who leaves one place or country to live in another.

**em·pha·size** (em' fə sīz') *v.* **em·pha·sized, em·pha·siz·ing.** to stress.

**em·ploy·er** (em ploi' ər) *n.* a person or business that hires a person for pay.

**en·chant·ed** (en chant' id) *adj.* greatly delighted; charmed; bewitched.

**en·close** (en klōz') *v.* **en·closed, en·clos·ing.** to surround.

**en·ter·prise** (en' tər prīz') *n.* a project or undertaking, especially one that is difficult or important.

**en·ter·pris·ing** (en' tər prī' zing) *adj.* showing energy and initiative; venturesome.

**en·ti·tle** (en tī′ təl) *v.* **en·ti·tled, en·ti·tling. 1.** to give a claim or right to; qualify. **2.** to give the title of; call.

**en·vi·ron·ment** (en vī′ rən mənt) *n.* surroundings, especially the earth, air, and water of our planet.

**e·rode** (i rōd′) *v.* **e·rod·ed, e·rod·ing.** to wear or wash away, especially by rain, wind, waves, flowing water, and the effects of freezing and thawing.

**er·rand** (ãr′ ənd) *n.* a short trip to do something, usually for someone else.

**e·rupt** (i rupt′) *v.* to throw forth something suddenly and violently.

**es·cort** (es kôrt′) *v.* to accompany as a courtesy, honor, or protection.

**erupt**

**es·say** (es′ ā) *n.* a short written composition on a particular subject.

**et cet·er·a** (et set′ ər ə) and so forth; and others. Abbreviated etc.

**e·ter·nal** (i tèrn′ əl) *adj.* **1.** forever the same; never changing. **2.** without beginning or end; lasting forever.

**e·vap·o·rate** (i vap′ ə rāt′) *v.* **e·vap·o·rat·ed, e·vap·o·rat·ing.** to change from liquid to gas, leaving behind what solids were contained.

**e·ven·tu·al·ly** (i ven′ chü ə lē) *adv.* in the end; finally.

**ev·i·dence** (ev′ ə dens) *n.* something that serves to prove or disprove a belief or conclusion.

**ex·alt·ed** (ig zôl′ tid) *adj.* raised in rank or position.

**ex·as·per·a·tion** (ig zas′ pə rā′ shən) *n.* the act or state of being greatly irritated or angry.

**ex·cel** (ek sel′) *v.* **ex·celled, ex·cel·ling.** to become better or greater than, as in ability or quality; outdo.

**ex·change** (eks chānj′) *n.* the act of giving one thing in return for another.

**ex·ert** (ig zèrt′) *v.* to make active use of. **to exert oneself.** to make a great effort; try hard.

**ex·hib·it** (eg zib′ it) *v.* to put on public display.

**ex·it** (eg′ zit, ek′ sit) *v.* to leave; go out; depart. —*n.* the way out.

**exhibit**

**ex·pand** (iks pand′) *v.* to make larger, as in size.

**ex·panse** (iks pans′) *n.* a wide, unbroken stretch or area.

→ **ex·pe·di·tion** (eks′ pə dish′ ən) *n.* a journey made for a specific purpose.

**ex·pose** (iks pōz′) *v.* **ex·posed, ex·pos·ing.** to leave open; uncover.

---

a **b**a**t**, ā **c**a**ke**, ä **f**a**ther**, är **c**a**r**, ãr **d**a**re**; e **hen**, ē **me**, èr **term**; i **bib**, ī **kite**, ir **clear**; o **top**, ō **rope**, ô **saw**, oi **coin**, ôr **fork**, ou **out**; u **sun**, u̇ **book**, ü **moon**, ū **cute**; ə **about**, tak**en**

**ex·tend** (iks tend') *v.* to continue in distance or time; stretch out.

**ex·te·ri·or** (eks tir' ē ər) *n.* the outer surface or part.

**ex·treme** (eks trēm') **1.** farthest. **2.** of the greatest or highest degree.

# F

**fal·ter** (fôl' tər) *v.* to act with hesitation or uncertainty.

**fath·om** (fath' əm) *n.* a unit of measure equal to six feet, used especially in nautical measurements, as for the depth of water.

**fa·tigue** (fə tēg') *n.* exhaustion.

**fer·tile** (fért' əl) *adj.* producing or able to produce crops abundantly.

**fi·an·cée** (fē' än sā') *n.* a woman to whom a man is engaged to be married.

**file** (fīl) *v.* **filed, fil·ing.** to hand in legally or officially.

**fil·i·gree**
(fil' ə grē') *n.*
**1.** anything ornamental, delicate, or fanciful, such as a pattern or design. **2.** delicate ornamental work of intertwined gold or silver wire.

**filigree**

**fi·nan·cial** (fi nan' shəl) *adj.* relating to money matters.

**flail** (flāl) *v.* **1.** to wave or swing, especially violently or quickly. **2.** to strike with a flail; thresh.

**flaw·less** (flô' lis) *adj.* without flaws; perfect.

**flood plain** (flud' plān') *n.* an area of flat land along a river subject to flooding, made by deposits of earth from floodwaters.

**flow·stone** (flō' stōn') *n.* a cave formation of minerals deposited in sheets or layers on the walls or floors.

**flu·id** (flü' id) *n.* **1.** any liquid. **2.** a substance, as a liquid or gas, that is capable of flowing, has no definite shape, and adapts itself to the shape of any container that confines it.

**fore·ground** (fôr' ground') *n.* the part of a picture or view nearest to a person's eye.

**for·lorn** (fôr lôrn') *adj.* abandoned, deserted.

**for·ma·tion** (fôr mā' shən) *n.* something formed or shaped.

**for·mu·la** (fôr' myə lə) *n.* **1.** recipe or prescription. **2.** a set method for doing something; fixed rule.

**for·ty-nin·er** (fôr' tē nī' nər) *n.* a person who went to California seeking gold in the gold rush of 1849.

**forty-niner**

**foun·da·tion** (foun dā' shən) *n.* something serving as a base or support.

**foun·der** (foun' dər) *n.* a person who founds, starts, or sets up something.—*v.* to fill with water and sink.

**frag·ment** (frag' mənt) *n.* a part broken off; small piece.

**fran·ti·cal·ly** (fran′ tik lē) *adv.* with a feeling of great excitement brought about by worry, fear, or anger.

**fren·zied** (fren′ zēd) *adj.* marked by great emotion or excitement; frantic.

**frig·ate** (frig′ it) *n.* formerly, a three-masted, square-rigged sailing warship.

frigate

**frilled** (frild) *adj.* ornamental trim of lace or fabric.

**fron·tier** (frun tir′) *n.* the settled border of a country lying along the border of unsettled or undeveloped territory.

**fur·row** (fėr′ ō) *n.* a long narrow groove or channel.

# G

**gad·get** (gaj′ it) *n.* a small mechanical device.

**gal·ax·y** (gal′ ək sē) *n., pl.* **gal·ax·ies.** any of the vast groupings of stars, dust, and gases scattered throughout the universe.

**gap·ing** (gā′ ping) *adv.* opened wide; yawning.

**gar·ment** (gär′ mənt) *n.* an article of clothing.

**gaze** (gāz) *v.* **gazed, gaz·ing.** to look long and steadily, as in admiration or wonder.

**gear** (gir) *n.* **1.** any equipment used for a specific purpose. **2.** a wheel having a toothed edge designed to fit into the teeth of another similar wheel.

**gen·er·a·tion** (jen′ ə rā′ shən) *n.* a group of individuals born at about the same time.

**gen·er·os·i·ty** (jen′ ə ros′ ə tē) *n., pl.* **gen·er·os·i·ties.** willingness to give or share freely.

**gen·u·ine** (jen′ ū in) *adj.* actually what it seems or appears to be; real.

**ge·og·ra·phy** (jē og′ rə fē) *n., pl.* **ge·og·ra·phies.** the study of the earth's climate, surface, and resources, and of how people make use of the earth.

**ge·ol·o·gist** (jē ol′ ə jist) *n.* a scientist who studies the earth's structure and composition.

**gilt** (gilt) *adj.* covered with gold or having a golden color.

**gim·crack** (jim′ krak′) *n.* a gaudy, useless object; trifle.

**gir·dle** (gėrd′ əl) *n.* a belt or band worn around the waist.

**glee** (glē) *n.* joy or delight; merriment.

**glint** (glint) *v.* to shine; gleam.

---

a **bat**, ā **cake**, ä **father**, är **car**, ãr **dare**; e **hen**, ē **me**, ėr **term**; i **bib**, ī **kite**, ir **clear**; o **top**, ō **rope**, ô **saw**, oi **coin**, ôr **fork**, ou **out**; u **sun**, ù **book**, ü **moon**, ū **cute**; ə **about, taken**

**gloom** (glüm) *n.* **1.** complete or partial darkness; dimness. **2.** a depressing or dismal atmosphere.

**goat·ee** (gō tē')
*n.* a small
pointed beard.

goatee

**goods** (gu̇dz) *n.
pl.* things that
are sold; mer-
chandise;
wares.

**gorge** (gôrj) *n.* a deep, narrow opening or passage between steep and rocky sides of walls or mountains.

**grade** (grād) *n.* **1.** the slope of a road or railroad track. **2.** any one of the divisions of study in an elementary or high school.

**grad·u·al·ly** (graj' ü əl lē) *adv.* moving or changing slowly or by degrees.

**Grand Can·yon** (grand' kan' yən) *n.* a large canyon on the upper Colorado River, in northwestern Arizona, re-garded as one of the most spectacular natural wonders of the world.

**grat·er** (grā' tər) *n.* a kitchen utensil
having sharp,
raised edges
used to grate
vegetables,
cheese, spices,
and other foods.

grater

**grav·i·ty** (grav' ə tē) *n., pl.* **grav·i·ties.** the force that pulls things toward the center of the earth.

**grease·wood** (grēs' wu̇d') *n.* a stiff, prickly shrub with narrow leaves, growing in the western United States.

**Great De·pres·sion** (grāt' di presh' ən) *n.* a period of severe reduction in business activity and high unemploy-ment lasting from 1929 to 1939.

**green·horn** (grēn' hôrn') *n. Informal.* an inexperienced person; person with-out training.

**grim·y** (grī' mē) *adj.* full or covered with dirt; filthy.

**grope** (grōp) *v.* **groped, grop·ing.** to feel about with the hands.

**gross** (grōs) *n.* total amount, as of in-come, before deductions.

**grot·to** (grot' ō) *n., pl.* **grot·toes, grot· tos.** cave.

**guar·an·tee** (gar' ən tē') *v.* **guar·an· teed, guar·an·tee·ing.** to assure the quality of.

**gym·nast** (jim'
nast) *n.* a per-
son skilled in
gymnastics,
physical exer-
cises designed
to develop
strength, agility,
coordination,
and balance.

**gymnast**

**gyp·sum** (jip' səm) *n.* a common min-eral used especially in cements, in plaster of Paris, and as a fertilizer.

# H

**hai·ku** (hī' kü) *n.* a form of Japanese poetry containing seventeen sylla-bles, usually about a subject from nature.

**ham·mock** (ham′ ək) *n.* a swinging bed made from a long piece of canvas, leather, or netting hung between two supports, such as trees or poles.

**Ha·wai·i** (hə wī′ ē) *n.* **1.** the fiftieth state of the United States. **2.** the largest island in the group of islands that makes up the state of Hawaii.

**hawk·er** (hô′ kər) *n.* a person who offers goods for sale by calling out in public.

**hay·rick** (hā′ rik′) *n.* a pile of hay stacked outdoors; haystack.

**head·quar·ters** (hed′ kwôr′ tərz) *n. pl.* **1.** any center of operations, as of a business; main office. **2.** the center of operations from which a commanding officer, chief, or other leader issues orders.

**heave** (hēv) *v.* **heaved, heav·ing.** to rise and swell; bulge.

**he·ro** (hir′ ō) *n., pl.* **he·roes.** a person who is looked up to and admired for bravery and other noble qualities.

**he·ro·ic** (hi rō′ ik) *adj.* of or like a hero; courageous.

**hes·i·tant·ly** (hez′ ə tənt lē) *adv.* in an uncertain way.

**hoar** (hôr) *n.* frost.

**hob·ble** (hob′ əl) *v.* **hob·bled, hob·bling.** to tie the front legs or hind legs of a horse to prevent it from moving far.

**hoist** (hoist) *v.* to lift or pull up, especially by means of ropes and pulleys or a crane.

**home·stead** (hōm′ sted′) *n.* **1.** 160 acres of public land granted by the United States government to a settler for farming. **2.** a house with its buildings and the land they are on.

**ho·ri·zon** (hə rī′ zən) *n.* the line where the sky and the earth or sea seem to meet.

**horn** (hôrn) *n.* a hard, permanent growth on the head of various hoofed animals, including sheep, cattle, and antelopes.

**horn spoon** (hôrn′ spün) *n.* a small container like a trough, made from a section of cow horn, and used for careful washing tests in gold mining.

**horn spoon**

**host** (hōst) *n.* a person who receives or entertains others as guests.

**hov·er** (huv′ ər) *v.* to remain suspended in the air over or around a particular spot.

**hu·man·i·ty** (hū man′ ə tē) *n., pl.* **hu·man·i·ties.** human beings as a group; the human race.

**hu·mil·i·a·ting** (hū mil′ ē ā ting) *adj.* made to seem foolish or worthless; embarrassing.

---

a **bat**, ā **cake**, ä **father**, är **car**, âr **dare**; e **hen**, ē **me**, ėr **term**; i **bib**, ī **kite**, ir **clear**; o **top**, ō **rope**, ô **saw**, oi **coin**, ôr **fork**, ou **out**; u **sun**, u̇ **book**, ü **moon**, ū **cute**; ə **about, taken**

**hu·mus** (hū′ məs) *n.* a dark substance in the soil, made up of decayed animal or vegetable matter and containing nitrogen and other plant nutrients.

**hur·ri·cane** (hėr′ ə kān′) *n.* a storm with violent winds of more than 75 miles an hour that spin around a calm center and are accompanied by heavy rain, high tides, and flooding in coastal regions.

**hurricane**

**hur·tle** (hėrt′ əl) *v.* **hur·tled, hur·tling. 1.** to move with clattering and crashing; rush noisily or violently. **2.** to dash or drive violently; rush suddenly.

**hys·ter·ics** (his tãr′ iks) *n. pl.* a fit of uncontrollable emotion, especially of laughing and crying at the same time.

# I

**i·den·ti·ty** (ī den′ tə tē) *n., pl.* **i·den·ti·ties. 1.** the fact of being a certain person or thing; being who one is. **2.** a person's sense of being different from other persons; individuality.

**im·me·mo·ri·al** (im′ ə môr′ ē əl) *adj.* going back beyond memory or record; ancient.

**im·pres·sion** (im presh′ ən) *n.* an influence produced on the mind or feelings.

**im·pulse** (im′ puls) *n.* a force or feeling that makes a person act without planning or thinking.

**in·cli·na·tion** (in′ klə nā′ shən) *n.* a natural tendency; bent.

**in·cred·i·ble** (in kred′ ə bəl) *adj.* hard or impossible to believe.

**in·di·ca·tion** (in di kā′ shən) *n.* a sign; something that indicates or points out.

**in·dig·nant** (in dig′ nənt) *adj.* angry at something unjust or unfair.

**in·do·lent** (in′ dəl ənt) *adj.* having or showing a dislike of work or effort; lazy.

**in·fan·cy** (in′ fən sē) *n., pl.* **in·fan·cies.** the condition of being in the earliest period of life; babyhood.

**in·fe·ri·or** (in fir′ ē ər) *adj.* of poor quality; below average.

**in·gen·ious** (in jēn′ yəs) *adj.* having creative ability; imaginative; inventive.

**i·ni·tia·tive** (i nish′ ə tiv′) *n.* the ability to take a first step in doing something.

**in·quire** (in kwīr′) *v.* **in·quired, in·quir·ing.** to ask about.

**in·scrip·tion** (in skrip′ shən) *n.* a message or note written on something.

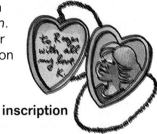
**inscription**

**in·spired** (in spīrd′) *adj.* stimulated, stirred.

**in·tent** (in tent′) *adj.* firmly directed or fixed.

**in·tent·ly** (in tent′ lē) *adv.* in a fixed or firmly directed way; with undivided attention.

**in·ter·cept** (in′ tər sept′) *v.* to seize or stop on the way.

**in·ter·cep·tion** (in′ tər sep′ shən) *n.* the act of intercepting, seizing, or stopping something on the way.

**in·ter·sec·tion** (in′ tər sek′ shən, in′ tər sek′ shən) *n.* place where two roads or pathways meet.

**intersection**

**in·ter·view** (in′ tər vū′) *n.* a meeting between a writer or reporter and a person from whom information is wanted, or a broadcast or published report resulting from such a meeting.

**in·tri·guing** (in trēg′ ing) *adj.* arousing the curiosity of; fascinating.

**in·trude** (in trüd′) *v.* **in·trud·ed, in·trud·ing.** to enter without being asked or wanted.

**in·vert·ed** (in vėrt′ id) *adj.* turned upside down.

**in·vest·ment** (in vest′ mənt) *n.* sum of money that is invested, or put into a business, to obtain profit.

**is·sue** (ish′ ü) *v.* **is·sued, is·su·ing.** to go or come out; flow out; pour forth.

# J

**jade** (jād) *n.* a hard stone that is commonly deep green to greenish-white in color and is used for jewelry and carved ornaments.

**jar** (jär) *n.* a shake or sudden movement; shock; jolt.

**jerk·y** (jėr′ kē) *n.* meat, usually beef, that has been cut into strips and dried.

**jour·nal** (jėrn′ əl) *n.* a record or account of events or experiences, especially one written every day.

**Juan de Fu·ca plate** (hwän de fü′ kä plāt) *n.* a tectonic plate in the northern Pacific Ocean, named after the Greek explorer whose name was also given to the waterway between Vancouver Island and the state of Washington.

**junc·tion** (jungk′ shən) *n.* a place or station where railroad lines meet or cross.

**junk** (jungk) *n.* a large, flat-bottomed sailing vessel developed in China, having a square prow and squarely-stretched sails.

**junk**

a **bat**, ā **cake**, ä **father**, är **car**, âr **dare**; e **hen**, ē **me**, ėr **term**; i **bib**, ī **kite**, ir **clear**; o **top**, ō **rope**, ô **saw**, oi **coin**, ôr **fork**, ou **out**; u **sun**, u̇ **book**, ü **moon**, ū **cute**; ə **about**, **taken**

# K

**ki·mo·no** (ki mō' nə) *n.* a loose robe or gown tied with a sash, worn by Japanese men and women.

kimono

**kin·dle** (kin' dəl) *v.* **kin·dled, kin·dling.** to make bright or glowing.

**knoll** (nōl) *n.* a small, rounded hill or mound.

# L

**lac·quer** (lak' ər) *n.* any of various kinds of varnish made from the resin of the lacquer tree. Lacquer takes a hard, high polish and is used for coating articles of wood.

**lad·en** (lād' ən) *adj.* loaded.

**lair** (lãr) *n.* a home or resting place, especially of a wild animal.

**land·la·dy** (land' lā' dē) *n., pl.* **land·la·dies.** a woman who owns apartments or houses occupied by tenants.

**land·mark** (land' märk') *n.* an object in a landscape that is familiar or striking and serves as a guide.

**land·scape** (land' skāp') *n.* a stretch or expanse of scenery that can be viewed from one point or place.

**lank·y** (lang' kē) *adj.* ungracefully tall and slim.

**lar·i·at** (lãr' ē ət) *n.* a long rope with a loop at one end, used for roping livestock; lasso.

**launch** (lônch) *v.* **1.** to push or propel by force into the air. **2.** to put a boat or ship into the water.

**la·va** (lä' və, lav' ə) *n.* melted rock that flows from a volcano or a crack in the earth's surface.

**lean-to** (lēn' tü') *n.* a shed or building having a roof that slopes in one direction, supported by the wall of a building against which it is built.

**lean-to**

**lec·ture** (lek' chər) *n.* a prepared talk on a particular subject given for the purpose of instruction.

**ledge** (lej) *n.* **1.** a narrow shelf of rock jutting out from the side of a mountain or other natural formation. **2.** a narrow shelf, such as a window ledge.

**le·gal lim·it** (lē' gəl lim' it) *n.* the greatest amount or extent that something may be acquired or done under the law.

**le·gion** (lē' jən) *n.* **1.** a vast number of persons or things. **2.** a military unit in the army of ancient Rome, having from 3,000 to 6,000 infantrymen and from 300 to 700 cavalrymen.

**lei·sure** (lē' zhər, lezh' ər) *n.* free time.

**Le·o·nid** (lē' ə nid) *n., pl.* **Le·o·nids, Le·on·i·des.** a shower of meteorites that seem to come from the area around the constellation Leo.

**Le·the** (lē′ thē) *n.* *Greek and Roman Mythology.* a river in the Underworld whose water, when drunk, caused a person to forget the past.

**Li·be·ri·a** (lī bir′ ē ə) *n.* a country on the west coast of Africa, founded in 1822 by freed black slaves from the United States.

**li·chen** (lī′ kən) *n.* any of a large group of plants without flowers found in all parts of the world, usually growing on tree trunks, rocks, or the ground.

lichen

**lime·stone** (līm′ stōn′) *n.* a rock consisting mostly of calcium carbonate from the skeletons and shells of sea creatures.

**lob** (lob) *v.* **lobbed, lob·bing.** to hit or throw a ball in a high, slow arc.

**lob·by** (lob′ ē) *n., pl.* **lob·bies.** an entrance hall or large public room, as in a hotel or theater.

**lock** (lok) *n.* a tuft or strand of hair.

**lof·ty** (lôf′ tē) *adj.* at a great height; towering.

**long·boat** (long′ bōt′) *n.* the longest and strongest boat carried by a sailing ship.

**loom** (lüm) *v.* to appear dimly or vaguely.

**loy·al** (loi′ əl) *adj.* **1.** faithful in one's allegiance to one's king, government, or country. **2.** faithful in one's friendship, devotion, or regard.

**lunge** (lunj) *v.* **lunged, lung·ing.** to move suddenly forward; lurch.

**lux·u·ri·ous·ly** (lug zhür′ ē əs lē, luk shür′ ē əs lē) *adv.* in a very restful, easy, or relaxed manner.

# M

**mag·ma** (mag′ mə) *n., pl.* **mag·mas, mag·ma·ta.** melted rock that exists beneath the surface of the earth and from which lava and igneous rocks are formed.

**man·age·ment** (man′ ij mənt) *n.* the act of directing or guiding affairs.

**Man·dan In·di·ans** (man′ dan) a tribe of the Sioux Indian nation.

**ma·neu·ver** (mə nü′ vər) *v.* **1.** to move or manage skillfully. **2.** to cause troops or ships to perform maneuvers.

**man·tle** (man′ təl) *n.* the layer of the earth's interior between the crust and the core.

**mar·ket** (mär′ kit) *n.* **1.** demand for something. **2.** open space or building where food products or goods are bought and sold.

---

a bat, ā cake, ä father, är car, âr dare; e hen, ē me, ėr term; i bib, ī kite, ir clear; o top, ō rope, ô saw, oi coin, ôr fork, ou out; u sun, u̇ book, ü moon, ū cute; ə about, taken

**mar·vel** (mär′ vəl) *v.* to be filled with wonder and amazement.

**mar·vel·ous** (mär′ və ləs) *adj.* causing wonder or astonishment.

**Mau·na Ke·a** (mou′ nə kā′ ə) *n.* an extinct volcano on the island of Hawaii, 13,784 feet (4201 meters) high.

**maze** (māz) *n.* a confusing network of paths or passageways, usually bordered by high walls, through which it is difficult to find one's way.

**maze**

**me·an·der** (mē an′ dər) *v.* to follow a winding course.

**me·chan·i·cal** (mi kan′ i kəl) *adj.* of or involving machines.

**mech·a·nism** (mek′ ə niz′ əm) *n.* the working parts of a machine.

**me·di·a·tor** (mē′ dē ā′ tər) *n.* a person or group that settles differences by coming between disagreeing or opposing parties.

**mem·o·rize** (mem′ ə rīz′) *v.* **mem·o·rized, mem·o·riz·ing.** to learn by heart.

**mem·o·ry banks** (mem′ ər ē bangks) *n. pl.* sections of a computer's or robot's brain where information is recorded and stored.

**men·tal** (men′ təl) *adj.* **1.** performed by the mind. **2.** of or relating to the mind.

**mer·chan·dise** (mèr′ chən dīz′, mèr′ chən dīs′) *n.* articles bought and sold.

**me·sa** (mā′ sə) *n.* a flat-topped hill or mountain with steep sides descending to the plain below; high plateau.

**met·a·phor** (met′ ə fôr′) *n.* a way of expressing something in which one object or idea is compared with another in order to suggest a similarity between the two.

**mil·dew** (mil′ dü′) *n.* any of various kinds of fungus that grow on moist areas, appearing as a fuzzy powder or fuzzy down.

**mind-bog·gling** (mīnd′ bog′ ling) *adj.* astounding; overwhelming.

**mind·ful** (mīnd′ fəl) *adj.* conscious; aware.

**min·er·al** (min′ ər əl) *n.* any natural substance that is neither animal nor vegetable and has a definite chemical composition.

**min·i·a·ture** (min′ ē ə chər, min′ ə chər) *adj.* greatly reduced in size; very small.

**Mi·nos** (mī′ nəs) *n. Greek Legend.* a king of Crete who built the labyrinth and kept the Minotaur in it.

**Minos**

**mir·a·cle** (mir′ ə kəl) *n.* an amazing or marvelous happening or thing.

**mir·ror** (mir′ ər) *v.* to reflect or picture.

**mis·chie·vous·ly** (mis′ chə vəs lē) *adv.* playfully but harmfully doing something.

**mis·for·tune** (mis fôr′ chən) *n.* bad luck; unfortunate occurrence.

**mis·giv·ing** (mis giv′ ing) *n.* a feeling of doubt or uneasiness.

**mis·hap** (mis′ hap) *n.* an unfortunate accident.

**mne·mon·ic** (ni mon′ ik) *n.* something, such as a formula or phrase, that helps a person remember something.

**mod·el** (mod′ əl) *v.* to serve as a model, a person or thing that serves as an example or standard for imitation or comparison.

**mod·er·ate** (mod′ ər it) *adj.* kept within reasonable limits; not going to extremes.

**mod·est** (mod′ ist) *adj.* not boastful or forward.

**mol·ten** (mōlt′ ən) *adj.* melted by heat.

**mo·ti·vate** (mō′ tə vāt) *v.* **mo·ti·vat·ed, mo·ti·vat·ing.** to provide with a goal that causes a person to act.

**murk·y** (mėr′ kē) *adj.* dark, gloomy, or cloudy.

**mus·lin** (muz′ lin) *n.* a cotton fabric.

**mus·ty** (mus′ tē) *adj.* **1.** out-of-date; old-fashioned. **2.** having a stale or moldy odor or taste.

**myth** (mith) *n.* a traditional or legendary story that expresses the belief of a particular people. Myths often offer explanations for natural happenings that are not understood.

# N

**na·tive** (nā′ tiv) *adj.* **1.** living or growing in a particular place. **2.** belonging to a particular place or country.

**ne·go·ti·at·ing** (ni gō′ shē ā′ ting) *adj.* bringing about or arranging the terms of an agreement.

**net** (net) *n.* the amount, as of income, that remains after all deductions or allowances have been made.

**niche** (nich) *n.* a recess or hollow in a wall for a statue, vase, or the like.

**nim·bly** (nim′ blē) *adv.* lightly and quickly.

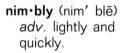

**niche**

**Nobel Prize for Literature** a prize established by Alfred Nobel, to be awarded each year for accomplishment in the field of literature.

**no·tion** (nō′ shən) *n.* mental image; idea.

**nut·meg** (nut′ meg′) *n.* a hard, aromatic seed of an evergreen tree, dried and ground and used as a spice.

# O

**o·bliged** (ə blījd′) *adj.* placed under an obligation, as for a favor or service; grateful.

---

a **bat**, ā **cake**, ä **father**, är **car**, ãr **dare**; e **hen**, ē **me**, ėr **term**; i **bib**, ī **kite**, ir **clear**; o **top**, ō **rope**, ô **saw**, oi **coin**, ôr **fork**, ou **out**; u **sun**, u̇ **book**, ü **moon**, ū **cute**; ə **about**, taken

**ob·vi·ous·ly** (ob′ vē əs lē) *adv.* in a way that can be easily seen or understood; evidently.

**odd job** (od′ job′) *n.* an occasional, usually small task or job.

**Ogla·la Sioux** (ôg′ lä lä sü′) an Indian group within the Teton tribe of the Sioux Indians. The Oglala Sioux lived in what today is the state of Wyoming.

**op·po·nent** (ə pō′ nənt) *n.* a person who opposes, fights, or competes with another.

**op·por·tu·ni·ty** (op′ ər tü′ nə tē) *n.*, *pl.* **op·por·tu·ni·ties.** a time or circumstance favorable for a particular purpose.

**or·gan·i·za·tion** (ôr′ gən ī zā′ shən) *n.* a group of persons united for a particular purpose.

otter

**ot·ter** (ot′ ər) *n.* a furry, web-footed water animal related to and resembling the weasel and mink.

**out·crop·ping** (out′ krop′ ing) *n.* rock sticking out from the surface of the ground.

**o·ver·whelm** (ō′ vər welm′) *v.* to overcome or overpower completely.

**ox·bow lake** (oks′ bō lāk′) *n.* a small lake or pond formed by a river that has straightened its meandering bed, so that a former bend, or oxbow, becomes separated from the river.

# P

**pad·dock** (pad′ ək) *n.* a small field in which an animal can graze and exercise.

**pan·el** (pan′ əl) *n.* a section of a door, cabinet, or other surface, set off from the surrounding surface by being raised, recessed, or bordered.

**pan·ic-strick·en** (pan′ ik strik′ ən) *adj.* overcome by a terrible, uncontrollable fear.

**pan·to·mime** (pan′ tə mīm′) *v.* **pan·to·mimed, pan·to·mim·ing.** to tell a story without speech, using only gestures, body movements, and facial expressions.

**par·a·lyze** (pãr′ ə līz′) *v.* **par·a·lyzed, par·a·lyz·ing. 1.** to make helpless, powerless, or inactive. **2.** to affect with paralysis, the loss of the power of motion or feeling in a part of the body.

**parch** (pärch) *v.* **1.** to make very thirsty. **2.** to make very dry or shriveled.

**par·tic·i·pate** (pär tis′ ə pāt′) *v.* **par·tic·i·pat·ed, par·tic·i·pat·ing.** to take part in.

**pay** (pā) *v.* **paid** or **payed, pay·ing.** to give (money) in return for services or goods. **to pay out.** to let out by slackening, as a rope or line.

**pea jack·et** (pē′ jak′ it) *n.* a short, usually dark-blue coat of thick woolen cloth, worn especially by sailors.

pea jacket

**peer** (pir) *v.* to look closely or searchingly, as in an effort to see clearly.

**Pe·le** (pā′ lā) *n. Hawaiian Mythology.* goddess of volcanoes.

**pen·e·trat·ing** (pen′ ə trā′ ting) *adj.* passing through or into, especially by force.

**per·il** (pãr′ əl) *n.* danger.

**per·mit** (pər mit′) *v.* **per·mit·ted, per·mit·ting.** to allow.

**per·plex·i·ty** (pər plek′ sə tē) *n., pl.* **per·plex·i·ties.** the state of being filled with uncertainty; confusion.

**per·sua·sion** (pər swā′ zhən) *n.* the act of convincing someone to do or believe something.

**peter out** (pē′ tər out′) *v. Informal.* to become less and less until it disappears.

**pic·ca·lil·li** (pik′ ə lil′ ē) *n.* a relish of East Indian origin made of such things as chopped pickles, onions, and tomatoes, with hot spices.

**pick·et** (pik′ it) *v.* **1.** to fasten to a picket, a pointed stake driven into the ground to secure something. **2.** to act as a picket, or protestor, outside an establishment.

**pip·ing** (pī′ ping) *n.* **1.** a loud, shrill sound. **2.** a system of pipes.

**plas·toid** (plas′ toid) *adj.* having the nature or appearance of plastic.

**pla·teau** (pla tō′) *n.* an area of land raised above the surrounding land.

**plaza**

**pla·za** (plä′ zə, plaz′ ə) *n.* a public square or open space in a city or town.

**plight** (plīt) *n.* situation or condition, especially one that is bad.

**plod** (plod) *v.* **plod·ded, plod·ding.** to walk or move slowly or heavily; trudge.

**pneu·mo·nia** (nü mōn′ yə, nū mōn′ yə) *n.* an inflammation of the lungs caused by an infection.

**poise** (poiz) *v.* **poised, pois.ing.** to hold in balance.

**Po·li·a·hu** (pô lē ä′ hū) *n. Hawaiian Mythology.* goddess of snow.

**pol·lute** (pə lüt′) *v.* **pol·lut·ed, pol·lut·ing.** to make impure or dirty.

**po·ny ex·press** (pō′ nē eks pres′) *n.* a postal service in which mail was carried in relays by riders on horseback. The pony express ran between Missouri and California from 1860 to 1861.

**por·ce·lain** (pôr′ sə lin) *n.* a fine ceramic material that is hard and white.

**port·a·ble** (pôr′ tə bəl) *adj.* that can be carried easily by hand.

---

a **bat**, ā **cake**, ä **father**, är **car**, ãr **dare**; e **hen**, ē **me**, ėr **term**; i **bib**, ī **kite**, ir **clear**; o **top**, ō **rope**, ô **saw**, oi **coin**, ôr **fork**, ou **out**; u **sun**, ù **book**, ü **moon**, ū **cute**; ə **about**, **taken**

**por·trait** (pôr′ trit) *n.* a painting or photograph of a person, showing only the face and upper portion of the body.

portrait

**po·si·tion** (pə zish′ ən) *v.* to put in a particular place or arrangement.

**prai·rie** (prãr′ ē) *n.* a large, level or gently rolling grassland without trees.

**prai·rie schoon·er** (prãr′ ē skü′ nər) *n.* a covered wagon used by pioneers in crossing the prairies westward to the Pacific Ocean.

**pres·sure** (presh′ ər) *n.* the force exerted by one thing upon another.

**prim·i·tive** (prim′ i tiv) *adj.* simple or crude; characteristic of an early stage of development.

**prim·ly** (prim′ lē) *adv.* in a neat, precise, or proper manner.

**prin·ci·pal** (prin′ sə pəl) *adj.* the first or greatest in importance.

**pri·va·cy** (prī′ və sē) *n.*, *pl.* **pri·va·cies.** the state or condition of being secluded; isolated.

**pro·ces·sion** (prə sesh′ ən) *n.* a group of persons moving along in a formal, ceremonious manner.

**pro·fes·sion** (prə fesh′ ən) *n.* an occupation, usually one that requires special training.

**pro·fes·sion·al** (prə fesh′ ən əl) *adj.* **1.** undertaken or engaged in by professionals rather than amateurs. **2.** of or relating to a profession or a person in a profession.

**pro·fes·sor** (prə fes′ ər) *n.* teacher of the highest rank in a college, university, or other institution of higher education.

**pro·file** (prō′ fīl) *n.* **1.** a brief biographical sketch. **2.** a side view, especially of a human face or head.

**prof·it** (prof′ it) *n.* the amount remaining after all the costs of a business have been paid.

**pro·pose** (prə′ pōz) *v.* **pro·posed, pro·pos·ing.** to put forward for consideration; suggest.

**pub·lic·i·ty** (pu blis′ ə tē) *n.* information about a person or thing presented in order to attract notice or public attention.

**pub·lish** (pub′ lish) *v.* to produce and offer printed material for sale to the public.

**pub·lish·er** (pub′ li shər) *n.* a person or company whose business is the publishing of books, magazines, newspapers, and the like.

**pur·suit** (pər süt′) *n.* the act of following in order to overtake.

**put·ter** (put′ ər) *v.* to work or act in an aimless or useless way.

# Q

**qual·i·fi·ca·tion** (kwol′ ə fi kā′ shən) *n.* any ability or knowledge that makes a person fit for a certain job or office.

**quar·ry** (kwôr′ ē, kwor′ ē) *n.*, *pl.* **quar·ries.** a pursued or searched for person or thing.

**quar·ter sec·tion** (kwôr′ tər sek′ shən) *n.* a piece of land, usually square, containing 160 acres.

**ques·tion·naire** (kwes′ chə nãr′) *n.* a written or printed form consisting of a list of questions, used to get information or a sample of public opinion.

# R

**rage** (rāj) *n.* violent or uncontrolled anger; fury.

**ra·pids** (rap′ idz) *n. pl.* a part of a river where the current is swift, caused by a steep descent of the riverbed.

**rapids**

**rate** (rāt) *n.* price or charge for a service.

**rav·en·ous·ly** (rav′ ə nəs lē) *adv.* with a feeling of great hunger.

**raw·hide** (rô′ hīd′) *n.* the untanned hide of cattle or other animals.

**rea·son·a·ble** (rē′ zə nə bəl, rēz′ nə bəl) *adj.* **1.** not too expensive. **2.** showing or using good sense or judgment; not foolish.

**re·cede** (ri sēd′) *v.* **re·ced·ed, re·ced·ing.** to move back or away.

**rec·i·ta·tion** (res′ ə tā′ shən) *n.* the act of reciting a lesson in class.

**re·cite** (ri sīt′) *v.* **re·cit·ed, re·cit·ing.** to repeat from memory.

**re·cline** (ri klīn′) *v.* **re·clined, re·clin·ing.** to lie back or down.

**rec·om·men·da·tion** (rek′ ə men dā′ shən) *n.* the act of speaking favorably of something or someone.

**ref·er·ee** (ref′ ə rē′) *n.* an official in certain sports and games who interprets and enforces the rules.

**referee**

**reg·is·ter** (rej′ is tər) *n.* a book containing a formal or official record or list of names, facts, or events.

**reign** (rān) *v.* to hold or use the power of a monarch or other ruler.

**rel·a·tive** (rel′ ə tiv) *n.* a person, such as a cousin or an aunt, connected by family ties.

**re·li·a·ble** (ri lī′ ə bəl) *adj.* that can be depended on with confidence; trustworthy.

**re·lief** (ri lēf′) *n.* the projection of figures and designs from a surface in sculpture, drawing, painting, and the like.

**re·search** (ri sèrch′, rē′ sèrch) *n., pl.* **re·search·es.** a study or investigation in a particular field, usually for the purpose of learning new facts or making new interpretations.

---

a bat, ā cake, ä father, är car, âr dare; e hen, ē me, èr term; i bib, ī kite, ir clear; o top, ō rope, ô saw, oi coin, ôr fork, ou out; u sun, ů book, ü moon, ū cute; ə about, taken

**res·i·due** (rez' ə dü) *n.* a substance that remains at the end of a separating process.

**re·sign** (ri zīn') *v.* to give up voluntarily, as a job, position, or office.

**res·in** (rez' in) *n.* any of various yellow or brown sticky substances that come from certain trees, such as pine and balsam, and are used especially to improve paints and plastics and to make glue and rubber.

**re·sist** (ri zist') *v.* to withstand the action of effect of.

**rif·fle** (rif' əl) *v.* **rif·fled, rif·fling. 1.** to bend the edges slightly and slip the pages of (a book, magazine) quickly out from under the thumb. **2.** to shuffle (cards) by bending the edges slightly, so that the two divisions of the deck slide into each other.

**rig·or** (rig' ər) *n.* severity; harshness.

**roil** (roil) *v.* **1.** to make (liquid) muddy or unsettled by stirring up sediment. **2.** to disturb or vex (someone).

**rou·tine** (rü tēn') *n.* part of a performance in some sports, such as gymnastics or figure skating.

**ru·in·a·tion** (rü' i nā' shən) *n.* ruin; destruction; downfall.

# S

**sage·brush** (sāj' brush') *n.* a shrub that grows on the dry plains of western North America. It has silvery white leaves and small yellow or white flowers.

**sal·a·ry** (sal' ə rē) *n., pl.* **sal·a·ries.** a sum of money paid to someone for regular work.

**salt·pe·ter** (sôlt' pē' tər) *n.* a colorless or white crystalline salt, used especially in gunpowder and explosives, fertilizers, and medicine.

**sa·lute** (sə lüt') *v.* **sa·lut·ed, sa·lut·ing.** to honor or show respect for in a particular way, as by raising the right hand to the forehead.

**Sa·mos** (sā' mäs) *n.* a Greek island in the Aegean Sea, near the western coast of Turkey.

**sam·u·rai** (sam' ü rī') *n., pl.* **sam·u·rai.** in feudal Japan, a member of the warrior class.

**scale mod·el** (skāl mo' dəl) *n.* a representation or reproduction of something, constructed to scale so that every feature, though smaller, is proportional to that which it represents.

**scarce** (skârs) *adj.* difficult to get or find.

**scar·let** (skär' lit) *n.* a bright red or orange-red color.

**schol·ar** (skol' ər) *n.* a person having much knowledge of, or considered to be an authority in, a particular field.

**sculp·ture** (skulp' chər) *n.* a figure or design made by carving in stone, or casting in bronze or other metal.

**sculpture**

**scyth·ing** (sī' <u>thing</u>) *n.* a cutting, scraping sound.

554

**sear·ing** (sir′ ing) *adj.* extremely hot; scorching.

**sec·tor** (sek′ tər) *n.* a particular division or part; a particular area.

**se·cure·ly** (si kūr′ lē) *adv.* not likely to give way; firmly, tightly.

**sedge** (sedj) *n.* marsh or wetlands plant with spikelike clusters of tiny green flowers.

**sed·i·ment** (sed′ ə mənt) *n.* matter that settles to the bottom of a liquid; dregs.

**seethe** (sēth) *v.* **seethed, seeth·ing.** to be very disturbed or agitated; rile up.

**seg·ment** (seg′ mənt) *n.* a part into which something is divided; section.

**Sem·i·nole** (sem′ ə nōl) *n.* a member of a tribe of North American Indians, originally living in Florida. Most of this tribe now lives in Oklahoma.

**sen·try** (sen′ trē) *n., pl.* **sen·tries.** a person, especially a soldier, stationed to keep watch and alert others of danger; guard.

**sentry**

**se·rene·ly** (sə rēn′ lē) *adv.* in a calm and peaceful manner.

**ses·a·me** (ses′ ə mē) *n.* a small, oval seed of a tropical plant native to India, used mainly in baked goods and candies.

**shaft** (shaft) *n.* a deep passage, usually vertical, from ground level to an underground excavation.

**sheath** (shēth) *n.* a case for the blade of a sword, knife, or the like.

**sheathe** (shēth) *v.* **sheathed, sheath·ing. 1.** to enclose or protect in a case or covering. **2.** to put into a sheath.

**sheer** (shir) *adj.* **1.** straight up and down; very steep. **2.** very thin; almost transparent.

**shel·ter** (shel′ tər) *n.* something that covers or protects from weather or danger.

**sho·gun** (shō′ gən, shō′ gün) *n.* any of the hereditary administrative and political rulers of Japan from 1192 to 1867.

**shorn** (shôrn) *adj.* cut or clipped with shears, scissors, or a similar sharp instrument.

**Sic·i·ly** (sis′ ə lē) *n.* an island in the Mediterranean Sea, off the southwestern tip of Italy.

**side-wheel·er** (sīd′ hwē′ lər) *n.* a steamboat having a paddle wheel on each side.

**silt** (silt) *n.* very fine particles of earth, sand, or clay, carried by moving water and deposited as sediment.

a bat, ā cake, ä father, är car, ār dare; e hen, ē me, ėr term; i bib, ī kite, ir clear; o top, ō rope, ô saw, oi coin, ôr fork, ou out; u sun, u̇ book, ü moon, ū cute; ə about, taken

**sin·ew** (sin′ ū) *n.* a strong cord or band of tissue that attaches a muscle to a bone or other part of the body.

**sink·hole** (singk′ hōl′) *n.* a hole worn straight down in rock, especially limestone, by dripping water.

**site** (sīt) *n.* **1.** the position or location of a town, city, building, or the like. **2.** the place where something happened.

**skein** (skān) *n.* a continuous strand of yarn coiled in a bundle.

**slab** (slab) *n.* a broad, flat, and usually thick piece of some material.

**sleek** (slēk) *adj.* smooth and glossy.

**slith·er** (slith′ ər) *v.* to move along with a sliding or gliding motion.

**slo·gan** (slō′ gən) *n.* a phrase used in advertising a particular product or service.

**slope** (slōp) *n.* a stretch of ground that is not flat or level.

**slough** (slou) *n.* a place full of soft, deep mud.

**soar** (sôr) *v.* to fly upward or rise high into the air.

**sod** (sod) *n.* **1.** a piece of the grassy surface of the ground, usually cut in a square or strip. **2.** the surface of the ground, especially when covered with grass.

**so·lil·o·quize** (sə lil′ ə kwīz′) *v.* **so·lil·o·quized, so·lil·o·quiz·ing.** to talk to oneself.

**sound bar·ri·er** (sound′ bar′ ē ər) *n.* a sudden, sharp increase in resistance which the air presents to an aircraft as its speed nears the speed of sound. A loud, explosive noise is created when the aircraft reaches or exceeds this barrier.

**spec·tac·u·lar** (spek tak′ yə lər) *adj.* impressive.

**spell·bound** (spel′ bound′) *adj.* held as if by a spell; entranced.

**spe·lunk·ing** (spi lung′ king) *n.* the act or process of exploring caves.

**spire** (spīr) *n.* a tall structure that tapers to a point, usually built on the top of a tower.

**sports·man·ship** (spôrts′ mən ship′) *n.* conduct worthy of a sportsman, such as fair play or the ability to accept defeat graciously.

**sprawl** (sprôl) *v.* to lie or sit with the limbs spread out in an awkward or careless manner.

**square-rig·ger** (skwãr′ rig′ ər) *n.* a ship having square sails as its principal sails.

**sta·lac·tite** (stə lak′ tīt) *n.* an icicle-shaped formation hanging from the roof or sides of a cave that is composed of calcium carbonate deposited by dripping water.

**stalactite**

**sta·lag·mite** (stə lag′ mīt) *n.* a deposit of calcium carbonate, similar to a cone, built up on the floor of a cave by water dripping from the roof of the cave.

**stalk** (stôk) *n.* the main stem of a plant.

**stal·lion** (stal′ yən) *n.* a male horse, especially one used for breeding.

**stave** (stāv) *n.* any long, narrow strip of wood, such as that which forms the sides of a barrel.

**ster·i·lized** (stãr′ ə līzd′) *adj.* made free of bacteria and dirt.

**stern·ly** (stèrn′ lē) *adv.* in a severe or strict manner.

**stock** (stok) *n.* shares in a company.

**stock cer·tif·i·cate** (stok′ sər tif′ ə kit) *n.* an official document issued by a company to a stockholder as evidence of his ownership of a particular number of shares.

**stock·hold·er** (stok′ hōl′ dər) *n.* a person who owns stock in a company or corporation; shareholder.

**stow** (stō) *v.* to put or pack away.

**strict** (strikt) *adj.* **1.** closely enforced or followed. **2.** following rules or regulations in a rigid, exact manner.

**stur·dy** (stèr′ dē) *adj.* strong; stout.

**Styx** (stiks) *n.* *Greek Mythology.* the river surrounding the Underworld, across which the dead were ferried in a boat.

**sub·merge** (səb mèrg′) *v.* **sub·merged, sub·merg·ing.** to sink out of sight by going beneath the surface of a liquid.

**sub·side** (səb sīd′) *v.* **sub·sid·ed, sub·sid·ing.** to sink to a lower level.

**sul·fur** (sul′ fər) *n.* a yellow nonmetallic element occurring in both free and combined forms. Sulfur is very abundant in nature and is used to make sulfuric acid and process rubber.

**su·pe·ri·or** (sə pir′ ē ər) *adj.* higher in rank or status.

**sup·ply** (sə plī′) *n.*, *pl.* **sup·plies. 1.** the quantity of something available for sale at a certain price at a given time. **2.** the amount available for use; stock.

**sur·vey** (sèr′ vā) *n.* a detailed study or investigation.—*v.* to view or examine as a whole.

**survey**

**sus·pend** (sə spend′) *v.* to attach from above and hang down.

**sus·pend·ed** (sə spen′ did) *adj.* held in place by, or as if by, attachment from above.

---

a **bat**, ā **cake**, ä **father**, är **car**, ãr **dare**; e **hen**, ē **me**, èr **term**; i **bib**, ī **kite**, ir **clear**; o **top**, ō **rope**, ô **saw**, oi **coin**, ôr **fork**, ou **out**; u **sun**, u̇ **book**, ü **moon**, ū **cute**; ə **about, taken**

**swamp** (swomp) *n.* an area of low-lying land flooded with water and usually covered with dense vegetation such as grasses, trees, and shrubs.

**swell** (swel) *n.* an unbroken wave or waves; billow.

**swift** (swift) *adj.* moving or able to move with great speed; fleet.

**syn·di·cate** (sin′ di kit) *n.* **1.** an organization that sells material, such as articles and photographs, for publication in a number of newspapers or periodicals at the same time. **2.** association of individuals or companies formed to carry out a business purpose, especially one requiring a large amount of money.

**sys·tem** (sis′ təm) *n.* a group of things or parts related or combined in such a way as to form a whole.

# T

**tal·is·man** (tal′ is mən) *n.* an engraved stone, ring, or other object believed to have magic power.

**tal·low** (tal′ ō) *n.* the fat from cattle and sheep, used chiefly for making candles, soap, and margarine.

**tar·nished** (tär′ nisht) *adj.* dulled or discolored, as by exposure to air or dirt; made less bright.

**tart** (tärt) *adj.* sharp in taste; not sweet; sour.

**team·ster** (tēm′ stər) *n.* **1.** a person whose work is driving a team of horses or other animals. **2.** a person whose work is driving a truck.

**tec·ton·ic plate** (tek ton′ ik plāt′) *n.* any of approximately twenty large rock masses that, side-to-side, make up the earth's crust. The plates are constantly moving and colliding with each other, and sometimes causing earthquakes and volcanic eruptions along the edges.

**ter·raced** (tãr′ ist) *adj.* formed into a terrace or terraces. A terrace is a raised, level platform of earth with a vertical or sloping front or side, especially one of a series of such levels placed one above the other up the side of a hill.

**thresh·old** (thresh′ hōld′, thresh′ ōld) *n.* a piece of wood, stone, or metal that forms the bottom of a door frame.

**throb** (throb) *v.* **throbbed, throb·bing.** to beat heavily and fast, as the heart; pound.

**tid·al wave** (tī′ dəl wāv′) *n.* a huge, powerful ocean wave caused by an underwater earthquake.

**tidal wave**

**tinge** (tinj) *v.* to color slightly; tint.

**tink·er** (ting′ kər) *v.* to work in an unskillful or clumsy manner.

**top·notch** (top′ noch′) *adj.* *Informal.* first-rate; superior.

**trag·e·dy** (traj′ ə dē) *n., pl.* **trag·e·dies. 1.** a sad, dreadful, or disastrous event. **2.** a drama in which life is viewed or treated seriously, usually having a sad ending.

**trans·con·ti·nen·tal** (trans′ kon tə nent′ əl) *adj.* that crosses a continent.

**trans·for·ma·tion** (trans′ fər mā′ shən) *n.* the act of changing in shape, form, or appearance.

**trot** (trot) *n.* the gait of a horse or other four-legged animal, between a walk and a gallop.

**trus·tee** (trus tē′) *n.* a person or organization that manages the property or affairs of another person, company, or institution.

**tu·ber·cu·lo·sis** (tü bėr′ kyə lō′ sis, tū bėr′ kyə lō′ sis) *n.* an infectious disease caused by a bacterium that may affect any organ of the body, especially the lungs or joints. It is characterized by the formation of small swellings on the affected parts.

**tu·mul·tu·ous** (tü mul′ chü əs) *adj.* excited and noisy.

**typ·i·cal** (tip′ i kəl) *adj.* regular; ordinary; usual; showing the qualities of a particular type.

# U

**un·con·scious** (un kon′ shəs) *adj.* temporarily unable to sense things.

**Un·der·ground Rail·road** (un′ dər ground′ rāl′ rōd′) *n.* before slavery was abolished, a secret system of helping escaped American slaves to freedom by transporting them to Canada or the Free States.

**un·en·dur·a·ble** (un′ en dūr′ ə bəl, un′ ən dür′ ə bəl) *adj.* that cannot be endured; unbearable.

**un·fet·ter** (un fet′ ər) *v.* to free or liberate.

**un·furl** (un fėrl′) *v.* to open or spread out.

**unfurl**

**un·trod·den** (un trod′ ən) *adj.* not walked or stepped upon.

**ur·gent·ly** (ėr′ jent lē) *adv.* insistently, pleadingly.

# V

**va·cant** (vā′ kənt) *adj.* unoccupied; empty.

**vague** (vāg) *adj.* not definitely or clearly expressed.

**van·ish·ing cream** (van′ ish ing krēm′) *n.* a cream that, when applied, vanishes into the skin.

**veer** (vir) *v.* to change the direction or course of.

**ven·ture** (ven′ chər) *v.* **ven·tured, ven·tur·ing.** to expose to risk or danger.

---

a bat, ā cake, ä father, är car, âr dare; e hen, ē me, ėr term; i bib, ī kite, ir clear; o top, ō rope, ô saw, oi coin, ôr fork, ou out; u sun, u̇ book, ü moon, ū cute; ə about, taken

**ve·ran·da** (və ran' də) *n.* an open porch, usually roofed, extending along one or more sides of a house.

**veranda**

**verge** (vėrj) *n.* the edge or border of something.

**vi·brate** (vī' brāt) *v.* **vi·brat·ed, vi·brat· ing.** to move back and forth rapidly.

**vi·sor** (vī' zər) *n.* the projecting brim on the front of a cap, designed to shade the eyes from the sun.

**visor**

**vol·ca·no** (vol kā' nō) *n., pl.* **vol·ca· noes, vol·ca·nos.** a cone-shaped hill or mountain around an opening in the surface of the earth, through which molten rock, gases, and rock fragments are forced out.

# W

**wane** (wān) *v.* **waned, wan·ing. 1.** to draw to a close. **2.** to become less or smaller, as in size, brightness, or strength.

**wave·let** (wāv' lit) *n.* a small wave.

**wend** (wend) *v.* to make (one's way); go on (one's way).

**where·with·al** (hwãr' with ôl') *n.* necessary means or resources, especially money.

**wis·dom** (wiz' dəm) *n.* knowledge and good judgment based on experience.

**wit** (wit) *n.* the ability to make clever, amusing, or striking comments about persons, things, or situations.

**with·er·ing** (with' ər ing) *adj.* scornful; contemptuous.

**wran·gler** (rang' glər) *n.* in the western United States, one who herds or tends horses or other livestock; cowboy.

**wreathe** (rēth) *v.* **wreathed, wreath·ing.** to encircle; envelope; cover.

# Y

**yoke** (yōk) *n.* a wooden frame consisting of a long, curved bar fitted with two hoops by which two work animals are joined together.

**yore** (yôr) *adv.* **of yore.** of long ago; in the past.

# Z

**ze·nith** (zē' nith) *n.* **1.** the point in the heavens directly above the place where a person stands. **2.** the highest or greatest point.

---

a bat, ā cake, ä father, är car, ãr dare; e hen, ē me, ėr term; i bib, ī kite, ir clear; o top, ō rope, ô saw, oi coin, ôr fork, ou out; u sun, u̇ book, ü moon, ū cute; ə about, taken